Dictionary of

Financial World Publishing
IFS House
4-9 Burgate Lane
Canterbury
Kent
CT1 2XJ
United Kingdom

T 01227 818687
F 01227 479641
E editorial@ifslearning.com
W www.ifslearning.com

Typeset by Kevin O'Connor

Printed in Spain

ISBN 0-85297-574-0

FINANCIAL WORLD Publishing
THE CHARTERED INSTITUTE OF BANKERS

Preface

This book is intended to provide access to the terms of trade finance for students and professionals in the growing world of internatonal trade, and its interaction with banking and the stock exchange. It should also assist private investors and people who read financial journals and the financial pages of daily newspapers. Like its companion volume, the *Dictionary of International Accounting Terms*, it does not limit itself merely to well-established terms. It also includes definitions of the everyday jargon, acronyms and newly adopted words (many from the United States) that are now common in national and international financial dealings.

The Dictionary of International Business Terms is one of a series of publications complied from The CIB's unique database of dictionary definitions that relate to various aspects of finance and their applications. As a result, some definitions appear in more than one book – as they should to maintain a comprehensive coverage of the subject within a single self-contained volume. The dictionaries in the series published to date include:

Dictionary of International Accounting Terms
0-85297-575-9
Dictionary of International Banking and Finance Terms
0-85297-632-1
Dictionary of International Business Terms
0-85297-574-0
Dictionary of International Insurance and Finance Terms
0-85297-631-3
Dictionary of International Investment and Finance Terms
0-85297-577-5
Dictionary of International Trade Finance
0-85297-576-7

John O E Clark

John O E Clark is a writer and editor who regularly contributes to dictionaries, encyclopedias and other types of information books for publication in Britain and abroad. He specializes in explaining technical subjects to students and other non-experts, and to people whose first language is not necessarily English.

A

AAA Also called triple-A, the highest corporate security rating as issued by the US credit-rating companies Moody and Standard and Poor.

AAR Abbreviation of ***against all risks***.

abandonment Act of passing ownership of insured property to the insurer in the event of total loss. It takes place in certain circumstances, if the loss is unavoidable or the cost of repair exceeds the value of the property. In the latter case, the property is written off. Abandonment occurs most in marine insurance when a vessel is declared to be dangerous or unseaworthy.

abatement Reduction. The term is used in the USA to describe the cancellation, in whole or in part, of a government levy.

above par Normally used to describe a share that has a market value above its denomination or ***par value***.

above-the-line Describing items that are included in the ***profit and loss account*** of a business (as distinct from the ***appropriation account***).

Abschlag German for discount.

absenteeism Absence from work for no valid reason.

absolute advantage Argument in favour of international trade, put forward by Adam Smith (1723-90). Absolute advantage applies where, for example, two countries can both produce two commodities they need, but country A is more efficient at producing commodity X and country B is more efficient at producing commodity Y. They would therefore both profit by concentrating on the particular commodity each produces best, and trading them.

absolute liability Legal principle that a party that causes loss or harm is liable, whether or not it acted with wrongful intent or negligently. It is also called strict liability.

absolute quota Limit, imposed by government, on the amount of goods that may be imported in a particular period.

absorption Use of ***absorption rates*** to allocate a company's overhead to its production. It is a method used in ***absorption costing***.

absorption costing Method of costing a product that assigns a fixed *manufacturing overhead* as well as material and labour costs as a product cost to the units being produced.

absorption rate In an *absorption costing*, the rate is determined before an accounting period so that overheads can be charged to a company's production. It is equal to the budgeted overhead divided by the budgeted production.

abusive tax shelter Type of limited partnership in the USA that, according to the Internal Revenue Service, claims illegal deductions of tax, usually by inflating the real value of property that has been purchased.

ACAS Abbreviation of *Advisory Conciliation and Arbitration Service*.

accelerated accrual In calculating an employee's pension, the use of an accrual rate with a denominator of less than 60. For example, an employee with 50 years' service would receive 100% of his or her final salary if the denominator is set at 50.

accelerated depreciation Practice of depreciating an asset at a rate greater than the actual decline in its value in order to obtain tax concessions. It need not occur throughout the life of an asset; a substantial proportion of its total value is often written off in the first year, and reduced allowances for depreciation are made thereafter.

accelerated tariff elimination Speeding up of the reduction in tariffs, usually resulting from trade agreements between nations. Total elimination of tariffs results in a free-trade situation.

acceleration Increase in the rate of a price trend or, if a borrower defaults on a deal, the action of the lender when demanding early repayment.

accelerator principle Theory that growth in production is directly related to the level of investment. If consumer demand increases, for example, a company is likely to invest in more equipment, thereby accelerating the current economic growth.

acceptable use policy (AUP) System that restricts the use to which a computer network may be put, particularly used by commercial organizations.

acceptance Written irrevocable promise to pay, thus equivalent to a *promissory note*. A bank-endorsed ***bill of exchange***, for example, is guaranteed. *See also* ***banker's acceptance***.

acceptance credit Way of financing a sale to a foreign buyer in which a commercial or merchant bank provides credit to the foreign creditworthy importer, who can draw a ***bill of exchange*** against the credit. The bank charges an acceptance commission.

acceptance financing *See **acceptance credit**.*

acceptance for honour Alternative term for ***acceptance supra protest***.

acceptance supra protest Situation that occurs when a bill of exchange is turned down (or protested) and is then accepted by another party, thereby saving the honour of the drawer.

accepted bill of exchange Also known as trade acceptance, a draft for payment that does not involve a bank, presented by an importer to an exporter.

accepting bank Bank or other financial institution that endorses a time draft or sight draft for immediate payment. *See **acceptance house**.*

accepting house Also known as an accepting bank or, in the USA, as an acceptance house, a financial institution whose business is concerned mainly with negotiation of ***bills of exchange***, by either guaranteeing them or accepting them. It usually operates in much the same way as a commercial bank.

Accepting Houses Committee Committee that represents the London ***accepting houses*** and large ***merchant banks***. Its members get preferential terms on bills sold to the Bank of England.

acceptor Person who accepts either the terms of a contract or a ***bill of exchange***. When a bill of exchange is accepted, the drawee becomes the acceptor.

Access Credit card company in the UK owned jointly by Lloyds TSB, HSBC and NatWest banks.

access control list (ACL) Means by which access to a computer network security system is controlled. It lists the services available and the hosts allowed to use them.

accommodation Money that is lent for a short period.

accommodation bill ***Bill of exchange*** signed by one person in order to help another to raise a loan. The signatory (or accommodation party) is acting as guarantor, and normally does not expect to pay the bill when it falls due. Accommodation bills are also known as kites, windbills or windmills.

accommodating transactions In international trade, below-the-line items employed to offset any imbalances (such as those caused by a country's trade deficit).

accommodation payment Euphemism for a bribe.

accord Term often used in the USA to denote any form of agreement, especially between companies, the business communities of different countries or the governments of two countries.

accord and satisfaction When one party has discharged its obligations under a contract, it may elect to release the other party from its obligations. When this is done in return for a new consideration, the release is known as accord and satisfaction.

accord de participation French for ***profit sharing***.

account (a/c, acc or **acct.)** In general terms, any note kept of a financial transaction, often also referred to as *accounts*. There are two more specific meanings:

1. In banking, it designates an arrangement made to deposit money with a bank, building society or other financial institution. There are various types of such accounts, with different conditions of withdrawal, rates of interest, minimum deposits, and so on.
2. On the ***London Stock Exchange***, it is a period of two weeks (usually extended to three weeks when bank holidays occur) in which trading is carried out. Broadly, transactions are made in the two weeks of the account and the relevant paperwork is carried out during the following week, followed by payments (settlements) made on the sixth business day after the end of the account. This method of working allows transactions to be made with deferred payment, enabling speculation to take place.

accountability Requirement to give an account when requested. For example, a company's directors are accountable to its shareholders (which is why they publish an annual report and accounts, as required by the UK Companies Act).

accountant Any person practising accountancy, whether qualified or not. The term may be prefixed by various others, that denote the specialism of the accountant (such as cost accountant, management accountant), that accountant's position within a company (such as chief accountant), or his or her professional qualifications (such as certified accountant, Certified Public Accountant, Chartered Accountant).

account day Monday ten days or six business days after the end of each stock exchange ***account***, on which all settlements must be made. It is also known as settlement date or day.

account executive Advertising agency employee who is in total charge of a client's account and its fulfilment. In the USA, it is an alternative term for a stockbroker.

accounting exposure Risk arising from the translation of assets and liabilities into foreign currency. It is also known as translation exposure.

accounting system Any method of recording and evaluating a company's accounting transactions.

accounts An alternative term for a company's ***books of account*** or the ***profit and loss account*** together with the ***balance sheet***.

accounts analysis Analysis of a company's annual accounts to determine its profitability and whether its performance is accurately reflected in its share price.

account stated Legally binding account that shows an agreed balance between two parties, one of whom owes the other.

accreditation of prior learning (APL) Method of scoring the performance of students in terms of what they achieve in each of several small units into which a course is subdivided.

accredited Describing somebody who is authorized to act on behalf of a company or other person.

accreditief Dutch for ***letter of credit***.

accreditif French for ***letter of credit***.

accrual Gradual increase in something by addition over a period of time (and not resulting from a specific transaction). *See also* ***accrued charge***.

accrued charge Also called accrued liability, a charge that has not been accounted for or paid. For example, demand for rent made in arrears must appear on the accounts as an accrued charge, because the service had already been used but not paid for. *See* ***accrual***.

accrued interest Interest payment that is due, but not yet received.

accumulated depreciation Total value of an asset that has been written off so far. It is also known as accrued depreciation, aggregate depreciation and allowance for depreciation.

accumulated profits Also called accumulated earnings, the amount shown in the ***appropriation account*** that can be carried forward (after allowing for reserves and paying items such as dividends and taxes).

accumulating ordinary shares Shares that are issued instead of dividend (equal in value to the dividend less tax) and held in trust for the investor.

accumulation unit In unit trusts or life assurance, a unit for which the dividend is ploughed back into the investment, to produce higher earnings.

ACH Abbreviation of ***automated clearing house***.

acid-test ratio Ratio of a company's assets (excluding stock) to its current liabilities. It is also called the liquid or liquidity ratio or the quick ratio (because it gives a quick assessment of a company's financial state).

ACK In computing, abbreviation of acknowledgement, sent as a message to confirm the arrival of error-free data.

ACEP Abbreviation of ***Advisory Committee on Export Policy***.

ACL Abbreviation of ***access control list***.

acquired advantage Theory in trade that postulates that technology provides more advantage in the production of goods than do available resources.

acquisition Take-over of control of one company by another or by an individual. The purchase of an equity stake in the target company is the usual method of acquisition.

acquisition accounting Procedures introduced after a company has been taken over. The acquired company's results, including tangible and intangible assets (excluding goodwill) are taken into the consolidated profit and loss account only from the date of the take-over.

acquisitive Describing a company that is always on the lookout to grow by taking over other companies.

across the board tariff reductions Agreement between the members of the ***General Agreement on Tariffs and Trade (GATT)*** to make a fixed percentage reduction in tariffs in all member countries.

actionnaire Holder of shares in a French public company (*société anonyme*).

ACTPN Abbreviation of ***Advisory Committee on Trade Policy and Negotiations***.

add-on market *See aftermarket.*

ADEF Abbreviation of *Agence d'Evaluation Financiére.*

ADS Abbreviation of *Agent/Distributor Service.*

ad valorem Latin for according to the value. In taxation, it indicates that tax is calculated as a percentage of the value of the transaction, rather than being charged at a fixed rate. For example, value added tax (VAT) is paid as a percentage of the value of the goods or services sold.

advance corporation tax (ACT) In the UK, corporation tax is levied in two parts. The first part is levied on the distribution of profits and is known as advance corporation tax. The second half is estimated on the company's earnings. *See also* ***corporation tax.***

Advisory Committee on Export Policy (ACEP) US organization that resolves disputes between federal agencies, chaired by the US Department of Commerce.

Advisory Committee on Trade Policy and Negotiations (ACTPN) Committee appointed by the US president to advise on trade policy and related matters, such as trade agreements.

Advisory, Conciliation and Arbitration Service (ACAS) Organization established in the UK in 1975 to prevent or settle industrial disputes. It is an independent body used by companies, individual people and trade unions.

advice note Note from a supplier giving details of goods ordered or delivered. It may accompany or precede the actual shipment, and precedes the invoice. *See also* ***delivery note.***

AFBD Abbreviation of *Association of Future Brokers and Dealers.*

affidavit Statement or declaration made in writing and witnessed by a commissioner for oaths (such as a solicitor), often used in legal proceedings.

affiliate US term for a company that is directly or indirectly controlled by another company or individual in a different country. *See also* ***affiliated company.***

affiliated company Company that is associated in some way with another company. Of no legal standing in the UK, the term has confusingly two opposite meanings in the USA. It may be a company that controls another company, or a company that is controlled by another company.

affirmation of contract Express or implicit affirmation of the terms of a contract that makes the contract legally binding even if it involves misrepresentation by the other party.

affirmative action program US scheme designed to avoid or discourage discrimination in employment, equivalent to equal opportunities employment in the UK.

affreightment Carriage of goods by sea.

afloats Commodities loaded and secured on board ship, ready for the voyage.

after date Term written on a ***bill of exchange*** to indicate that the bill will become due a certain (specified) period after the date on the bill. It might, for example, read: "60 days after date, we promise to pay…"

after-hours trading Trading in shares that takes place after a stock exchange has closed (usually at about 16.30), treated by the exchange as having taken place on the following day.

aftermarket Trading in stocks and shares after they have made their initial debut on the market. The term may also refer to the market in components and services that arises after a product has been sold, which is also known as the add-on market.

after-sales service Acts performed by a manufacturer or supplier after the goods have been sold, such as repair, maintenance work or perhaps training. After-sales service packages are frequently put together as inducements to buy, especially in the sale of branded capital goods.

after sight Written on a bill of exchange, a term that indicates that the period for which the bill is drawn is to be calculated from the date on which the acceptor first saw (or accepted) it. This date is normally written on the bill by the acceptor.

AG Abbreviation of ***Aktiengesellschaft***.

against all risks (AAR) In marine insurance, a term that indicates that a vessel and its cargo have been insured against all insurable eventualities. It is roughly equivalent to fully comprehensive insurance of motor vehicles.

aged creditors analysis Method of listing unpaid bills that have been received with the most overdue at the top of the list (which should be paid first).

aged debtors analysis Method of listing unpaid invoices that are owing with the most overdue at the top of the list, so that these can be vigorously pursued. In the USA, the system is described as an ageing schedule or as ageing accounts receivable.

ageism Discrimination against people (especially in employment) because of their age.

Agence d'Evaluation Financiére (ADEF) Principal *rating agency* in France.

agency Person or company that represents another in a particular field, or a contractual arrangement by which one party agrees to represent another, the agent's word becoming binding in the affairs of the other as if the latter had acted on his or her own behalf.

agency bill Bill of exchange that is drawn on, and accepted by, the London branch of a foreign bank.

agency broker Correct (formal) name for a ***stockbroker***.

agency loan Loan from the European Investment Bank which may be allocated among various projects. Such loans are made only to public organizations.

agency of necessity Situation that arises when an agent acts to safeguard the principal's interests, without the principal's permission. It can only arise when (a) the principal cannot be reached, (b) there is a contract of agency already in existence between the two parties, and (c) immediate action is absolutely necessary. If these conditions exist, the agent's actions are legally binding on the principal.

agenda List of matters to be discussed at a meeting. It can constitute a legal document.

agent Person or company that has entered into a contract of *agency* with another party and acts as its representative, usually in buying and selling goods and services.

agent de change Stockbroker on the Bourse in Paris.

agent de cambio y bolsa Stockbroker on the Madrid Stock Exchange.

agent di cambio Italian for stockbroker.

Agent/Distributor Service (ADS) US organization that, for a fee, helps to find foreign representatives for US exporters.

agent for exporter Authorized forwarding agent of an exporting company.

agent's lien Right of an agent in certain circumstances to retain the property of the principal (for example, in lieu of payment).

aggregate Sum total.

aggregate demand In any economy, the total level of demand (i.e., consumer spending, company investment spending and net foreign revenue).

aggregation risk When trading in securities takes place in more than one market, the possible multiplying of risk.

agio Commission or charge made by a bank or bureau de change in return for converting cash from one currency to another.

AGM Abbreviation of ***annual general meeting***.

agreement Verbal or written contract between two or more parties to explain the way in which they intend to act in respect of each other.

agribusiness Industry that encompasses and includes farming and all commercial aspects of agriculture.

agricultural disarmament Reduction in protectionist practices, such as subsidies, in agriculture.

Agricultural Marketing Service (AMS) Service that the US Department of Agriculture provides by guaranteeing contract specifications of products exported to overseas buyers.

Agricultural Mortgage Corporation (AMC) Organization established by the Bank of England in 1928 to provide long-term loans to farmers, using their land as security.

AIBD Abbreviation of ***Association of International Bond Dealers***.

AIM Abbreviation of ***Alternative Investment Market***.

aims Company's long-term intentions, from which it sets its objectives, often expressed as a ***mission statement***.

air freight Goods carried by air, particularly by one of the air cargo companies.

Airline Users Committee UK organizaion established in 1973 to represent consumers' interests, particularly to the Civil Aviation Authority.

air transport licence Licence that a UK airline must obtain (from the

Civil Aviation Authority) in order to operate charter or scheduled flights.

air waybill (AWB) Document that accompanies goods shipped by air, itemizing the goods and constituting evidence of a contract to make the shipment.

airworthiness certificate Document, issued by the Civil Aviation Authority, that must be held in respect of every UK aircraft used as public transport.

AITC Abbreviation of ***Association of Investment Trust Managers***.

ajustabonos Mexican Stock Exchange bonds that pay a fixed yield above the rate of inflation.

Akkreditiv German for ***letter of credit***.

Aktie German for share.

Aktiebolager (Aktb) Swedish for joint stock company.

Aktiengesellschaft (AG) German for stock company, in practice meaning a public limited company (equivalent to the UK plc). The term is also used in Austria and Switzerland.

Aktieselskabet (Akts) Designation of a Danish or Swedish joint stock company.

Aktionär German for shareholder.

á la criée French for ***open outcry***, one of the methods of quotation on a French stock exchange.

alienation of assets Sale, by a borrower, of assets that have been used as security to obtain the loan, usually precluded by the loan agreement.

aliquot Small assay sample taken from gold bullion.

Allfinanz German term for an institution that conducts both banking and insurance business.

all-in Including everything, most often used to describe a price or service.

allocation under lines of credit Finance provided by Canada's Export Development Corporation to foreign importers of Canadian goods and services.

allocative efficiency Efficiency with which funds are split between various competing demands on them.

allocatur Certificate, for tax purposes, that approves the costs incurred in an action (such as liquidation).

allonge Slip of paper attached to a ***bill of exchange*** that provides extra space for noting endorsements. Allonges were most useful when bills of exchange were moved freely from one holder to another, but are now less common.

All Ordinaries Share Price Index Often shortened to All Ordinaries, a weighted index of 250 companies that trade on the Australian Stock Exchange.

allotment Broadly, the sharing out of something, usually funds, among a group of people. *See* ***allotment of shares***.

allotment note Signed document from a seaman to the master of a ship authorizing the master to pay all or part of his wages to his bank or members of his family. *See also* ***letter of allotment***.

allotment of shares When a company issues shares by publishing a prospectus and inviting applications, allotment is the assignment of shares to each applicant. If the issue is oversubscribed, shares are allotted in proportion to the quantity requested and so applicants do not always receive the number of shares originally requested.

allowance Money that is allotted (allowed) to individuals for a specific reason, or a provision made for unusual or uncertain events; or it is the amount deducted for one of various reasons before income is established for tax purposes.

ALM Abbreviation of ***Association of Lloyd's Members***.

alpha Stock Exchange categorization of the top 100 most actively traded shares with a large capitalization value. *See also* ***beta; delta; gamma***.

alphabet brokers Popular term for the leading US insurance brokers, which are usually referred to by their initials (e.g. A & A = Alexander & Alexander, J & H = Johnson & Higgins).

alpha cooefficient Measure of the volatility in the price of a share against that of all shares (i.e. ignoring overall market trends).

alpha stock *See* ***alpha***.

Alternative Investment Market (AIM) Replacement for the UK Unlisted Securities Market, which closed at the end of 1996, aimed at helping smaller companies to raise capital.

AMC Abbreviation of *Agricultural Mortgage Corporation*.

American Stock Exchange (AMEX) One of New York's two stock exchanges, which deals mainly in the shares of younger and smaller companies. It is also known as the Little Board or the Curb Exchange. Larger companies are listed on the *New York Stock Exchange (NYSE)*.

AMEX Abbreviation of *American Stock Exchange*.

AMH Abbreviation of *automated materials handling*.

AMS Abbreviation of *Agricultural Marketing Service*.

annual general meeting (AGM) Shareholders' meeting, required by law to be held yearly by every public company. An AGM is normally used to discuss the annual report and accounts, to announce dividends and to elect auditors and directors. This is often the only opportunity that shareholders have to air their views.

annual report Document required under UK company law to be released every year by public companies, describing the company's activities during the previous year. It usually includes the balance sheet for that year. It may be combined with the annual accounts as the annual report and accounts.

anti-trust laws US legislation that was enacted to prevent the formation of monopolies. It is similar to the *Monopolies and Mergers Act 1965* in the UK.

APACS Abbreviation of *Association of Payment Clearance Services*.

APL Abbreviation of *accreditation of prior learning*.

appropriation account Company account that shows net profits (current and carried forward) and how they are split between dividends and reserves. In the USA, it may be an account set aside to accommodate funds that have been authorized for a particular purpose.

APT Abbreviation of *Automated Pit Trading*.

arb Colloquial abbreviation of *arbitrageur*.

arbitrage Practice of dealing on two markets almost simultaneously in order to profit from differing exchange rates. Arbitrage may take place when dealing in commodities, bills of exchange or currencies. It also occurs in situations in which prices and returns are fixed and in this sense arbitrage may be contrasted with speculation, in that there is little risk involved.

arbitrageur (US **arbitrager**) Person who practises ***arbitrage***. In the USA, the term is sometimes shortened to arb.

arbitration In disputes arising out of a contract, the parties involved may either go to court or appoint somebody (an arbitrator) to settle the dispute. The agreement to go to arbitration does not preclude either of the parties taking legal proceedings if it desires.

arbitration clause Clause in a contract, particularly between an importer and an exporter or an employer and a trade union, that details the procedure to be taken to settle disputes. *See* ***arbitration***.

arithmetic mean Average; the total of a series of values divided by the number of values.

arithmetic progression Numerical series in which consecutive terms have a common difference. If the nth term of such a progression is given by $[a + (n - 1)d]$, the sum of n terms is $n[2a + (n - 1)d]/2$ (where a is the first term and d is the common difference).

arm's length Describing a transaction negotiated and entered into by unrelated parties, each of whom acts in his or her own best interest using fair market values. It is assumed that, unless there is a related party disclosure, all transactions described in financial statements are conducted at arm's length.

arrangement Generally, the settlement of any financial matter. More specifically, a deed of arrangement is an agreement between a debtor and some or all of his or her creditors, reached in order to avoid the debtor's bankruptcy. Arrangement may be encountered in various forms: as a letter of licence, deed of inspectorship, assignment of property or deed of composition. It may take place either before or after a bankruptcy petition has been presented to the courts.

arrears Money owed but not yet paid.

arrears of dividends Owed but unpaid share dividends, which must be shown in a company's accounts.

arrived ship Vessel that has arrived at the agreed port (either for loading or unloading, and notified to the person responsible for the cargo).

Article 65 Japanese legislation (part of the Securities and Exchange Act 1948) that prohibits banks from owning more than 5% of any company. It also prevents Japanese banks from acting as an issuing house or dealing in shares (although they may do so abroad through subsidiaries).

articled clerk Type of apprentice, usually working in one of the professions, such as accounting or law.

articles of association Legally-required document that sets up the internal regulations for a limited company's operation and which states, among other things, the powers of directors. It is submitted, along with the ***memorandum of association***, to the Registrar of Companies, where it is available for public scrutiny.

ASC Abbreviation of ***Australian Securities Commission***.

A shares Shares with rights different from those legally attached to ordinary shares. There are also B shares, C shares, and so on. The term is frequently used for ***non-voting shares***.

Asian option Also termed an average rate option, an option that is settled in terms of the difference between the strike price of a security and its average market value (over an agreed period).

asked price US term for ***offer price***.

as per advice Term normally found as a note on a ***bill of exchange***, indicating that the drawee has already been notified that the bill has been drawn on him or her.

assay Testing of metal or ore to determine the proportion of precious metal it contains. Assay most often applies to metals used in coinage, and to gold and silver. After assay metals are stamped with a hallmark or assay mark.

assay master Official who is responsible for an ***assay***.

assembly line Method of manufacture in which components or sub-assemblies are joined to make the final product. Generally the workers remain in one place, repeatedly performing the same tasks, alongside a moving conveyor belt.

assented In a situation where a company is threatened with a take-over, assented stocks or shares are those whose owner is in agreement with the take-over. In these circumstances, there may arise separate markets in assented and non-assented stock. Assented stock may also be stock whose owner is in agreement with a proposed change in the conditions of issue.

assessment Act of calculating value.

asset Something that belongs to a person or company and which has value, an economic resource (for example buildings, plant, stock and accounts receivable). There are several types of assets for business purposes, and they are usually classified in terms of their availability for exchange. Examples include ***tangible*** and ***intangible assets***, and long-term (US long-lived or noncurrent) and short-term (or current) assets.

asset allocation Allocation of investments, such as stocks and shares, to make up an investment portfolio.

asset-backed fund Fund consisting of investments that are related to ***tangible assets*** (such as property or shares), so that the investment participates in growth and can be regarded as a hedge against inflation.

asset cover Measure of a company's solvency equal to the ratio of net assets to debt. High asset cover implies that a company is more than marginally solvent.

asset-led marketing Type of marketing based on a company's strengths (such as its brand name), and not merely what customers want.

asset management Broadly, the efficient control and exploitation of a company's assets, most commonly used to describe the management of any fund by a fund manager.

assets employed Value of a company's assets less its current liabilities, equal to the sum of long-term assets and working capital.

asset stripping Practice (which is normally frowned upon) whereby a company is bought merely so that the buyer may sell off its assets for immediate gain. It is also known colloquially as unbundling.

asset structure Balance between a company's long-term (fixed) assets and its short-term (current) assets.

asset turnover Way of measuring a company's ability to produce sales turnover from its assets, equal to sales divided by net assets.

asset value Value of a company's assets less its liabilities. It is often divided by the number of issued ordinary shares and expressed as the asset value per share, theoretically payable to shareholders if the company were to be wound up.

assignment Legal transfer of a property, right or obligation from one party to another. Assignment most commonly takes place where a contract is involved. Acknowledging it is also called an assignment, or deed of assignment.

assignment of lease Transfer a lease to a sub-lessee, which does not remove the liability of the original lessee to the lessor under the terms of the original lease.

assignment of letter of credit Transfer of the proceeds of a ***letter of credit*** (or part of them) to another person (assignee) as advised by the beneficiary to the bank, which promises to pay the proceeds to the assignee before paying the balance to the original beneficiary.

assisted areas Parts of the UK in which companies receive government grants as an incentive to locate there.

associate company Also termed an associated company, a company that is partly owned by another, which has a stake of more than 105 but less than 50%. *See also* ***holding company***.

associated company *See* ***associate company***.

associate director Director who is a member of a company's board but lacks full voting powers. The position is normally held by able but comparatively junior managers; it rewards their enthusiasm and reinforces their commitment without giving them real power.

associated operation Operation that is somehow linked to another within a company. Such operations may, for example, manufacture similar products or use similar production methods.

associated undertaking Business entity that does not have company status but is considered as part of a group when compiling company accounts.

association Group of people or companies that share a common interest. For example, a trade association is a group of companies operating in the business, that come together to provide information and services to each other. The term is also used for the formation of a new company.

Association for Payment Clearing Services (APACS) Organization established in 1985 for managing and controlling the main payment clearing systems and methods of money transmission in the UK.

Association of Futures Brokers and Dealers (AFBD) Former self-regulating organization, established in 1986, which regulated the activities of brokers and dealers on the London futures market. In 1991 it became part of the ***Securities and Futures Association (SFA)***.

Association of International Bond Dealers (AIBD) Organization, established in Zurich in 1969, which in 1991 changed its name to the ***International Securities Market Association (ISMA)***.

Association of Investment Trust Managers (AITC) Organization

A

established in the UK in 1932 to represent investment trusts to the London financial organizations, government departments (and the Inland Revenue) and, more recently, the European Commission.

Association of Lloyd's Members (ALM) Unofficial voluntary organization of Lloyd's external members, which represents them to the market authorities.

Association of Unit Trusts and Investment Funds (AUTIF) Organization established in 1959, when it was known as the Association of Unit Trust Managers. It is a trade association of 138 financial institutions that deal in unit trusts.

AST Abbreviation of ***Automated Screen Trading***.

ASX Abbreviation of ***Australian Stock Exchange***.

as-you-like option Also termed a call-or-put option, an ***option*** whose form can be changed to another form, at the holder's choice and within a certain time limit.

ATA convention International convention that permits commercial travellers to take samples and so on into a country temporarily without paying duty. They use a temporary admission carnet for this purpose.

at best Instruction to a broker to buy or sell shares or commodities at the best price available.

at call Money at call has been borrowed but must be repaid on demand.

at limit Instruction to a broker to buy or sell shares or commodities with a limit on the upper and lower prices.

at par Equal; indicating a share price equal to the paid-up or nominal value.

ATS Abbreviation of ***automated trade system***.

at short notice Describing money that is borrowed for a very short period of time, say 24 or 48 hours, usually at a low interest rate.

at sight Note on a ***bill of exchange*** that indicates that the payment is due on presentation of the bill.

at-the-money option Call or put option where the price of the security on the market is the same as the ***exercise price***.

Athens Stock Exchange Only stock exchange in Greece, established in 1876, and now converted to electronic trading.

attachment Laying legal claim to the assets of a borrower (or debtor) by the lender (or creditor) because the borrower has failed to make repayments on time.

attorney In the UK, somebody who is legally authorized to act for another (i.e., who holds the power of attorney), or a person practising at the bar. In the USA, however, the term is more often used to denote a lawyer.

at warehouse Describing goods or commodities that are waiting at a warehouse either to be bought or delivered to a customer. A price at warehouse (or ex-warehouse) does not normally include freight charges.

auction Method of selling goods, property or land in public. The auctioneer acts as an agent for the seller, offers the goods and normally sells to the highest bidder (for which service the auctioneer charges a commission). After the item is knocked down, the auctioneer is also an agent of the buyer. An advertisement for an auction is not legally an offer for sale but an invitation to attend.

auctioneer *See* ***auction***.

auction system Order-driven stock exchange system in which brokers and dealers bid for stock using open outcry (or an auction), as on the New York Stock Exchange.

audit Examination of a company's accounts. It is a legal requirement in the UK that the accounts of limited companies over a certain size (and certain other organizations) be scrutinized annually by an independent auditor. This is termed a statutory audit, from which small companies (with a turnover of not more than £90,000 and not more than £1.4 million on the balance sheet) are exempt.

auditor Person appointed by a company or other organization to carry out an ***audit***. In the UK, in order to act as an external auditor he or she must be registered or a member of a recognized supervisory body.

auditors' report Report produced by external auditors appointed to audit a company's accounts, giving an opinion of the financial statements. Under the UK Companies Act 1985, it has to be filed with the accounts at the Registrar of Companies. In the USA, an auditor's report is sometimes called the accountant's report.

audit trail System by means of which each stage of a transaction is formally documented and recorded, so that they can be examined during an audit.

au jour le jour French for ***overnight money***.

Aufgeld German for ***premium***.

Aufsichtsrat German for the supervisory board (of a company).

AUP Abbreviation of ***acceptable use policy***.

Ausgabe German for ***issue***.

Austraclear Australian clearing house that deals with commercial paper.

Australian Securities Commission (ASC) Organization that supervises the trading in securities in Australia.

Australian Stock Exchange (ASX) Organization established in 1987 by the amalgamation of the previous six state stock exchanges in Australia, which in 1990 converted to total electronic trading (using SEATS: Stock Exchange Automated Screen Trading System).

authentication Statement that something is true, such as an auditor's signature on a company's accounts.

AUTIF Abbreviation of ***Association of Unit Trusts and Investment Funds***.

authority Broadly, the given power to act in a certain way. For example, an agent receives authority to act in such a way on behalf of his or her principal.

authorized capital Amount of a company's capital, as stated in its memorandum of association. It is thus the limit of what the company can issue as shares. It is also sometimes called nominal capital.

authorized capital stock Another term for ***authorized capital***.

authorized cheque signatory Director or member of staff who has the authority to sign cheques on behalf of an organization (such as a company or association). Usually the risk of fraud is reduced by requiring two authorized signatures on every cheque.

authorized foreign exchange bank Bank authorized by the Japanese Ministry of Finance to make short-term borrowings or loans in foreign currencies.

authorized share capital Alternative term for ***authorized capital***.

automated clearing house (ACH) Computer system used by the US Customs Service for making electronic transfer of funds (instead of using cheques or cash) for paying duty and taxes on imported goods.

Automated Pit Trading (APT) Computerized trading system that initially supplemented the open outcry market at the London International Financial Futures Exchange (LIFFE). Its main use was after 1620 hours (when the floor market closed) until 1800 hours (when the exchange closed).

Automated Screen Trading (AST) Computerized trading system that can operate 24 hours a day worldwide, now introduced in most of the world's major stock exchanges.

automated trade system (ATS) First automated screen trading system, introduced in 1989 for the New Zealand Futures and Options Exchange.

automatic materials handling (AMH) Computerized system designed to move materials and components from one location to another in a factory or warehouse.

autonomous group working Team of workers within an organization that has a set task delegated to it, and has the power to decide how it does it.

aval Guarantee given by a bank at a customer's request that a ***bill of exchange*** will be paid on presentation.

avant-bourse Swiss for stock exchange.

average *See **arithmetic mean**.*

average due date Date on which several payments due at different times can be paid together, to settle the whole debt.

average rate of return (ARR) Average annual profit (on an investment) expressed as a percentage of the sum invested. It is equal to 100 times the profit per annum divided by the capital outlay.

average rate option Alternative term for ***Asian option***.

averaging Practice of buying more of a share if its price falls below that originally paid for it (thus reducing the average cost per share).

avoirdupois System of weights used in the UK and the USA (such as ounces and pounds), now being replaced by the metric system (such as grams and kilograms). The largest weights in each system are the long ton (avoirdupois: 2240 lb) and the tonne (metric: 1000 kg) which, coincidentally, are almost exactly equivalent.

avoir fiscal French for a tax credit equal to 50% of a dividend, allowed to foreign holders of French securities.

award Decision of an arbitrator (*see* ***arbitration***).

AWB Abbreviation of ***air waybill***.

azione Italian for share.

B

B1 visa Visa required on a non-American's passport in order that he or she may enter the USA to do business.

back door System by which the Bank of England purchases Treasury bills at the market rate, rather than assist discount houses by lending cash to them directly, in order to inject funds into the money market.

backed note Receiving note that authorizes a ship's master to take goods on board. It is endorsed by a shipbroker and is proof that freight will be (or has been) paid.

backfreight Freight for the return of cargo paid by the consignor when goods are not delivered through the consignor's own fault, or are refused by the consignee.

Background Notes Information about the trade and economic status of major trading partners published by the US Department of State.

backhander Informal term for a bribe or unofficial payment for favours or work done.

back-in Poison pill tactic sometimes used by the shareholders of a company threatened by a hostile take-over in which the shareholders sell their holdings back to the company at a price agreed by the board.

backing away Failure of a securities dealer to carry through a deal at the price he or she quoted. It is usually frowned upon in all markets.

back month On financial futures markets, those contracts that are being traded for the month that is farthest in the future.

back office Department of a financial services institution that does the "paper work", i.e., the documentation of transactions carried out by the front office.

backroom Informal term for ***back office***.

back-to-back credit Form of credit by which a finance house acts as an intermediary between a foreign seller and a foreign buyer, concealing the identity of the seller. The seller passes to the finance house the documents relevant to the sale and the house reissues them to the buyer in its own name.

back-to-back loan Loan in one currency matched by another loan in another currency, usually to get round exchange controls or high interest rates.

back to the knitting Colloquial term indicating that a company should return to activities it does best (and not diversify).

back-up credit Guaranteed credit from a bank or banks that backs a note issuer or Euronotes, used when any of the notes do not get purchased.

backwardation In a commodity market, the situation in which the future price is lower than the spot price, because of excessive present demand, which is expected to fall with the passage of time. It is opposite, in commodity terms, to ***contango***. In stock markets, backwardation is the situation in which the highest bid price is higher than the lowest offer price, making it theoretically possible to buy from one market maker and sell to another immediately, at a profit.

backward integration Amalgamation of a company that operates at one stage of production with another that is located farther back in the chain. For example, a manufacturing company amalgamates with a company that provides raw materials.

backward vertical integration Also called upstream vertical integration, situation in which a producer buys out its supplier.

BACS Abbreviation of ***Bankers Automated Clearing House***.

bad debt Debt that has not been, and is not expected to be, paid. Such losses are practically unavoidable in business (and allowances are almost always made for such instances), although some bad debts may be sold to a factoring company, which attempts to recover the debt on its own account. In company accounts, bad debts are written off to the profit and loss account or to a provision for bad and doubtful debts.

badge engineering Use of different brand names to sell identical products (but not necessarily at the same price).

badges of trade Criteria that distinguish between trading and investment. For example, dealings on the commodity market are usually regarded as trade for UK tax purposes, whereas dealings in securities may not be.

bagged cargo Goods loaded in sacks and possibly also onto pallets before being loaded into a container for shipment.

bagging the street Concealment of information about the sale of stock from dealers and specialists by institutional investors or brokers. Such information may include reasons why the stock is being sold off, and the number and price of the shares in question.

bailment Act of placing goods into somebody else's care. The person who places the goods is the bailor and must be the rightful owner. The person who receives the goods is the bailee.

BAK Abbreviation of ***Bundesaufsichtamt für das Kreditwesen***.

balance of payments (BOP) Account of all recorded financial exchanges made between the residents of a country and those of other countries. The balance of payments is divided into the current and capital accounts. The current account takes stock of all visible and invisible trade (the ***balance of trade*** is part of the balance of payments current account), and the capital account includes all movements of capital in or out of the country.

balance of trade (BOT) Also known as the visible balance, the difference in value between a country's visible imports and visible exports. When the value of visible imports total is more than the value of visible exports, it is known as an adverse balance of trade. *See* ***balance of payments***.

balance sheet Statement that shows the financial position of a company in respect of its assets and liabilities at a certain time, often the last day of its accounting period, which must be included in the company's financial accounts. It must also give a true and fair view of the company's affairs. After listing the fixed and current assets, and the liabilities (part 1), the statement indicates how they were financed (part 2). The totals of parts 1 and 2 should be equal – they must balance. The balance sheet should also show the corresponding figures for the previous accounting period. In the USA, a balance sheet is sometimes known as a statement of financial condition or position.

balance ticket Alternative term for ***certification of transfer***.

Baldridge Award Prestigious award that recognizes quality in a USA-based company.

balloon Large, irregular part-payment during the period of a loan, or (in the USA) a large final repayment of a loan.

ballot Although in general terms a ballot is a method of voting by marking a paper, in finance it more specifically refers to a method of allotting shares to applicants in the event of a share issue being oversubscribed. All applicants are entered for a ballot and those drawn at random receive some or all of the shares applied for.

Baltic Exchange One of the oldest centres for chartering freight (by sea or air). Located in London, it has more than 700 members who are concerned with freight handling.

Baltic freight index In the US *Journal of Commerce*, a daily listing of price trends for chartering ships to carry freight.

Baltic International Freight Futures Exchange (BIFFEX) Facility for the purchase and sale of freight futures, transferred to the ***London Futures and Options Exchange*** in 1991.

bancassurance Use of the same distribution channel to sell both banking and insurance products.

bank bill Instruction to a bank to pay somebody a certain sum of money; i.e., a ***bill of exchange*** that a bank has accepted. The term is normally employed in transactions involving foreign currencies. In the USA, the term normally refers to a banknote.

bank draft Alternative term for ***banker's draft***.

banker's acceptance US term for a draft ***bill of exchange*** that is drawn on a bank and accepted by it. It is equivalent to the UK term acceptance.

Bankers Automated Clearing Services Ltd (BACS) Company established in 1986 whose name is based on its previous title, Bankers Automated Clearing House. It processes automated credits, direct debits and standing orders, as well as other types of payments.

banker's draft Also called a bank draft, a cheque drawn on a bank by itself. A banker's draft must be honoured, because it is drawn on the bank itself rather than on the debtor's account. The debtor must pay the bank the sum drawn in advance.

Bank for International Settlements (BIS) International bank that acts as agent and trustee for various international organizations. It is also a clearing house for interbank transactions using European currency. The Bank of England is the agent of BIS in London. BIS was originally established in Basle, Switzerland, for dealing with German war reparations after World War I.

bank holiday Public holiday in the UK, when banks do not open. Payments that fall due on a bank holiday are carried over to the following day, except on Christmas Day and Good Friday, when they become due the day before.

banking covenant Formal agreement between a bank and a company borrowing from it, defining limits within which the company can act (for example, it may put a ceiling on any borrowing from another source).

Banking Directives Directives of the EU that are aimed at streamlining banking practice across European borders. For example, the Second Directive of 1989 allows banks to operate in any country as long as they are authorized in their own. In 1993 this facility was extended to companies dealing in investment products.

Bank Insurance Fund (BIF) Organization that offers insurance to US banks to cover all deposits up to $100,000. It was established in 1933 as the Federal Deposit Insurance Corporation.

Bank of Documentary Credit Insurance (BDCI) Organization that provides guarantees against losses to Canadian banks that finance export business. It is part of the Canadian Export Development Corporation.

Bank of England Central bank of the UK. Founded in 1694, it now has various functions including the supervision of other banks, managing monetary policy, and acting as a banker's bank and lender of the last resort. It also issues banknotes in the UK.

Bank of France Central bank of France. Founded in 1800, it changed composition in 1994 (following the Maastricht Treaty) to give it a higher degree of autonomy in formulating monetary policy.

Bank of Japan Central bank of Japan. It manages monetary policy and acts as lender of last resort; it also issues banknotes. The supervision of other banks, however, is undertaken by the Banking Bureau.

Bank of Scotland Commercial bank in Scotland which, while not a central bank, issues its own banknotes.

bank rate Official rate of interest charged by the central banks as lender of the last resort. The term has fallen out of use in the UK, to be replaced by ***minimum lending rate***.

bankruptcy State of an individual or unincorporated body that is unable to pay debts, as determined by the court. A similar situation involving a limited company is termed ***insolvency***.

banque d'affaires French for ***merchant bank***.

Banque Française du Commerce Exterieur (BFCE) Organization owned by the French government that provides export credits at preferential rates of interest.

Barclaycard Plastic card issued by Barclays Bank that functions as a cash card, cheque card and credit card with a pre-set spending limit. As well as Barclays banks, any bank in the Visa organization will accept the card for over-the-counter cash withdrawals.

bar code Data recorded as a series of wide and narrow lines that can be read instantly using a laser scanner. It is most commonly used for pricing goods for sale and effecting stock control.

Bardepot West German regulation in force until the 1970s that required German borrowers on foreign markets to deposit part of the proceeds at the Bundesbank (where it earned no interest). It was a measure to control a balance of payments surplus.

bareboat charter Type of ship charter in which the hirer pays all expenses during the charter period.

bargain In Stock Exchange jargon, any deal struck that involves the buying and selling of shares.

Bargeld German for cash.

barker card Card placed on a shelf in a retail outlet to advertise a product. It is also known as a shelf-talker.

barrier to entry Set of economic and other conditions that make it difficult to set up a business, i.e. to enter the market.

BARs Abbreviation of ***buy American restrictions***.

base currency Currency that forms the basis of an exchange rate. For example, a foreign currency may be quoted in terms of the pound sterling or the US dollar, which are base currencies.

base date *See* ***base year***.

base period Time period selected as the base for an index number series. The index for a base period is usually 100, and changes in prior or subsequent periods are expressed relative to it.

base year Sometimes known as the base date, the time from which an index (e.g., the *Financial Times* All Share Index) is calculated.

basis point Unit used to measure the rate of change of investment payments for bonds or notes. Each basis point is equal to 0.01 per cent.

basket of currencies Group of currencies against which the value of some other currency is measured.

Basle Concordat Also known as the Basle Statement, an agreement made in 1975 (revised 1983) that acts as a basis of cooperation between the central banks of the EU.

BBA Abbreviation of ***British Bankers Association***.

BDCI Abbreviation of ***Bank of Documentary Credit Insurance***.

bear Stock exchange dealer or analyst who believes that prices or investment values will go down.

bear closing Situation that occurs when a dealer has sold shares or commodities he or she does not yet own and then buys them back, at a lower price, thus making a profit.

bearer Somebody who holds a bill, cheque or certificate.

bearer bill Also called a bearer note, a bill of exchange, cheque or other negotiable instrument that is payable to the bearer (or is endorsed in blank).

bearer bond Bond that is payable to the bearer, rather than to a specific, named person.

bearer note *See* ***bearer bill***.

bearer securities Securities that are payable to the bearer and are thus easily transferable.

bearer scrip Temporary document that acknowledges acceptance of an offer form and cheque for a new issue, exchanged for a bearer bond when the bond is available (or when all instalments have been paid).

bearer stocks Like bearer bonds, securities that are payable to the bearer, not to a named holder.

bear hug In corporate finance, an informal term for notice given to the board of a target company that a take-over bid is imminent.

bear market Condition in which share prices are falling.

bear position Position of an investor whose sales exceed his or her purchases, and who therefore stands to gain in a falling or bear market.

bear raid Vigorous selling in concert in order to force down the price of a particular commodity or share.

bear squeeze Situation in which bears who have been selling short are faced with a price rise rather than a fall.

bed-and-breakfast deal Transaction used to minimize the impact of capital gains tax. A shareholder sells his or her holding after trading closes for the day, for tax purposes. Next morning, the shareholder buys back his or her holding. The US term for a bed-and-breakfast deal is swap.

bells and whistles Extras added to a financial product to make it more attractive. Options are a typical incentive.

below par Describing a share price that has fallen below the nominal value at which the share was issued.

below-the-line Describing items, included in a company's accounts, that refer to the distribution of profits. For example, dividends are included in below-the-line accounts.

below the market Describing a price that is lower than the usual market price.

beneficial owner When a shareholding is held by a nominee such as a stockbroker, the nominee's name appears on the register of shareholders. The real owner is known as the beneficial owner.

BES Abbreviation of ***Business Expansion Scheme***.

Besloten Vennootschap (BV) Dutch equivalent of a private limited company (Ltd).

best execution rule Requirement that a stockbroker must obtain the lowest available price when buying securities for a client and the highest possible price when selling.

best price Order to buy or sell something at the best price available at the time.

beta Describing a second-line share, as opposed to the less numerous highly capitalized ***alpha*** (first-line) or more numerous gamma (third-line) shares.

beta factor Also called the beta coefficient, a measurement of the volatility of a company's shares, i.e. how sensitive the stock is to market fluctuations. The beta is denoted in figures, e.g. 1.5, which means that the share price will rise by 15% in a market that has risen 10%. Shares that underperform are rated below 1.

bet the ranch To take a substantial risk in a stock exchange dealing or other financial transaction.

BFCE Abbreviation of ***Banque Française du Commerce Exterieur***.

bid Offer to buy something (e.g. shares) at a certain price. A seller may make a certain offer and a prospective buyer may make a bid. The bid cancels out the offer. More specifically, a bid is an offer by one company to buy the shares of another; a take-over bid.

bidding ring Group of stock market or antique dealers who act in concert to drive prices up or down. The practice is illegal.

bid-offer spread Difference between the bid price and the offer price offered by a market-maker.

bid price Price a market-maker is prepared to pay to buy securities.

bid rate Rate of interest offered for deposits. It is also short for London Offer Bid Rate.

BIDS Abbreviation of ***British Institute of Dealers in Securities***.

BIF Abbreviation of ***Bank Insurance Fund***.

BIFFEX Abbreviation of ***Baltic International Freight Futures Exchange***.

Big Bang Popular term for the deregulation of the London Stock Exchange on 27 October 1986. Among the changes implemented were the admission of foreign institutions as members of the exchange, the abandonment of rigid distinctions between stockbrokers, jobbers and bankers, and the abolition of fixed commissions.

bigger fool theory Justification for buying shares that are overpriced, which assumes that there is always a bigger fool somewhere in the market who will buy them from you at an even higher price.

BIIBA Abbreviation of ***British Insurance and Investment Brokers Association***.

bill Term with four possible meanings:

1. It is a list of charges to be paid for goods or services. In this sense the usual US term is check.
2. It is a document, isued by a bank, promising to pay somebody a certain amount of money. It is in this sense that the US meaning of the term is banknote.
3. It is a document describing goods, most often used in dealings with customs.
4. It is short for ***bill of exchange***.

bill broker Person or company that buys or sells bills of exchange, either on their own account or as an intermediary.

bill of exchange Document that indicates that one party (the drawee) agrees to pay a certain sum of money on demand or on a specified date to another party (the drawer). Two familiar bills of exchange are cheques and banknotes.

bill of imprest Order that entitles its bearer to have money paid in advance.

bill of lading Document that details the transfer of goods from a (foreign) supplier to a buyer. It may be used as a document of title.

bill of sale Document that certifies the transfer of goods (but not real estate) to another person. Goods transferred in this way may not become the property of the receiving party but may be redeemed when the bill is paid.

bill of sight Document that is passed to a customs inspector by an importer who is unable to describe imported goods in detail. When the goods are landed, a full description must be given, known as perfecting the sight.

bill rate Rate at which a ***bill of exchange*** is discounted.

bills in a set Foreign bills of exchange are normally made out in triplicate and sent to the drawee separately to prevent loss. These copies are known as bills in a set.

BIMBO Abbreviation of buy-in management buy-out, a type of management buy-out that involves also ***venture capital*** from outside.

BIS Abbreviation of ***Bank for International Settlements***.

black To forbid or boycott trade in certain goods or with certain trading partners.

black book Company's pre-planned strategy to be put into action in the event of a hostile take-over bid.

black economy Illegal economic activity conducted largely for cash by companies and people who pay no taxes on the proceeds.

blacklist List of companies, products or people that are undesirable and to be avoided. In the USA the term means more specifically the denial of work to certain people on the grounds of their past beliefs or actions.

black market Illegal market that usually deals in scarce or stolen goods.

Such markets frequently come into existence in wartime because the goods concerned are rationed or in very short supply, or because the market is exceptionally high – in which case counterfeit or imitation goods often appear. Trading is often in kind, one valued commodity being exchanged for another. *See also* ***grey market***.

blank bill ***Bill of exchange*** on which the payee is not specified.

blank transfer In the transfer of shares, a transfer form that is left blank as regards the name of the transferee. For example, if shares are to be put up as security to a mortgage, the transfer form will be left blank, because the mortgagor has the right to complete the transfer form and sell the shares if the mortgagee defaults.

blocked currency Currency that may not be removed from a country, sometimes for political reasons.

blue chip Describing an investment that is regarded as extremely safe, without being gilt-edged. It also describes a company whose shares are regarded as an extremely safe investment.

board of directors Decision-making group consisting of all the directors of a company, who are legally responsible for their actions. The board of directors is specifically charged with the management of the company, and in the case of a public limited company (plc) is elected by the shareholders at the company's annual general meeting (AGM). In the USA, the board of directors draws up company policy and appoints executives to run the company. It is sometimes known simply as "the board".

Board of Inland Revenue *See* ***Inland Revenue***.

Board of Trade UK committee whose main responsibilities included commercial relations with other countries, supervision of shipping, publication of statistics about UK industry, and acting as a go-between for the government with UK industry. In 1972 it was incorporated into the new ***Department of Trade and Industry (DTI)***.

boiler room Little-known firm of brokers or dealers that sells securities over the telephone.

bolsa Spanish for ***stock exchange***.

Bolsa de Valores de Lisbon Lisbon Stock Exchange.

Bolsa Mexicana de Valores Mexican Stock Exchange.

Bombay Stock Exchange India's oldest stock exchange which, along with others, is regulated by the Securities and Exchange Board of India.

bona fide Latin for in good faith. It usually appears in reference to contracts, especially contracts of insurance. The term is also used simply to mean honest or trustworthy.

bona vacantia Describing goods with no obvious owner or claimant, such as the estate of somebody who dies without making a will. Another example is property that remains in the hands of a liquidator after the creditors have been paid. In law it belongs to the Crown.

bond Term with three meanings:

1. It is a security issued at a fixed rate by central government, local authorities or occasionally by private companies. It is essentially a contract to repay money borrowed, and as such represents a debt. Normally, bonds are issued in series with the same denominations and conditions of repayment. It is also known as a fixed-interest security.
2. It refers to the importing of goods from abroad. If dutiable goods are imported and duty is not paid immediately, the goods are placed in a bonded warehouse (i.e. they are held in bond) until all customs formalities are concluded.
3. It is a from tie or agreement between individuals. "My word is my bond" is the motto of the London Stock Exchange.

bonded goods *See* ***bond*** *(2)*.

bonded stores Stores to be used on board ship and held in bond (with no duty paid on them).

bonded warehouse Warehouse for goods on which no excise duty need be paid until the goods are removed. *See* ***bond*** *(2)*.

bond note Document that indicates that imported goods held in bond may be released, because all import formalities have been completed.

bon du trésor French for ***Treasury bill*** or ***bond***.

bond washing Practice of buying bonds ***cum dividend*** and selling them ***ex dividend*** (dividend stripping), to reduce the rate of tax payable on the transaction. The dividend on the bond becomes a capital gain, on which a lower rate of tax is payable than if tax were paid on the proceeds as dividend income. Because of changes in the tax laws in the UK, there is no longer scope for this kind of manoeuvring, although it still happens in the USA.

bonus Additional payment, usually applied to a premium paid in addition to normal salary or wages.

bonus dividend Unexpected extra dividend paid to a shareholder.

bonus issue Issue of shares made by a company wishing to reduce the average price of its shares. Shareholders receive a number of extra shares in proportion to the number they already hold. It is also known as a capitalization issue.

booking centre US term for a financial organization with headquarters overseas. Transactions recorded there can take advantage of any lower tax rates.

book-keeping Practice of keeping records of financial transactions, and analysing them if required. It may be done manually or with the aid of a computer program.

book runner Bank or other financial institution that is responsible for the documentation and management of an issue of a security or syndicated loan.

books of account Company's books in which business transactions are recorded, often consisting of journals, ledgers and various other records of accounts. They are normally held to be legal documents and should indicate the financial position of the business at any time.

book value Also called written-down value, the value shown in a company's books for an asset or liability (or owner's equity), taking due account of any depreciation. Of a company as a whole, it is the amount by which total assets exceed total liabilities (i.e., the net assets).

boom Popular term for a period when employment, prices and general business activity are at a high level and resources are being used to the full.

bootstrap Term used mostly in the USA where take-over activity is more common, to describe a cash offer for a controlling interest in a company which, if accepted, is followed by another offer (usually at a lower price) for the remainder of the shares.

BOP Abbreviation of ***balance of payments***.

borrowed capital Capital in the form of a loan that is used to finance a business, on which interest has to be paid. It is also called debt capital or loan capital.

borrowing Most widely used in the sense of accepting money that is not one's own on the understanding that it will be repaid, usually with interest, at a later date. On the London Metal Exchange borrowing is the process of buying a metals contract due to be completed on a near date, and at the same time selling forward a contract for a date farther in the future.

borsa Italian for ***stock exchange***.

Borsa Valori Milan's main stock exchange.

Börse German for ***stock exchange***. The largest German exchange is in Frankfurt (see ***London Stock Exchange***). Borse is also a general term for stock exchange in many European countries.

Börsenvorstand Body that supervises the German stock exchange.

BOT Abbreviation of ***balance of trade***.

BOTB Abbreviation of ***British Overseas Trade Board***.

bottleneck Hold-up of anything from traffic or a factory's production line to the whole of a nation's economy. Most can be blamed on bad planning.

bottom fishing Practice of buying shares in a falling market in the expectation that the market will improve and the shares can be sold at a profit.

bottoming out Informal term for a very sudden and serious fall in market prices.

bottom line Last line of an account, showing either a profit or a loss. From this sense it has come into general usage to mean the "brutal truth".

bottomry bond Bond used to raise money by the master of a ship, who uses the ship and its cargo as security.

bought deal Acquisition of a subsidiary (using ***venture capital***) from a larger company with the intention of subjecting it to a management buy-out or other method of syndication.

bounty In a modern business context, a government subsidy given to aid particular industries. It make take the form of tax concessions or a cash handout.

bourse French for ***stock exchange***. The term is also used in Belgium and Switzerland, and in other European countries. *See also* ***Paris Bourse***.

boutique Fairly new type of financial services company that operates in much the same way as a High Street shop, into which customers may walk to seek investment advice and services. It is also known as a financial supermarket.

box spread Complex mixture of options consisting of a long-call option with a short-put option at the same exercise price and a short-call option with a long-put option, also at the same exercise price.

BRAD Abbreviation of ***British Rate and Data***.

Brady bonds Dollar-denominated, interest-bearing securities issued, in order to reschedule international debt, by Argentina, Venezuela and other South American countries in the 1990s. Collateral security was provided by interest-free US government securities. They were named after US Treasury Secretary Nicholas Brady, who devised them.

branded goods Goods packaged by the manufacturer with the brand name conspicuously displayed. They may often be sold at a higher price than others because of the selling power of the name.

branding Establishing an identity for a product that sets it apart from those of competitors.

brand leader Brand of a certain type of goods that has the largest share of the market. A brand leader may often be seen as a company's most valuable asset.

brand loyalty Marketing concept by which customers continually purchase certain goods which they identify by brand name (and associate with quality and value for money).

brand value Monetary value assigned to a company's brand name, classified as an intangible asset.

breach of contract Failure of one party to a contract to act according to its terms, for which the other party may sue.

breach of warranty of authority Action of an agent who exceeds his or her authority and is thereby liable (and not the principal).

break Sudden and substantial drop in prices after a slow steady rise.

break bulk Action of splitting a large shipment into smaller tranches for delivery to separate customers.

breakeven chart Graph on which combined fixed and variable costs are plotted against a range of activity and on which sales revenue is also plotted. The two curves intersect at the ***breakeven point***.

breakeven point Volume of production or sales at which total costs and total revenue are equal. It may be expressed (in terms of units) as fixed costs divided by the contribution per unit, or (in terms of sales) as selling price per unit times fixed costs, divided by the contribution per unit. *See also* ***breakeven chart***.

break-forward On the money market, a combination of a currency option contract and a forward-exchange contract, which can be broken at a pre-set fixed rate of exchange if exchange rates move in favour of the investor.

breakout What happens when a share or commodity price breaks a previously fixed, or at least stable, pattern.

break-up value Of an asset, its value assuming the company holding it will cease trading and that the asset will have to be sold in a hurry (perhaps following a successful take-over of the company).

Bretton Woods Agreement International agreement between the USA, Canada and the UK formulated at a conference held at Bretton Woods, New Hampshire, in 1944. It defined a new system of international monetary control that resulted in the setting up of the International Monetary Fund (IMF) and the International Bank for Reconstruction and Development (World Bank).

bribe Illicit payment made by one person (or organization) to another in order to gain rights or privileges that the recipient would not normally be entitled to. Offering or accepting a bribe is often a criminal offence.

bricks and mortar Informal name for the fixed assets of a company.

British Bankers Association (BBA) Organization established in 1919 by British banks with business in the UK and by members of the British Overseas Banks Association. In 1972 membership was extended to include foreign banks trading in the UK.

British Export Houses Association Organization formed by export houses in the UK for the provision of free advice to exporters seeking such services.

British Institute of Dealers in Securities (BIDS) Former trade association of companies that deal in over-the-counter securities.

British Institute of Management Organization established in 1964 to represent all the various kinds of managers, promote training courses and publish information.

British Insurance and Investment Brokers Association (BIIBA) Organization established in 1977 to represent registered insurance brokers and investment intermediaries, promote training and offer advice.

British Overseas Trade Board (BOTB) Organization that promotes UK exports and advises exporters on the complexities of overseas marketing. It is sponsored by the government and its head is the Secretary of State for Trade and Industry.

British Productivity Council Organization established in 1952 to represent managers and workers and stimulate better productivity throughout industry.

British Rate and Data (BRAD) Monthly publication that details advertising media and their costs.

British Standards Institute (BSI) Organization that sets standards of quality, safety and performance for a wide range of products.

British Venture Capital Association (BVCA) Trade association of companies that deal in ***venture capital***.

broadside Informal term for a publicity leaflet or handout.

broken stowage Cargo space that cannot be used because crates or cartons of various shapes and sizes cannot be packed closely together.

broker Broadly, an intermediary between a buyer and a seller, a mercantile agent. There are several forms of broker, the job title referring to what it is that a particular broker deals in; e.g. a stockbroker deals in stocks and shares. Most brokers' earnings take the form of commission. In the USA, a broker is more often known as a brokerage house.

brokerage Payment made to a broker for services rendered, also known as a broker's commission.

brokerage account US term for a stockbroker's record of an individual client's sales and purchases of securities.

brown goods Collective term for electrical household goods originally designed in wooden cabinets (such as radios and television sets). In North America the term often refers to durable goods of any sort.

Brussels Stock Exchange Centre of trading in local shares in Belgium (since the closure of the Antwerp Stock Exchange in 1997).

BSI Abbreviation of ***British Standards Institute***.

bubble Industry or trend with no substance to it. A bubble usually bursts with more-or-less disastrous consequences for those involved. Probably the most famous bubble was the South Sea Bubble, which burst in 1720.

bubble company Company formed with no real business to undertake. Some bubble companies have been set up for fraudulent purposes.

bucket shop Popular term for brokers of stocks, shares and commodities who are not recognized members of any exchange.

budget Plan that details expected future income and outgoings from an activity, normally over the span of a year. It is often referred to in controlling the activity. A budget is also the sum of money set aside for a given activity or project.

budgetary control Management of the activities of an organization with reference to an approved budget (so that spending is not allowed to exceed the budgeted amount).

budget deficit Budgetary imbalance, caused by excess of expenditure over revenue. In the case of the British government budgets, the deficit is generally funded by the authorization of an increase in the ***national debt***.

budget surplus Situation that arises when a government's revenue is larger than its expenditure.

buffer stock On the commodities markets, buffer stocks are held for release at certain strategic times in order to stabilize prices and markets.

building and loan association US organization roughly equivalent to a building society in the UK. It is also known as a savings and loan association.

building society Financial institution in the UK that accepts deposits, on which it pays interest, and lends money, originally only in the form of a mortgage to enable people to purchase property. Many building societies now issue cheque books and plastic cards, and so operate in much the same way as a bank.

built-in obsolescence Practice of manufacturers who design a product so that it needs to be replaced by the consumer in a relatively short time, resulting from either fast deterioration or changes in fashion.

bulk buying Purchasing in sufficient quantities to obtain a discount on the normal retail price (although capital is thereby locked up in stock that has to be held for a comparatively long time).

bulk cargo Cargo that is not bagged or crated (termed unbound cargo) before being carried aboard ship. It can be measured only in terms of volume or weight.

bulk-decreasing good Good that gets smaller (in terms of size and/or weight) while it is being manufactured, such as glass or metals.

bulk-increasing good Good that gets larger (in terms of size and/or weight) while it is being manufactured, such as furniture or soft drinks.

bull Stock exchange dealer or analyst who believes that prices or investment values will increase. On this conviction, the dealer buys now and profits later by selling at a higher price.

bulldog bond Sterling-denominated security issued by a foreign government for sale on the UK market.

bullet Final payment of a loan usually consisting of the whole principal (previous payments being of interest only). Or it is a security that pays a guaranteed (fixed) interest at a specific date.

bullion Bars or ingots of a precious metal (such as gold or silver), as opposed to coins.

bull market Situation in which share prices are rising.

bull position Position of an investor whose purchases exceed his or her sales, and therefore stands to gain in a rising, or bull, market.

Bundesaufsichtamt für das Kreditwesen (BAK) Federal Supervisory Office for Credit in Germany, which regulates banking and fund investments (such as unit trusts).

Bundesbank Full name Deutsche Bundesbank, the central bank of Germany, with headquarters in Frankfurt. It was established in 1957, when it replaced the Bank Deutscher Länder, founded in 1948.

bundling Practice of providing more than one product or service at once at an inclusive price (such as software with a computer or life assurance with a loan).

bunny bond Bond that has the option of yielding either interest or additional bonds instead of interest.

buoy dues Dues claimed by Trinity House from shipowners when using ports where there are buoys.

burden of debt When a debt is passed on to successive generations, the burden of debt is the interest payments on the accumulated debt.

bureau de change Office at which currencies may be exchanged on payment of a commission. Some bureaux offer additional services, such as the encashment of personal cheques.

burn rate When a company starts trading using ***venture capital***, the rate at which the company consumes capital in financing fixed overheads.

business cycle Fairly regular swings in economic activity (demand and output) that tend to repeat every few years.

business development loan UK government loan made for buying fixed assets such as plant and premises, usually over a five-year term.

business entity concept Idea that the activities of a business entity, and not of its owners, are the subject of financial accounting and reporting.

business environment Factors outside a company's control that nevertheless affect its performance. Such factors range from government policy to the activities of pressure groups.

Business Expansion Scheme (BES) Scheme introduced by the UK government in 1981 to help smaller unquoted companies to expand (by providing the means to raise the necessary capital) and to encourage investment in such companies (by providing incentives such as tax relief). In 1995 it was replaced by the similar ***Enterprise Investment Scheme***.

business objectives Targets set by a company's senior management that affect the running and decision making throughout the company.

business plan For a business that is just starting up, a document that gives details of costings, cash flows and marketing policy.

business school UK college of further education that offers qualifications (up to a masters degree) in various aspects of business management.

busted bond Bond whose issuer has defaulted on the loan raised to finance the issue. Valueless except as collectors' items, busted bonds are also called old bonds.

butterfly Complex type of option dealing in which two identical options are bought and sold at the same time as two others, one with a lower exercise price and one with a higher exercise price (all with the same expiry date).

buy American restrictions (BARs) Various restrictions on US companies purchasing foreign goods and services, arising from the Buy American Acts of 1933 and 1988.

buy-back A company that is originally financed by ***venture capital*** may pay back the capital invested either by seeking a quotation or by being taken over. In either case, it will be buying itself back from the venture capitalist.

buyer credit System in which a seller makes a cash contract with an overseas buyer, who pays up to 20% of the price and funds the rest through a long-term loan with a UK bank. The repayment of the loan to the bank is guaranteed by the ***Export Credits Guarantee Department (ECGD)***.

buyer's market Market in which there are too many sellers and not enough buyers, so that buyers are in a position to influence prices or conditions of purchase.

buyers over On the Stock Exchange, a condition in which there are more buyers than sellers. The opposite is sellers over.

buy forward To buy shares, commodities, and so on for delivery at a later date. In essence, buying forward is a gamble on the current price, i.e. that it will rise in the future and the buyer will then be able to sell at a profit.

buy-in Refers to a situation in which a seller of shares and so on fails to deliver on the agreed date, which sometimes happens if the seller is selling short. In this case the buyer is entitled to buy shares from another source and to charge the seller with any expenses incurred. This process is known as buying in. The term is also used for the purchase of more than 50% of a company's shares, in order to gain financial and managerial control.

buy on close Describing the practice of buying contracts on a financial futures market at a price within the closing range.

buy on opening Describing the practice of buying contracts on a financial futures market at a price within the opening range.

buyout Purchase of a major holding of a company's shares by its existing management.

buy side Informal term for the institutional investors on the New York Stock Exchange.

BV Abbreviation of ***Besloten Vennootschap***.

BVCA Abbreviation of ***British Venture Capital Association***.

by-product Secondary product from a process which, although not the main purpose of the operation, is capable of yielding revenue.

C

cabotage Term with three meanings:

1. Law that restricts coastal traffic to vessels of the country that owns the coast.
2. Permission for an air transport company to operate in a country other than the one in which it is registered.
3. Exclusive right of an air transport company to operate all routes within its own country.

CAC Abbreviation of ***Compagnie des Agents de Change***.

CACM Abbreviation of ***Central American Common Market***.

CAD Abbreviation of ***cash against documents***.

Cadbury Report A report published in the UK in 1992 by a committee chaired by Sir Adrian Cadbury. The committee was established by the ***Financial Reporting Council***, the Stock Exchange and the accountancy profession. The report recommended that the accounts of a company should contain a statement to the effect that the company's directors had or had not complied with a code of practice regarding the appointment of non-executive directors.

Cairns Group Non-official organization established in 1986 (at Cairns, Australia), consisting of agricultural exporting countries (mainly from eastern Asia, Australasia, Oceania and South America). They seek to reduce subsidies and take other measures of support for agriculture.

calendar spread Simultaneous sale and purchase (or vice versa) of an option at the same striking price but for different dates.

call Act of demanding payment for stocks or shares, or repayment of a debt. A lender may advance money on condition that it is repayable on call (i.e. without notice).

callable bond Bond that may be called for payment before its maturity date.

called-up share capital Face value of a company's shares that the shareholders have actually paid for.

call money Type of loan made by a bank, which must be repaid on demand. It is also known as money at call.

call option Option to buy shares, commodities or financial futures at an agreed price on or before a future agreed date.

call-or-put option Alternative term for ***as-you-like option***.

call-over Method of trading on a stock exchange whereby the securities listed are called out in order, and dealers make bids or offers for each security according to their instructions.

call-over price Price for a security verbally agreed at ***call-over***.

Calvo doctrine Legal principle, originating in Latin America, that in an international dispute over investments, jurisdiction lies in the investment's country of location (i.e. with the local courts).

Canada-US Free Trade Agreement 1989 Agreement between the USA and Canada designed to ensure the unimpeded flow of goods and services between the two countries.

Canadian International Trade Tribunal Government agency of Canada that is concerned with imports and duties on them.

cancellation Voiding of an agreement, either in due course (such as the discharge of a bill of exchange) or by defacement or mutilation of the document.

C & F Abbreviation of ***cost and freight***.

cannibalization Effect that the launch of a new product may have on sales of the existing brands of a company

cap Upper limit on a charge, such as an interest rate (which cannot then not rise above the limit despite financial trends that are adverse to the lender).

CAP Abbreviation of ***Code of Advertising Practice*** and ***Common Agricultural Policy***.

capacity Measure of the ability of a company to produce goods or provide services. For a manufacturing business it is the amount produced in unit time, which may be expressed in direct labour hours, machine hours or standard hours.

capacity utilization Extent to which a company uses its maximum capacity, expressed as a percentage and equal to 100 times the actual output in a given period divided by the full output capacity during the same period.

capital Imprecise term that, unqualified, generally refers to the resources of an organization or person (such as cash, equipment or skills), as contributed by the owners (i.e. the owners' equity). More precisely it is the total value of assets less liabilities.

capital account Part of the ***balance of payments***, which refers to international movements of capital, including government loans.

capital adequacy Legal requirement that a financial institution should have enough capital to meet all its obligations and fund the services it offers.

capital allowance Amount deducted from a company's profits before tax is calculated, to take into account depreciation of capital assets (such as vehicles, plant and machinery, and industrial buildings).

capital asset pricing model (CAPM) Method of weighing risk and return to achieve the best equity value of a company in planning its financial policy.

capital assets Another term for ***fixed assets***.

capital budget Budget detailing proposed outgoings to obtain long-term assets, i.e. a company's capital expenditure. It involves longer timescales than a cash budget. It is also known as a capital expenditure budget or capital investment budget.

capital clause In the memorandum of association of a company, the section that sets out details of the company's capital.

capital commitments Company expenditure committed to (under contract) but not paid by the date of the annual balance sheet.

capital costs Expenditure on capital goods, for example ***fixed assets*** such as plant, or on ***trade investments*** and ***current assets***. Capital costs are classed as below the line for accounting purposes. They are also known as capital expenditure, capital investment, investment costs or investment expenditure.

capital duty Former tax paid by UK companies on profits from new share issues. It ceased to be levied in 1988.

capital employed Capital that a company uses to finance its assets. It is taken to be the sum of the shareholders' funds, loans and deferred taxation.

capital expenditure Alternative term for ***capital costs***.

capital flight Also called flight capital, capital removed from a country that seems to be politically (or economically) unstable, and taken to a more stable environment.

capital gain Gain made from a capital transaction, such as the buying and selling of assets. It is the amount by which the proceeds exceed the cost.

capital gains tax (CGT) Tax paid on ***capital gains***. In the UK the rate of tax, which was introduced on 6 April 1965, depends on when the asset was acquired (before or after 31 March 1982 or after 6 April 1988). Rates of tax vary between 10% and 40%, depending on other income. Under US tax laws, a lower rate of capital gains tax is levied if the asset had been held for more than nine months before resale.

capital gearing Also called leverage, especially in the USA, the relationship between a company's funds derived from ordinary shares and long-term, fixed-interest rate funds such as preference shares and debentures. It is the ratio of the company's debts to total capital or shareholders' funds. High gearing, i.e. a high proportion of debt, generally represents a speculative investment.

capital goods Goods (such as machines) that are used for the production of other goods. Ships are sometimes regarded as capital goods.

capital growth Increase in the value of an investment over a period of time.

capital-intensive Describing a business in which capital is the most important and costly factor of production. Thus, an industry in which the major cost is the purchase and maintenance of machinery (fixed assets) is capital-intensive. *See also* ***capital/labour ratio***.

capitalization Conversion of a company's reserves into share capital by issuing more shares (a scrip issue); or the total amount of capital available to a company in the long term; or the process of providing such capital.

capitalization issue Alternative term for ***bonus issue***, also called a scrip issue.

capital/labour ratio Capital required to produce a good divided by the cost of labour involved. A capital-intensive product has a high capital/labour ratio.

capital levy Wealth tax; an additional tax on a person's accumulated assets.

capital loss A negative ***capital gain***, also called allowable capital loss.

capital market Market made up of the various sources of capital for (medium- or long-term) investment in new and already existing companies. In the UK it is centred on the ***London Stock Exchange*** and the ***Alternative Investment Market (AIM)***.

capital outlay Expenditure on fixed assets (such as machinery).

capital profit Capital generated by selling capital goods (fixed assets), rather than by trading.

capital ratio Bank's capital and reserves divided by its total assets, which generally has to be kept below a certain figure.

capital rationing Situation in which a company has to chose between equally attractive projects because it cannot finance all of them.

capital redemption reserve Reserve created by a company's buying its own shares with a resulting lowering of share capital and maintenance of the capital base.

capital reserve Profits from a company's trading that are set aside as part of its capital and so may not be repaid to shareholders until the company is wound up.

capital risk In a lending situation, the risk that the investment's capital amount may be less than its par value (even when it matures).

capital saturation Situation in a company or industry in which there is such a large capital/labour ratio that any increase in capital would have no significant positive effect on output.

capital structure Make-up of a company's borrowings in terms of the proportions of owners' equity, short-term debt and long-term debt. The complete financial structure includes also its assets and any other liabilities.

capital stock Value of all capital goods owned by a company (or an industry or even a nation), after ***depreciation*** has been taken into account.

CAPM Abbreviation of ***capital asset pricing model***.

capped floating rate note ***Floating rate note*** whose coupon has a pre-agreed maximum value.

captive Describing an investment services business that is owned by a financial institution that provides related servies (such as a car sales outlet that offers credit facilities being owned by a finance house).

captive fund Fund for ***venture capital*** held by a large financial services group.

captive market Market for goods or services that has no alternative source of supply (because it is served by a single company, in a monopoly position).

CAR Abbreviation of ***compound annual return***.

carat Unit for measuring the purity of gold. Pure gold is 24 carats; 18-carat gold is 18/24 gold and 6/24 another metal (such as copper or silver). Another carat is also a unit of mass for gemstones, equal to 200 milligrams.

cargo carrier Freight company; any transporter of cargo by land, sea or air.

Caribbean Common Market (CARICOM) Organization established in 1973, with headquarters in Georgetown, Guyana, by 13 English-speaking Caribbean countries for purposes of mutual trade.

Caribbean Free Trade Association (CARIFTA) Organization that set up a free trade area in the Caribbean, superseded in 1973 by the ***Caribbean Common Market (CARICOM)***.

CARICOM Abbreviation of ***Caribbean Common Market***.

CARIFTA Abbreviation of ***Caribbean Free Trade Association***.

carnet Internationally valid document that allows the passage of dutiable goods without duty having to be paid until the goods reach their destination.

carriage and insurance paid (CIP) Term indicating that carriage and insurance has been paid on transported goods to a named destination. For goods shipped by sea, the equivalent expression is cost, insurance and freight (CIF).

carriage paid to (CPT) Term indicating that carriage has been paid on transported goods to a named destination. For goods shipped by sea, the equivalent expression is cost and freight (C & F).

carrier Company whose business is to carry freight, often delivering directly to a customer's home. In the USA, the term also describes an exporter that allows another company's (non-competing) goods to be exported along with its own.

carry Money borrowed or lent in order to finance trading in ***futures***. The process of borrowing and lending in this way is known as carrying.

carrying market Commodity market that can accept a (durable) commodity in one month, store it, and then deliver it in a later month.

carry over To postpone payment on a bargain traded on a stock exchange from one settlement day to the next.

carry-over day First day of each (two-weekly) new ***account*** on the ***London Stock Exchange***, so-called because people who cannot pay for shares ordered from a stockbroker ask for payment to be carried over into the next accounting period.

cartel Group of companies that come together to monopolize a market, agreeing between them which company presides over which area of operation. Cartels are illegal in the UK and USA.

cascade tax Tax imposed at each stage of production. For example, a product may pass from one country to the next as each stage of production is carried out, and would thus attract several taxation stages, and the price of the finished product would therefore be higher than if it has been produced in one country.

case of need Particular type of endorsement made on a ***bill of exchange***. It is followed by the name of the person or company to whom the holder of the bill may apply in the event that it is not paid.

cash Ready money (legal tender such as coins and notes), or to convert something (such as a cheque) into ready money.

cash against documents (CAD) Method of payment for goods for export, whereby the documentation for a shipment is sent to an agent or bank at the destination. These are passed to the consignee, who makes the payment. The consignee is free to take delivery of the shipment when it arrives. Cash against documents is a process of payment that is also used by large UK investment houses.

cash and carry Popular term for a wholesale warehouse, from which retailers buy their goods and transport them away. More and more frequently, cash and carries are used by members of the general public.

cash and new On a stock exchange, a method of postponing payment on a bargain until the next settlement day. The investor begins with a bargain for which he or she would like to postpone payment. Towards the end of the account (period), a deal is made that is opposite to the first (i.e. the investor either buys or sells a similar instrument). The original position is then restored by yet another purchase or sale, to be settled on the next settlement day. In effect, the investor negates the original position and then returns to it in the next account.

cash budget Forward plan of expected day-to-day income and expenditure. It is generally calculated monthly, and is also known as cash-flow budget, cash-flow forecast, cash-flow projection or financial budget.

cash cow Product or aspect of business that continues to provide a healthy revenue after its initial launch, with relatively little extra investment.

cash deal Arrangement or transaction concluded with a cash payment. On the stock exchange, it is a deal to be completed on the next trading day.

cash dealing Stock exchange deals that must be settled on the following settlement day. Such bargains are said to be for cash settlement rather than account settlement.

cash discount Reduction in the price of goods or services in return for (prompt) payment in cash. Discounts allowed in this way are classified as expenditure. To the receiver of the discounts, they are regarded as revenue.

cash dividend Dividend paid in cash (rather than in shares).

cash flow Movement of money through a company from when it is received as income (or borrowing), to the time it leaves the company as payments (for example, for raw material, wages, and so on). A negative cash flow occurs when there is too little money coming in to pay for all the outgoings. Conversely, a positive cash flow occurs when a company receives income before it is due to pay outgoings.

cash-flow forecast Alternative name for ***cash budget***.

cash in advance (CIA) Method of payment in which the purchaser pays for goods or services before delivery.

cash on delivery (COD) Distribution system whereby the person in receipt of goods makes payment for them on the spot to the deliverer. Such a system is operated by the UK Post Office, where it is the postman or woman who takes receipt of payment.

cash position State of the finances of a person or business at a given time, particularly whether there are funds available (cash positive) or unavailable (cash negative).

cash price Price at which goods may be bought using cash (for which a discount may be given). It is usually different from, for example, the credit sale or hire purchase price, which usually includes interest.

cash with order (CWO) Terms of an agreement by which goods are supplied only if payment is made in cash at the time the order is placed.

CAT Abbreviation of ***computer-assisted trading***.

CATS Abbreviation of ***Certificate of Accrual on Treasury Securities***, a form of zero-coupon bond.

caveat emptor Latin for "buyer beware". In legal terms this maxim means that a buyer of goods should use his or her own common sense, and that the law is not prepared to aid someone who buys goods foolishly.

caveat subscriptor Latin for "signer beware", meaning that anyone who signs a document is bound by its contents, regardless of whether or not he or she has read it, or understands its legal implications.

CBI Abbreviation of ***Confederation of British Industry***.

CBOE Abbreviation of ***Chicago Board Options Exchange***.

CBOT Abbreviation of ***Chicago Board of Trade***.

CD Abbreviation of ***certificate of deposit***.

CDC Abbreviation of ***Commonwealth Development Corporation***.

CEDEL Abbreviation of ***Centrale de Livraison de Valeurs Mobilières***.

CEFTA Abbreviation of ***Central Europe Free Trade Association***.

Central African Customs and Economic Union (UDEAC) Union Douanière et Economique de l'Afrique Centrale, an organization established in 1966 to found a Central African common market with a common tariff. Its terms were revised in 1974.

Central American Common Market (CACM) Common market established in 1960 among Central American countries. It was revised beginning in 1973.

Central Arbitration Committee UK organization established in 1975 that settles wage claims and arbitrates in disputes about pay and terms of employment. It may also make awards to injured parties.

central bank Bank that carries out government economic policy, influences interest and exchange rates, monitors the activities of commercial and merchant banks, and usually issues currency. In this way it acts as the government's banker and is the lender of last resort to the banking system. In the UK it is the ***Bank of England*** and in the USA the ***Federal Reserve Banks***.

Centrale de Livraison de Valeurs Mobilières (CEDEL) Organization of international banks, established in Luxembourg in 1970 as a settlement system for trading in ***Eurobonds***. It acts as an agency for the collection of dividends and as a clearing house.

Central Europe Free Trade Association (CEFTA) Organization, similar to the ***European Free Trade Association (EFTA)***, formed by the Czech Republic, Hungary, Poland and Slovakia.

Central Gilts Office (CGO) Computerized book-entry transfer system for UK gilt-edged stock established in 1986 by the Bank of England and the Stock Exchange. It ensures automatic "same-day" payments for the electronic transfer of stock.

Central Government Borrowing Requirement (CGBR) Amount calculated by deducting private sector borrowing (by public companies and local authorities) from the ***Public Sector Borrowing Requirement (PSBR)***.

Central Moneymarkets Office (CMO) Method of electronic book-keeping, established in 1990, for transactions in negotiable instruments such as cheques and banker's drafts. Each member has a unique number and password, and is on-line to the CMO from his or her own premises.

Central Statistical Office (CSO) UK government department that collects and collates data about business, the economy and society. Its findings are published by the ***Stationery Office***.

CEO Abbreviation of chief executive officer. *See* ***chief executive***.

certificate of accrual on treasury securities (CATS) In the USA, ***zero-coupon bonds*** issued by the Treasury Department.

certificate of bonds Document issued to a registered bond holder confirming that the bonds are registered in his or her name.

certificate of damage Document, issued by a dock company, certifying that goods it has received were damaged on arrival.

 certificate of deposit (CD) Essentially, a document (originally issued by merchant banks) declaring that a certain sum had been deposited with a bank. Sterling certificates of deposit refer to long-term fixed deposits of sums over £10,000 and therefore offer high interest rates.

certificate of incorporation Document issued to a UK company when it has completed legal incorporation procedures and satisfied the requirements of the Companies Acts.

certificate of origin Import-export document that declares the country of origin of goods.

certificate of quality In the commodities market, a document that certifies that a commodity has passed a grading test, valid (for soft commodities) for six months.

certification of transfer Act of sending to the Stock Exchange a document certifying that a number of a company's shares have been handed in by their former shareholder and are lodged at its offices, prior to being sold and transferred to a new shareholder.

cesser clause In a charter agreement, a clause that absolves the charterer from responsibility for a cargo once it has been landed at its destination. *Cesser* is Latin for "to stop".

CET Abbreviation of *common external tariff*.

ceteris paribus Latin for "other things remaining equal". It is used in economic analysis to study the effects of economic variants while assuming that other factors remain the same.

CFTC Abbreviation of *Commodity Futures Trading Commission*.

CGBR Abbreviation of *Central Government Borrowing Requirement*.

Cge Pd Abbreviation of carriage paid.

CGO Abbreviation of *Central Gilts Office*.

CGT Abbreviation of *capital gains tax*.

CH Abbreviation of *corporate hospitality*.

chain store One of several shops under common ownership and in different locations, usually organized as branches of a main shop or head office. When holders of such a chain amalgamate with (or are taken over by) another chain, they do not necessarily change the names of the stores, so that apparently different retailers are in fact under one ownership.

chairman/chairperson Person who chairs a meeting, also sometimes called merely "chair". The name is also given to the most senior director of a company, full title Chairman of the Board of Directors.

chairman's report Also known as the chairman's statement, a statement by a company's chairman (the most senior director) giving an account of the company's activities during a given financial period and possibly its plans for the immediate future. It is addressed to members of the company (i.e., shareholders), published in the annual report and accounts., and often read out by the chairman at the company's ***annual general meeting (AGM)***.

chamber of commerce UK voluntary organization that promotes and represents the interests of those involved in commerce in a particular geographical area. Chambers of commerce in other countries may be state-aided. *See also* ***chamber of trade***.

chamber of shipping Organization similar to a ***chamber of commerce*** that represents the interests of shipowners and shippers.

chamber of trade Organization of retailers in a particular area that promotes their interests, particularly to local government. It is more limited in composition and purpose than a ***chamber of commerce***.

Chambre de Compensation des Instruments Financiers de Paris (CCIFP) Clearing house for the French financial futures exchange, the *Marché à Terme des Instruments Financiers* (MATIF).

champtery Illegal practice of paying the costs of a court case in which one is not involved, in return for a proportion of any damages awarded.

channel manager US term for a marketing manager of an international organization whose job is to keep down prices in a competitive market.

CHAPS Abbreviation of ***Clearing House Automated Payment System***.

Chaps & Town Clearing Company Limited Company established in 1985 to operate the UK's twice-daily same-day clearance system under the auspices of CHAPS (***Clearing House Automated Payment System***).

Chapter 7 Clause in US company law that provides for the winding up (liquidation) of a company that is unlikely to recover a viable financial position. It is part of the Federal Bankruptcy Act 1978.

Chapter 11 Clause in US company law that enables a company to continue to operate after it has been declared bankrupt (under the direction of the court), so that it may find a way to pay its creditors. It is part of the Federal Bankruptcy Act 1978 and roughly equivalent to the UK's administration.

charge Obligation to meet a debt, a debit to an account, or the process of debiting. It is also a legal interest in land agreed by a borrower to secure a loan that gives the chargee (often a bank or building society) a priority right to repayment when the land is sold. A creditor's interest in company property is also called charge and must be registered with the Registrar of Companies.

chargeable asset Asset that is liable to give rise to a charge for ***capital gains tax (CGT)***.

chargeable gain Any ***capital gain*** that results from disposing of an asset.

charge off Alternative term for ***write off***.

charges forward When goods are to be delivered, a notice that all carriage charges must be paid at the time the goods are delivered.

charging order Court order that allows a debtor's land, stocks, shares and interest under a trust to be "earmarked" for the creditor. If the debt is not repaid, the goods become the property of the creditor.

charter To rent an aircraft or vessel, or part of its cargo space, for a particular journey or period of time. As a noun, a charter is an authorization or grant in writing of a title, right or privilege. A person or organization with a charter usually has the word *chartered* in its name.

chartered agent Broker who finds space aboard ship for a particular cargo.

chartered company UK company that is incorporated by Royal Charter, originally for purposes of international trade. Unlike an ordinary company, it is treated in law as an individual person. Famous chartered companies of the past include the East India Company and the Hudson's Bay Company.

chartism Activities of a ***chartist***.

chartist Stock market or economic analyst who believes that trends (e.g. in price movements and so on) follow recognizable patterns and so predicts future trends with the aid of charts.

chattels Moveable property, as opposed to fixtures (property that cannot be moved).

cheap jack Person who buys goods at very low prices (e.g. from bankrupt companies or goods that are of poor quality) and sells them at below normal price, sometimes in the street, at a market or at a mock auction.

cheap money Also called easy money, money borrowed at a low rate of interest, usually consisting of funds made available by authorities wishing to encourage economic activity.

check sample Sample taken from a consignment of goods and examined to determine whether or not the consignment is acceptable.

Cheque and Credit Clearing Company Limited London-based organization established in 1985, part of the ***Association for Payment Clearing Services (APACS)***, which clears interbank cheques and paper credits in England and Wales (Scotland and Northern Ireland have their own clearing arrangements).

Chicago Board of Trade (CBOT) World's largest futures exchange, established in 1848, which today deals mainly in financial futures.

Chicago Board Options Exchange (CBOE) Major world market in options, established in 1973.

Chicago Stock Exchange Stock exchange established in 1882 to deal mainly in securities of banks, energy companies and railway companies. It became the USA's largest exchange in 1948 and changed its name to the Midwest Stock Exchange, reverting to its original name in 1993.

Chicago Mercantile Exchange (CME) Major world market in cash and futures, established in 1919, which today deals particularly commodities.

chief executive Also known as the chief executive officer (CEO), the person responsible for the day-to-day running of a company, usually the managing director.

chief executive officer (CEO) *See* ***chief executive***.

Chinese wall Artificial barrier erected in any business where confidentiality between departments is a legal requirement. The Chinese wall has become necessary since the ***Big Bang*** changed the ***London Stock Exchange*** to a dual capacity system in 1986. The purpose of the wall is to prevent ***insider dealing***.

Chinese water-torture tactic Popular term for the gradual take-over of a company by building up a majority shareholding from shares bought on the open market.

CHIPS Abbreviation of ***Clearing House Interbank Payments System***.

choice price When comparing different market-makers' bid-offer spreads on a futures market, an identical bid and offer price.

chose-in-action Legal term for a right that cannot be enforced by physical possession, such as a copyright or debt. *See also* ***chose-in-possession***.

chose-in-possession Legal term for an asset that can be secured by physical possession, such as a book. *See also* ***chose-in-action***.

churning Informal term for a broker's practice of buying and selling of stocks and shares solely in order to generate higher commission income. The practice is illegal in the USA if the activity is not in the client's best interest.

CIA Abbreviation of ***cash in advance***.

Cie Abbreviation of *Compagnie* (French for Company).

CIF Abbreviation of ***cost, insurance and freight***.

CIFI Abbreviation of ***cost, insurance, freight and interest***.

CIP Abbreviation of ***carriage and insurance paid***.

circuit breaker Mechanism that could automatically restrict trading in the stock, futures and options markets when prices rise above or fall below pre-set maxima and minima in one trading session.

circular letter of credit ***Letter of credit*** from a bank instructing other banks to pay the holder the sum stated on the production of satisfactory proof of identity.

circular transaction Reciprocal transactions between two companies merely to artificially inflate turnover in each other's accounts.

circulating assets Money used for a company to invest in assets for resale. When such assets have been sold, the capital raised returns to the company. They are also called circulating capital, current assets or floating assets.

circulating capital Alternative term for ***circulating assets.***

City, The Financial district of London, situated in the City of London. It covers an area of roughly one square mile and for this reason is also sometimes known as the Square Mile.

CKD Abbreviation of ***completely knocked down***.

claused bill *Bill of lading* that has endorsements (as opposed to a clean bill of lading).

Clayton Act Antitrust law passed in the USA in 1914 to maintain competition mainly by banning price discrimination among the buyers and sellers of commodities.

clean bill *Bill of exchange* that has no documents or special conditions attached.

clean bill of lading *Bill of lading* that does not include clauses referring to defective goods or their packaging (as opposed to a claused bill).

clean collection Method by which an exporter finances a sale by submitting a draft to the bank and instructing it to collect payment from the importer.

clean price Price of a gilt-edged security excluding any interest that may have accrued since the last payment of a dividend.

clear days For the term of a contract, days that exclude the days on which the contract starts and ends.

clearing Practice of organizing the payment of financial instruments (such as cheques). In the UK, commercial banks are usually members of the Banker's Clearing House, which settles their daily balance.

clearing house Financial institution that specializes in clearing debts between its members. The best-known type is a banker's clearing house, which clears cheques between the major banks.

Clearing House Automated Payments System (CHAPS) Organization established in 1985 as part of the *Association for Payment Clearing Services (APACS)*, that provides a guaranteed same-day electronic transfer of sterling funds within the UK.

Clearing House Interbank Payments System (CHIPS) US organization established in 1970 that provides on-line electronic transfer of funds in US dollars, mainly for international transactions.

clock card Also called a time card, a card on which an employee's time at work or time on a particular job is recorded. It is usually marked by a mechanical clock mechanism or electronically.

close company Company whose shares are held privately, by a few people (usually not more than five), and not traded on a stock exchange. The US term is closely-held company.

closed-end fund Fund with fixed capital, as opposed to an open-ended fund. Sums held by investment companies are closed-end funds (investment trusts).

closed indent Order for goods placed with an agent abroad that specifies the supplier from whom the goods are to be purchased.

closed shop Place of work where, by agreement between management and staff, it is compulsory for employees to belong to a ***trade union***. The ***Employment Act*** 1988 made it illegal to enforce total union membership.

closely-held company US term for a ***close company***.

close out Counterbalancing transactions in two or more financial instruments that leaves the investor neither in credit nor in debt (a net zero position).

closing price Price of shares at the close of trading each day on a stock exchange.

closing purchase Purchase of an option that closes an ***open position***.

closing range On a financial futures market, the highest and lowest prices recorded during the close.

closing rate Rate at the close of business for the day for the foreign exchange of spot money.

closing sale On an options market, a transaction in which an option is sold in order to close a position.

cluster sample Comparatively small representative sample of potential customers for a product.

CME Abbreviation of ***Chicago Mercantile Exchange***.

CMEA Abbreviation of ***Council for Mutual Economic Assistance***.

CMO Abbreviation of ***Central Moneymarkets Office*** and ***collateralized mortgage obligation***.

CNAR Abbreviation of ***compound net annual rate***.

Co Abbreviation of ***Company***.

c/o Abbreviation of ***cash with order***.

COB Abbreviation of ***Commission des Opérations de Bourse***.

COD Abbreviation of ***cash on delivery***.

Code of Advertising Practice (CAP) UK Advertising Standards Authority publication that defines what is acceptable in an advertisement.

code of conduct Also called code of practice, the norm of behaviour expected from the members of a group, organization or business community.

co-determination System for industrial democracy within large companies in Germany. The board of directors of such a company (defined as one with 2000 or more employees) must have equal numbers of representatives from staff and the employer (management).

coemption Legal term for ***cornering the market***.

co-financing Providing finance for projects in developing countries from a commercial bank and a major international institution such as the World Bank.

cold calling Sales practice of approaching a potential customer, by mail, telephone or in person, without any prior introduction.

collar In return for a premium, an option that guarantees a borrower a fixed maximum interest (cap) and fixed minimum interest (floor) for a loan.

collateral Alternative term for ***security*** put up for a loan.

collateral agreement Contract or agreement running in parallel with an existing one.

collateralized mortgage obligation (CMO) US bond secured against a portfolio of mortgages issued by the Federal Home Loan Mortgage Corporation.

collateral security In addition to the borrower's personal security, a second security for a loan.

collections Payment method in which an importer and exporter agree to employ the exporter's bank to handle payment for goods.

collective Group of people working together towards a common aim.

collective bargaining Practice of workers in trade unions electing representatives to bargain on their behalf with management on such issues as wage levels and working conditions.

collective ownership Ownership, of e.g. a business or property, with all the gains being equally divided among the members of the collective.

combat pay US term for danger money.

come to market US term describing a new issue (of stocks etc.).

COMECON Abbreviation of ***Council for Mutual Economic Assistance***.

COMEX Abbreviation of ***Commodity Exchange of New York***. The New York copper price is also commonly referred to as *comex*. *See* ***New York Mercantile Exchange (NYMEX)***.

comfort letter Independent auditor's letter that guarantees that information in a new company's prospectus has remained unchanged between the preparation of the prospectus and its distribution. It is a legal requirement in the USA.

Comisión Nacional del Mercado de Valores *See* ***Madrid Stock Exchange***.

commercial bill Bill of exchange that is not a Treasury bill.

commercial invoice Bill for goods dispatched by a seller to a buyer, often used by government to determine the value of goods for assessment of customs duty.

commercial paper (CP) Corporate debt in a tradable form. In the USA, the commercial paper is a short-term, non-bank market in which firms lend money to each other without the intervention of a financial intermediary.

commingling Combining in the same shipment, in such a way that they cannot easily be separated, articles that attract different rates of customs duty. Unless the shipper or his agent separates them, the highest rate of duty applicable to any one item will be applied to the whole consignment.

commission Money paid for the services of an agent or other intermediary, usually as a percentage of the sum involved in the transaction.

commission agent Agent who is paid a ***commission***, usually calculated as a percentage of the value of purchases or sales made overseas.

commission broker Dealer on the US stock exchange who buys or sells securities (for the public) in return for a commission.

Commission des Opérations de Bourse (COB) Official supervisory organization, established in 1967, of French stock exchanges. Belgium has a similar organization of the same name.

Commissione Nazionale per le Società e le Borsa (CONSOB) Official supervisory organization, established in 1974, of Italian stock exchanges.

commitment fee Bank charge for keeping loan facilities available for a customer (even if they are not used).

committee of inspection Committee made up of a bankrupt company's creditors that directs the company's winding-up, either in the hands of a receiver or a liquidator.

commodity Raw materials and foods, especially goods such as cocoa, coffee, jute, potatoes, tea, and so on, that can be traded on a commodity market; or (in economics) any tangible good that is traded. Primary products and raw materials used in industrial processing and manufacture are also sometimes known as commodities.

commodity broker Broker who deals in commodities, usually in a commodity market.

Commodity Credit Corporation (CCC) Organization established in 1933 as an agency of the US to finance government farm programmes. In 1939 it was transferred to, and made part of, the US Department of Agriculture.

commodity exchange Commodity market on which actuals and futures are traded.

Commodity Exchange of New York (COMEX) Commodity market in metals established in 1870 which, together with the *London Metal Exchange*, has a leading role in the world. It deals mainly in futures contracts and in 1994 merged with the *New York Mercantile Exchange (NYMEX)*.

Commodity Futures Trading Commission (CFTC) US organization established in 1974 that regulates the country's commodity futures exchanges, particularly in agricultural products and derivatives.

commodity market Market on which commodities are traded.

Common Agricultural Policy (CAP) EU agreement on farming that aims to protect farmers of member countries, e.g. by subsidizing their produce and setting minimum prices.

Common Budget Funds available to the European Commission, mainly to intervene to support the *Common Agricultural Policy (CAP)*.

common carrier Legal status of a person or organization that offers to ship goods for anybody who will pay for the service.

common external tariff (CET) Import tariff charged by all members of a trading community (such as the EU) on goods being imported from non-member states.

common market Any market organization among countries that have a common external tariff (unlike a free-trade area). The EU is a modern example.

common ownership Economic principle that everyone who produces certain goods and services is an equal owner of the means of production.

common shares US term for equity shares, with a stated face value that does not relate to the true value.

common stock US term for *ordinary shares*.

Commonwealth Development Corporation (CDC) UK public organization established in 1948 to help the economic development of overseas countries, particularly new members of the Commonwealth and particularly with agriculture.

Compagnie des Agents de Change (CAC) Professional association to which French stockbrokers belong.

Companies Act 1985 Chief legislation that applies to companies in the UK. It deals with all aspects of company law from setting up a company, running it and winding it up.

Companies Act 1989 Legislation enacted to make UK company law conform to that of the EU.

Companies House Informal name of *Companies Registration Office*.

Companies Registration Office Known informally as Companies House (or sometimes Company's House), the location of the office of the Registrar of Companies, in Cardiff, Wales. It contains a register of all UK companies, listing the names of its directors and shareholders as well as copies of its latest balance sheet.

company Enterprise that has been legally incorporated to produce certain goods or provide certain services, or to transact any other type of business. There are strict legal requirements of a company, as set out in the Companies Acts.

company doctor Person who is brought into a company, usually at board level, that is on the brink of liquidation. A company doctor often has powers to administer very strong medicine in order to put the company back on its feet.

company limited by guarantee Company whose members are liable only up to the amount they guarantee to make available in the event of the company being wound up. The guarantors may or may not hold shares in addition. Charities and educational establishments are the most common organizations that form companies limited by guarantee.

company limited by shares Usual type of company, in which the members' liability is limited to their share holding. *See also* ***limited company***.

company seal Common seal that must legally be applied to certain documents and which every limited company must possess.

company secretary Person who is responsible for ensuring that his or her company complies with company law. He or she is an officer of the company but need not be a director.

Company Security (Insider Dealing) Act 1985 UK law that made ***insider dealing*** illegal.

company union Method of trade union representation in Japan where every employee of a company is automatically a member of the union, which is run by the company itself.

comparative advantage Economic state of being more efficient in one activity than in another, relative to a different country. For example, a country is able to produce cars twice as efficiently as another, but produces aircraft ten times more efficiently. In a free market, this country should export aircraft and import cars, and it is said that, in the production of aircraft, it has a comparative advantage over the other country.

compensation for loss of office Sum paid to a senior executive (usually a director) when he or she leaves a company's employment. It may be effectively a redundancy payment following a successful take-over, or it may be instead of or as well as a pension.

competition analysis Process of gathering and assessing information about corporate competition.

Competition Act 1980 UK legislation that allowed the ***Monopolies and Mergers Commission*** to investigate anti-competitive practices (such as refusal to supply goods or services to certain customers or purchase goods or services from certain suppliers).

competitive market Open market in which goods and services are freely offered for sale by any number of sellers to anybody willing to buy, at prices agreed between them.

competitive pricing Setting a price on goods and services based on what competitors charge for the same or similar products. Sellers in a strong market position (perhaps because of a well-known brand name) can force others to sell at a discount in order to make significant sales. In a market where buyers perceive all products to be similar, no seller dare set a price higher than the competition.

complaints procedure Method of dealing with (i.e. resolving) complaints from customers or clients and passing on the results to management (so that the fundamental cause can be dealt with and similar complaints do not occur in future).

complementary goods Two goods that are related to each other in such a way that when demand for one increases, demand for the other rises at the same time. For example, cameras and photographic film are complementary goods, as are cars and petrol.

completely knocked down (CKD) Describing goods that are unassembled or disassembled for shipment or storage.

compliance cost Cost to a company of complying with regulations, such as keeping records for ***Customs and Excise*** (for value added tax, VAT) or the ***Inland Revenue*** (for income tax etc.).

compliance officer Person whose job is to ensure that a company and its staff adhere to rules and regulation as they affect securities and other financial dealings.

composite currency peg Type of exchange rate system in which a country pegs its currencies to a basket of currencies of its main trading partners.

compound annual return (CAR) Total return on a sum invested or lent over a period of a year, including the return on interest previously accrued.

compound interest Rate of interest calculated by adding interest previously paid to the capital sum plus previous interest payment. After n years a sum S invested at x per cent compound interest is worth $S[(100 + n)/100]^n$. *See also* ***simple interest***.

compound net annual rate (CNAR) Return, after deduction of tax at the basic rate, of interest from a deposit or investment that includes the return on interest previously accrued.

C

compound option Option to buy an option at a pre-agreed price and date.

comptroller Mainly US term for the chief financial officer of a group of companies or the financial director of a single company. The title should not be confused with that of controller, who is the chief accounting executive, although not all companies preserve the distinction. Both titles are pronounced in the same manner.

compulsory liquidation Liquidation of a company that has become insolvent. In this case, the Official Receiver (in the UK) is initially in charge of the disposal of the company's assets.

computer-assisted trading (CAT) Method of trading in which brokers and traders use computers on, e.g., the foreign exchange market or the stock exchange.

concentration ratio Measure of the make-up of a market in terms of the sizes of companies (expressed as capital employed, number of staff or annual turnover). For example, the market may be dominated by a large number of small companies or a small number of large ones.

concentration risk Risk in dealing in securities if they are concentrated in any one market sector or mostly only one type of security is held.

concern Alternative term for a business or company.

concert party Group of people who come together secretly to act "in concert", that is, to orchestrate a market in the group's favour. For example, two or more people may form a concert party to buy shares in a company in order to effect a take-over. Such action is illegal.

concession Allowance made to somebody who otherwise would have to pay; or the right to use somebody else's property as part of a business.

conciliation Attempt to get disputing parties to settle their differences. In the UK it may be done through the ***Advisory, Conciliation and Arbitration Service (ACAS)***.

conditional bill of sale ***Bill of sale*** by which the owner of the goods transferred retains the right to repossess them.

conditional endorsement Endorsement on a ***bill of exchange*** on which the endorser has added a condition, which has to be fulfilled before the endorser receives the proceeds of the bill. The condition does not affect the paying banker, who can ignore it.

conditional sale agreement Agreement by which goods are paid for in instalments and, although the buyer may have possession of the goods, the legal property in them remains with the seller until payment is complete.

conditions of employment Amount of pay, hours of work and paid holidays as detailed in a contract of employment (or, less formally, in a letter of appointment).

Confederation of British Industry (CBI) Independent organization established in 1965 by combing the British Employers Confederation, the Federation of British Industry and the National Association of British Manufacturers. It represents industry in consultations with the government and promotes the activities of industry in the UK.

conference In international trade, effectively a cartel of shipping companies carrying certain cargoes between certain destinations.

confirmation Method an auditor uses to get evidence from a third party of the accuracy of information provided by a client. A positive confirmation is requested whether the balance figure, for example, is correct or incorrect. The return of a negative confirmation is requested only in the event that the figures are incorrect.

confirmed letter of credit Letter of credit issued by a foreign bank, with its validity confirmed by a home bank (thus guaranteeing payment).

confirming house Type of export house that acts for foreign buyers, who use it like a UK office. The house places orders with UK exporters and thereby effectively becomes the buyer.

conflict of interest Situation in which the interest of a person or company in one role conflicts with the interests in another role. Such occurrences can be minimized by using a ***Chinese wall***.

conglomerate Very large public company that is extremely diverse and probably international in its operations.

conglomerate merger Merger between companies whose business interests are not connected.

conseil d'administration French for board of directors.

Consensus Common name for the ***International Agreement for Guidelines on Officially Supported Export Credit***.

consensus-based decision making Japanese tradition of waiting until all key staff agree before enacting a management decision.

consideration In most forms of contract, the agreement is made binding by the promise or payment of a sum of money or other favour from one party to the other. Such a payment or favour is known as a consideration. The term is also used informally for any kind of payment.

consignee Person or company to which goods are sent.

consignment Shipment of goods sent or delivered at the same time, usually to an agent for selling on to somebody else (the consignee). *See also* ***on consignment***.

consignment note Document sent with a consignment of goods, to be signed by the consignee or his agent upon receipt of the goods. It may also be known as a waybill.

consignment stock Stock held by an agent or dealer that legally belongs to somebody else. The dealer can, in law, sell it or return it unsold to the rightful owner.

consignor Person or company that dispatches goods (to a consignee).

CONSOB Abbreviation of ***Commissione Nazionale per le Società e le Borsa***.

Consol Abbreviation of Consolidated Stock or Consolidated Loan, a form of fixed-interest government security that has no redemption date.

consolidation of capital Changing the nominal value of a company's shares (for example, by making every ten £1 shares equal to one £10 share).

consortium Group of companies that come together to bid for a certain project. It is usually dissolved after that one project is completed. It is similar to a ***syndicate***, but more short-term.

conspicuous consumption Consumer trend that involves the consumer buying goods (usually status symbols, such as sports cars, etc.), deriving satisfaction not from consumption of the goods themselves, but from being seen by other people to own them.

constant dollar plan *See* ***pound cost averaging***.

constant prices Expressing prices in terms of a base year so that figures can be compared without being affected by inflation.

constraint Something that prevents an organization from performing better. It may be a shortage of such things as labour, production capacity or raw materials, which must be remedied before performance levels can improve.

constructed value (CV) Method of arriving at the fair market value of something when there are no similar goods for comparison. It is arrived at by adding the cost of materials and production, and allowing for general expenses and profit. The cost of packaging may also be added.

consumable materials Also called consumables, materials that are used up in producing something, although not part of the prime cost (as are ***direct materials***), such as abrasives, cleaning agents and lubricating oil.

consumer Person who buys goods for consumption.

consumer credit Personal credit, such as a bank loan or incorporated into a hire-purchase agreement.

Consumer Credit Act 1974 Legislation in the UK that safeguards people who take out personal credit worth up to £15,000. It covers bank loans, credit cards, credit sale agreements, hire-purchase agreements and mortgages (bank overdrafts are excluded).

consumer durables Consumer goods of some technological sophistication that yield utility over a period of time, for example, clothing, cars, washing machines, and so on.

consumer goods Goods that are consumed in use, either over a short period (e.g. foodstuffs) or over a longer period, such as motor vehicle tyres (or even the motor vehicles themselves).

consumer loyalty Similar to goodwill, a difficult to measure asset based on a consumers' habitual purchase of certain goods or patronage of certain retail outlets.

consumer price index US term for ***retail price index***.

consumer resistance Reluctance of consumers to purchase a particular product. It may be because they do not like the "idea" of a particular new product (because of its colour, composition or advertising, for example), or because they remain loyal to an older competing product. The former may be overcome by the use of free samples or cheaper trial packs.

consumerism Policy that bases business decisions on the best interest of the consumer.

Consumers' Association Independent, non-profit making UK organization established in 1956 that tests goods and services and publishes the results in its monthly magazine *Which?* It also lobbies the government on consumer matters.

containerization Shipping of goods, by land, sea or air, in large metal containers.

contango Stock exchange term for a delayed settlement of a bargain from one account to the next. A premium then becomes payable. The term is also used more frequently in futures trading to mean the opposite of ***backwardation***.

Conti di Gruppo Italian for corporation.

contingency Allowance for a possible loss (or gain) written into a costing or account. The prudence concept requires that contingent losses, particularly, should be disclosed.

continuation Alternative term for ***contango***.

continuous stocktaking Also called perpetual inventory, continuous audit or continuous inventory, a way of keeping a record of stock which is changed whenever an item is added to or removed from the stock. It is most commonly used in retailing, where stock turnover is fast.

contract Legally binding agreement between two parties, or the act of forming such an agreement. It may be verbal or a ***contract in writing***.

contract bond Alternative term for a ***performance bond***.

contract by deed Type of contract that is binding only if made by deed (such as conditional bills of sale and mortgages of land).

contract in writing Written contract, required for various purposes such as bills of exchange, transfers of shares and credit sale or hire-purchase agreements.

contract note Also called a bought note or sold note, a document from a stockbroker that is evidence of a transaction to buy or sell shares. It must carry a transfer stamp and a contract stamp.

contract of affreightment Contract between a shipowner and a shipper relating to carriage of cargo by sea.

contract of employment Legally binding document that details the terms and conditions of somebody's job.

Contract of Employment Act 1963 UK legislation that made it obligatory for an employer to draw up and sign a contract of employment with each full-time permanent employee.

contract of novation New contract that replaces an existing one, usually retaining the same rights and liabilities, as when one partner in a partnership is replaced by another.

contribution Money earned or paid in addition to another sum, often used of extra profit that accrues once a product's break-even point has been reached.

controlling interest Holding of more than 50% in the voting shares of a company, necessary for a successful take-over. A director with more than 20% of the voting shares is also said to have a controlling interest.

convergence Aim, as detailed in the Maastricht Treaty, of bringing the currencies and economies of EU countries into line with each other, necessary before the introduction of a single currency and the *European Monetary Union (EMU)*.

convertible capital bond Financial instrument similar to ***convertible loan stock*** except that its conversion takes place in two stages: first to preference shares and then to ordinary shares.

convertible currency Currency that is easily exchangeable for another currency, with no limit.

convertible loan stock Loan stock with the right of conversion into preference shares or ordinary shares at some time in the future. Government stock that can be converted into new stock (instead of repayment) is also known as convertible loan stock.

convertibles Loan stock, bonds and debentures that can easily be converted into ordinary shares. In the USA they are known as converts.

convertible shares Alternative term for ***convertible loan stock***.

cooling-off period Period of ten days (in the UK) during which a person who has agreed to a certain form of contract (such as a credit sale or hire-purchase agreement) may withdraw from the agreement and have his or her money repaid. Such a period exists in order to minimize the effects of hard selling that some companies or their agents undertake.

cooperative Organization run by a group of people who each have a say in its management and a financial interest in its profitability. It may be a group of producers (such as farmers), consumers (in retail cooperatives) or the workers themselves (as in some Communist countries).

COP Abbreviation of ***cost of production***.

Copenhagen Stock Exchange Non-monopoly public limited company (since 1995) that runs the stock exchange in Copenhagen, using an electronic order-driven system.

core activities Activities that a company perceives as central to its business strategy and, as such, essential (as opposed to peripheral activities).

core workers Workers that are essential to a company's operation (skilled workers, craftsmen, technicians and managers), as opposed to freelance or peripheral workers.

cornering the market To build a virtual monopoly in particular goods or services, so that the monopolist is able to dictate price.

Corn Exchange London commodity exchange that deals in such commodities as cereals and animal foodstuffs.

Corp Abbreviation of *Corporation*.

corpocracy If a company is involved in several mergers, its management is at risk of becoming cumbersome and confused. The resulting corporation thus labours under a large and inefficient bureaucracy and is known informally as a corpocracy.

corporate advertising Advertising campaign whose aim is to promote the image of a company, rather than its products.

corporate bond Bond issued by a company or corporation, which most frequently occurs in the USA.

corporate finance Funding for a business or large corporation, usually from a bank.

corporate hospitality (CH) Hospitality extended to a company's most favoured clients (or potential clients) in the form of entertainment, for example tickets to the theatre or to prestigious sporting events.

corporate identity Identity of a company as displayed in the visual images it uses, for example its logos and colours, in such things as packaging, uniforms, stationery and vehicles.

corporate image View of a company as it is perceived by its staff, customers and the general public.

corporate licensing Alternative US term for *merchandising*.

corporate objectives Aims of a whole company, covering such subject areas as new products, production targets and sales targets.

corporate raider Somebody who buys enough shares of a target company to take it over or to sufficiently influence management to make changes that improve the share value of the company. The raider can then sell the shares at a profit.

corporate veil Protection against liability that is afforded to multiple shareholders in a company as opposed to one single owner.

corporate venturing Practice of a company in providing ***venture capital*** for another company. It is usually undertaken to give the investing company a potential foothold in a new (or related) market or field, or to lay the foundations for a possible take-over bid at some future date.

corporation Large company, usually with several subsidiary companies. In the USA, it is a company that has been incorporated under US law. The term is therefore a virtual synonym for company. It is often abbreviated to corp.

corporation tax (CT) Tax levied on a UK company's profits. The rate depends on the amount of profit, starting at 10% for companies whose profits are less than £10,000, rising to 20% for companies with profits of between £10,000 and £300,000, rising to 30% for companies making more than $1.5 million. *See also* ***advance corporation tax***.

corset Restriction applied by the ***Bank of England*** on the amount of credit a bank can extend to its customers, usually in an attempt to control inflation.

cost and freight (C & F) When exporting goods, a contract in which it is agreed that the exporter pays all costs up to the delivery point except for insurance.

cost-based pricing Pricing goods or services in terms of their production costs, as opposed to taking account of market conditions.

cost centre Specific operation within an organization that is charged separately for its own expenses (so that its costs can be accurately assessed).

costing Practice of working out how much a product will cost to produce, taking into account costs such as raw materials, labour, overheads, and so on. A frequent alternative term is costing-out.

cost, insurance and freight (CIF) Foreign trade contract that stipulates that the exporter pays all costs up to the delivery point, including insurance of the goods in transit.

cost, insurance, freight and interest (CIFI) Export contract, by which the exporter is bound to pay all costs to delivery, along with insurance of the goods in transit and interest on the value of the goods.

cost of capital Average of the costs to a company of its various kinds of capital (bonds, debentures, loans, shares, retained profit, and so on).

cost of goods sold (COGS) Cost of items that are produced (or bought) and then sold (or resold). For a given accounting period, it is the value of stock at the beginning of the period plus the cost of goods produced (or bought) minus the value of stock at the end of the period.

cost of living In national terms, the amount of money each person has to spend in order to buy food and accommodation.

cost of living index Officially termed the Index of Retail Prices, an index related to the spending of an average family on the goods and services they need. Goods considered include a "standard food basket", clothing, fuel, household goods and services, transport, drink and tobacco.

cost of production (COP) Cost of the materials and production process involved in producing a good, with an allowance for cost of sales (but no profit).

cost of sales Usually the expense incurred in making sales (such as the cost of advertising, wages of sales personnel, and so on). The term is also sometimes used to mean the ***cost of goods sold***.

cost-plus contract Type of sales contract under the terms of which a supplier of goods or services charges cost price plus an agreed percentage markup.

cost-plus pricing Method of pricing in which the buyer pays the cost of an item plus a commission to the seller, as with a ***cost-plus contract***. The term is also applied to a method of arriving at the selling price of goods or services by estimating the total cost to produce or provide them and then adding a percentage markup in order to make a profit.

cost-push inflation Type of inflation that results from price increases resulting from increased production costs.

Council for Mutual Economic Assistance (CMEA or **COMECOM)** Group of Communist bloc countries that combined in 1949 with the aim of producing a self-sufficient economic bloc that could be coordinated from a central point (and to consolidate Soviet influence in the area). Its members were: Bulgaria, Cuba, Czechoslovakia, East Germany,

C

Hungary, Mongolia, Poland, Romania, USSR and Vietnam. In 1991 is was superseded by the ***Organization for International Economic Cooperation*** (OIEC).

Council of Economic Advisors US agency within the Executive Office of the President that analyses the national economy and its various segments, advises the President on economic developments, appraises the economic programmes and policies of the federal government, recommends policies for economic growth and stability, and assists in the preparation of the annual Economic Report of the President to Congress.

Council of Ministers Main decision-making body of the EU, made up of one government minister from each of the member countries (the minister may change, depending on the matter in hand).

council tax Local-government UK tax levied on property according to its market value, with a lower level of tax for buildings with only one occupant. It was established in 1993-94 (when it replaced the community charge).

counterbid Bid that is made (e.g. during a take-over battle or an auction) against a previous bid, going one better.

counterclaim Claim for damages made by a defendant against a plaintiff, in the hope that the counterclaim will offset any damages payable to the plaintiff in the first action.

counterfoil Document kept as a record of a transaction, often attached to (and then detached from) a bond, certificate or cheque.

counterparty risk In trading securities, the risk that the counterparty to a sale or purchase may fail to fulfil his or her obligations.

countersign To sign a document that was previously signed by somebody else.

countertrading Barter; obtaining goods or services using means other than money.

countervailing credit Alternative term for ***back-to-back credit***.

countervailing duty (CVD) Extra charge imposed on imported goods to offset subsidies received by the exporter.

country of origin Country in which imported goods or services were originally made, which may affect the rate of duty applicable.

coupon Term with two meanings:

1. Document attached to a bond, which must be detached and sent to the paying party in order for the bond holder to receive interest payments. Each payment is detailed on the coupon for each payment period.
2. Alternative term for interest that is payable on a fixed-interest security.

coupon bond Alternative term for ***bearer bond***.

covenant Broadly, any form of agreement; or more specifically, an agreement taken out between two parties, stating that one party agrees to pay the other a series of fixed sums over a certain period of time.

cover Term with several meanings:

1. Any form of security (i.e. collateral).
2. In financial futures, the buying of contracts to offset a ***short position***.
3. Number of times a company could theoretically pay dividends to shareholders from its earnings.
4. To make enough money in selling products or services to pay for their production.
5. Constituent amount put up as margin per unit of quotation on a futures contract, which combined will dictate the margin.
6. Amount of money an insured person stands to receive from an insurer should he or she make a claim.

covered bear Also known as a protected bear, a dealer who sells shares or commodities he or she owns, hoping to buy them back later at a lower price (i.e. he or she is not taking the risk of short selling).

covered interest arbitrage Where there are interest rate differences between two countries, borrowing money in one currency (at the lower rate) and investing it in the other currency (at the higher rate), using the forward market to cover the exchange risk.

CP Abbreviation of ***commercial paper***.

CPT Abbreviation of ***carriage paid to***.

crash Informal term for a very severe drop in prices on securities, financial and commodities markets.

crawling peg Form of fixed exchange rate, in which the rate is allowed to fluctuate according to supply and demand but only within certain specified maximum and minimum rates. It is also known as a sliding peg.

credit Loan of money (made by a trader before requiring payment for goods or services); or a book-keeping balance that shows a profit (i.e., on the right-hand side of the account); or a person's or company's financial standing; or to add a sum to an account.

credit account Also called a charge account, an account offered by some retail stores and chains which allows a customer to purchase goods on the spot (usually by means of a plastic card) and to pay for them at the end of the accounting period or in instalments. Some credit accounts also charge interest.

credit agency Also called credit bureau, a company that gathers information on the creditworthiness of individuals and companies, and distributes this information when requested to those providing credit facilities.

credit balance Account balance showing that more money has been received than has been debited, and so the account concerned is in credit.

credit broker Person who introduces somebody wanting credit to somebody who can provide it. Some retailers who sell goods by means of credit sale agreements are licensed credit brokers.

credit bureau Alternative term for ***credit agency***.

credit control Method employed by a company to ensure that its debts are paid within a reasonable time. The person responsible for this activity is the credit controller.

credit controller *See* ***credit control***.

credit crunch Situation in which short credit becomes scarce and thus more expensive than long credit.

credit limit Maximum sum that a person or organization is prepared to lend (to a given borrower).

credit line US term for overdraft.

credit note Document, sometimes printed in red ink, issued to confirm the transfer of credit from one account to another. The term is also used for a note or document that confirms the availability of funds for future purchases (as when goods are paid for but later returned to the supplier).

creditor Person or company that lends or is owed money. In company accounting, creditors who are due to be paid within a year are classified as current creditors; creditors who are not due to be paid until after a year are classified as long-term liabilities.

creditor days Average number of days a company takes to pay its creditors.

creditors' meeting Meeting that confirms the appointment of a receiver to a company in liquidation.

credit rating Rating assigned to a person or company that assesses creditworthiness.

credit risk When a loan is made, the risk that the borrower will be unable (or unwilling) to repay the principal and any interest owing.

credit sale Purchase that is paid for at a future date, usually in instalments (i.e. using instalment credit).

credit sale agreement Contract that permits a buyer to pay for goods received by means of instalments paid over a period. Unlike a ***hire-purchase*** agreement, it confers ownership as soon as the contract is signed.

credit squeeze Action by banks and other lenders to restrict the extension of credit to customers, usually at the request of government to limit the money supply (and slow economic activity).

credit terms Time a supplier allows a creditor to pay his or her bills for goods or services delivered.

credit union In the UK, a non-profit making mutual organization that offers facilities for savings, makes small loans, and may provide basic personal insurance within a local area. In the USA, a member-owned, democratically governed, non-profit making cooperative that provides financial services to members and whose earnings are returned to the members.

creditworthy Describing a person who, from his or her record, is deemed willing and able to pay back credit. Thus a creditworthy person finds it easier to borrow (and to borrow larger sums) than somebody who is deemed to be a credit risk.

creeping take-over Gradual increase in a shareholding through open purchase on the stock exchange with the aim of acquiring enough shares to make a take-over bid.

CREST An electronic (and therefore paperless) system introduced to the London Stock Exchange in 1996 for processing shares for the securities market. It replaced ***TALISMAN*** and includes registration, purchase, sales and payment of dividends as they become due.

cross-border listing Practice of listing securities on exchanges in more than one country. Investors in one country can purchase shares in another country by using a broker who deals through a broker in the other country.

cross default Condition attached to a security or debt specifying that, should the borrower default on any other debt, it also counts as a default on the one with the cross-default condition.

crossed US term for ***backwardation*** in which a market-maker's offer price is lower than another's bid price.

crossing Purchase and sale of a bloc of securities by the same broker. In the USA, a crossed sale is termed a swash sale.

cross offer Situation in which an offer to sell is made at the same time (and at the same price) as an offer to purchase. The two offers "cross in the post" and there is deemed to be no contract.

cross rate Rate at which one currency may be exchanged for a second, expressed in terms of a third currency.

crown jewel tactic Strategy undertaken by a company that is threatened by take-over, in which it sells, or offers to sell, the best part of its business to somebody other than the raider (e.g. a ***white knight***), in order to make the target seem less desirable.

CSO Abbreviation of ***Central Statistical Office***.

CT Abbreviation of ***corporation tax***.

cum coupon Describing a security that is passed from one holder to another with ***coupon*** (enabling the holder to claim interest payments) attached. *See also* ***ex coupon***.

cum dividend Describing shares that are sold with the right of the new holder to claim the next dividend payment. It is sometimes abbreviated to cum div. *See also* ***ex dividend***.

cum new Describing shares that are sold with the right to claim participation in any outstanding scrip or rights issue. *See also* ***ex new***.

cumulative preference share Kind of ***preference share*** whose holder can claim any dividends not paid in earlier years, as long as the company has funds to pay them. Even then, eventual payment is guaranteed before payment to holders of ordinary shares.

Curb Exchange Term for the ***American Stock Exchange (AMEX)***.

currency bond Bond issued in a foreign country. It is repaid in the currency of that country.

currency clearings Clearings that take place daily in London in eight foreign currencies (Australian dollar, Canadian dollar, Deutschmark, Dutch guilder, French franc, Italian lira, Japanese yen and US dollar), managed by the Currency Clearings Committee, a part of the ***Association for Payment Clearing Services (APACS)***.

currency depreciation Extent to which a currency's value has fallen with respect to the value of other currencies. For a free-floating currency, this will depend on which other currency it is compared with.

currency exposure Risk of holding assets in a foreign currency. The risk is incurred because its value, relative to that of the host nation's currency, may fall. It is possible to hedge against currency exposure by selling foreign currency on the forward markets.

currency gyration *See* ***floating exchange rate***.

currency of a bill Time that elapses between the drawing of a ***bill of exchange*** and its becoming payable. For an after sight bill, the time begins on the date of acceptance.

currency option contract Contract that allows the purchaser of an option the right (if he or she wishes) to trade within a specified time period in a foreign currency at a pre-set rate of exchange.

currency swap Transaction in which one currency is exchanged for another at a fixed rate (for example, by buying on the spot market and selling on the forward market). It is a way of hedging against exchange exposure.

current assets Alternative name for ***circulating assets***.

current assets ratio Total of current assets, including stock-in-trade, divided by total of current liabilities. A test of a company's liquidity, it is also known as current ratio and working-capital ratio.

current expenditure Expenditure on assets for resale, such as raw materials, rather than fixed assets. It is also known as above-the-line expenditure.

current liability Money owed by a person or company that should be paid within a year of the date of the balance sheet (as opposed to a ***long-term liability***).

current ratio Alternative term for ***current assets ratio***.

current yield Dividend calculated as a percentage of the price paid for each share.

cushion bond Bond that can be called in before maturity (i.e. retired early).

custodian Somebody who holds an investor's securities and deals with all matters pertaining to them.

customer loyalty Tendency to make repeat purchases of a product (or a particular company's products), because of quality, after-sales service or the power of advertising.

customer satisfaction How well (or poorly) a product or service measures up to what the customer expects of it.

custom of trade Knowledge of the practices of a particular trade when interpreting the written (or sometimes unwritten) terms of a contract.

customs National authority charged with collecting duty levied on exports and imports. The term is also used to describe the area in which customs officials can examine goods entering or leaving a country. *See also next entry.*

Customs and Excise In full Her Majesty's Customs and Excise, UK government department charged with levying indirect taxes, including value added tax (VAT) and customs duty on goods imported into the UK or produced in the UK for home consumption (***excise duty***).

customs duty Duty levied on imports, either as a protectionist measure or simply to raise revenue.

customs tariff List of dutiable goods.

customs union Agreement between two or more nations to remove or standardize restrictions on mutual trade, and apply common duties, tariffs or quotas to countries outside the union.

cut a deal To agree on the basic principles of a contract. Negotiation or finalization of details usually follows.

cut-throat competition Situation in which producers reduce the prices of their goods, and keep them as low as possible until competitors are driven out of business.

CV Abbreviation of ***constructed value***.

CVD Abbreviation of ***countervailing duty***.

CWO Abbreviation of ***cash with order***.

cycle time Overall time taken (e.g. on a factory assembly line) until a job function or process repeats itself.

cyclical stocks Also called cyclicals, US term for shares in companies that are involved in basic industries, such as the provision or raw materials, metals, and so on. They are so called because their prices on the stock market tend to rise and fall with the ***business cycle***.

D

D/A Abbreviation of ***documents against acceptance***.

Dachgesellschaft German for ***holding company***.

danger money Also termed danger pay, employee bonus granted in return for working in dangerous conditions

dangerous goods Goods that could pose a risk to the health and safety of people or property, therefore requiring special care in handling and storage.

data privacy Business requirement to maintain the privacy of personal information relating the customers or staff. *See also next entry*.

Data Protection Act 1984 UK legislation that is designed to protect people whose personal details are held in a computer system. Businesses that hold such data have to register with the Data Protection Registrar.

date d'échéance French for ***redemption date***.

dated security Security, such as a ***bill of exchange*** or a ***bond***, that has a stated date for repayment (redemption date) of its nominal value. It may be described as short-dated or long-dated.

dawn raid Buying a significant number of a target company's shares at the start of the day's trading, or before the market becomes aware of what is happening, often at a price higher than normal. The purpose of a dawn raid is to give the buyer a strategic stake in the target company, from which he or she could launch a take-over bid.

DAX Abbreviation of ***Deutsche Aktienindex***.

day order Order given by an investor to a stockbroker that is valid only on the day it was given. A day order also specifies a price limit on the transaction envisaged. If not completed on the day in question, the transaction is automatically cancelled.

days of grace Period of three days still permitted in the UK for the payment of any bill of exchange except ***bills of sight***. Days of grace have been abolished in most other countries.

day-to-day loan Alternative US term for an overnight loan or day-to-day money, borrowed particularly by a financial institution that is temporarily illiquid. The money is lent by companies that wish to be paid interest on money earned in the previous day's trading. Interest rates on day-to-day loans are high and variable.

day trader Mainly US term for an investor who spends most of the day dealing on the stock market through the Internet.

DCF Abbreviation of ***discounted cash flow***.

DCR Abbreviation of ***domestic content requirements***.

dead-cat bounce Brief rise in the stock index of a falling market. The term refers to the supposed ability of a cat always to land on its feet: if a falling cat bounces, it must be dead.

dead freight Freight charged by a shipowner to a charterer who does not use all the cargo space on a ship (which the owner may otherwise have sold to somebody else).

dead in the water Describing a project that has failed completely, often before it is properly underway.

dead rent Rent payable to a mine-owner whether the lessee uses the mine or not.

dead stock Stock (inventory) that is not being sold or used. It should be got rid of (by selling at a discount or for salvage) and the space put to better use.

deadweight debt Debt that is not covered by or incurred in exchange for real assets. For example, part of the ***national debt*** taken on to pay for war is a deadweight debt.

dealer Anybody who is engaged in trading (usually on their own account) on a financial market; or an overseas agent who acts as an intermediary between an overseas exporter and a home importer.

dear money Describing money that is difficult to find for borrowing or investment and even then at only very high interest rates.

death duty Also called estate duty, a former tax levied in the UK until 1975 on the estate of someone who has died. It was superseded by capital transfer tax, which was itself replaced in 1986 by ***inheritance tax***.

death valley days Colloquial term for the "dry" days on the financial markets – days on which little trading takes place.

debenture Long-term loan to a company made at a fixed rate of interest and usually with a specified maturity date, generally between 10 and 40 years. Debenture holders are numbered with the company's creditors, and in the event of liquidation have preferential claims on the company. Debentures may be treated as tradable securities.

debit note Notification sent to a customer that a supplier is about the debit the client's account with a certain sum. Debit notes are normally issued only in unusual circumstances, as when the client has been charged too little for goods or services delivered.

debt Sum of money, or value of goods or services, owed by one person, group or company to another. Debts arise because the seller allows the purchaser ***credit***. Assignable debts may be transferred in whole from one per son to another. In commerce, especially in the USA, the term is also used to describe the whole of a company's long-term borrowings.

debt buy-back In international trading, an arrangement whereby a debtor nation buys back its debt at a discount for cash.

debt collecting Business of a company or organization that collects debts on behalf of other companies or individuals. *See also* ***factoring***.

debt-equity swap Method by which a lender (such as a bank) disposes of a loan to a Third World country by converting it into a holding of equity in a company in that country. ***Venture capital*** may also be provided in exchange for equity in the company being financed.

debt forgiveness In international finance, writing off part of a nation's debt, or selling the debt to a third party for a large discount.

debt instrument Written promise to pay a debt; or a medium for obtaining a (usually short-term) loan.

debt market Market (such as the New York Bonds Exchange) in which debt securities are bought and sold.

debtor (dr) Person or company that owes money, goods or services to another.

debtor days Average time customers who buy goods or services on credit take to pay for them.

debt rescheduling When a debtor has difficulties making repayments, a method by which the lender defers interest or repayments, extends the loan period, or agrees to a completely new loan.

debt service ratio In international finance, a nation's annual repayments on its foreign debt divided by the value of its exports (in hard currency).

debt servicing Payment of interest on a debt.

debt swap *See* ***debt-equity swap***.

debt-to-equity ratio A company may finance itself through borrowing or through shareholder investment, depending on current interest rates. The proportion of each is its debt-to-equity ratio, or ***gearing***.

debut Arrival on the stock market of the shares of a newly listed company and the first day's trading in that company's stock.

decentralization Distribution of the constituent part of a company or government to a variety of geographical locations. The advantages include the availability of cheaper labour (that is likely to be offset initially by the cost of relocating key personnel), increased efficiency and, in the case of government, the provision of incentives to industry to consider non-metropolitan locations.

deck cargo Cargo that is stored on the deck of a ship (as opposed to being stowed as belly cargo).

declaration of solvency Formal statement by a company's directors that it seeks voluntary liquidation but that it expects to pay its creditors within at least 12 months.

de-diversification Shedding of interest in companies acquired in the process of ***diversification***, so as to reduce the variety of business in which the company engages.

deductive value Value of imported goods deduced by customs, based on their resale price (less certain expenses).

deed Document that records an agreement or transaction and may bear the seals of the parties concerned to testify to its validity.

deed of assignment *See* ***assignment***.

deed of inspectorship Method of handing over an insolvent business to its creditors, who appoint inspectors to wind it up or continue running it as a going concern.

deed of partnership Legal agreement that details the rights and responsibilities of partners and how profits or losses of the partnership should be apportioned.

deed of transfer Legal document that gives authority to registrars of securities to transfer them from the seller to the buyer.

deed of variation Legal document that amends the terms of a will after the death of its author (all beneficiaries have to agree to the changes).

deep discount stock Also called zero-coupon stock, loan stock issued at a greater discount than other stock of the issuer, providing lower (or zero) interest.

deep market Financial market in which many transactions can take place without affecting the price of the underlying financial instrument.

deep pocket Description of a company or person who seems to have plenty of money (and may therefore be worth suing). A deep-pocket view of some subsidiaries is that they may have access to more funds than an independent company of a similar size. A subsidiary may thus be able to call upon the greater resources of its parent company to engage in competition with independents in its sector.

default Failure to comply with the terms set out in a contract. Legal proceedings generally follow if the matter cannot be settled amicably (*see* ***default notice***).

default notice Notice issued by a lender to a borrower who is in default of a loan subject to the ***Consumer Credit Act 1974***. If the notice is not complied with, the lender can seek an ***enforcement order***.

defeasance Condition built into the wording of a deed that renders the deed void if the condition is complied with. The term is also used for any annulment or act that renders something null and void, such as the removal from a company's balance sheet liabilities that have no right to early repayment.

defence bonds UK government securities, in £5 units, sold between 1939 and 1964 to pay for spending on World War II. They paid a tax-free bonus at maturity, but there was a limit to the number of bonds that any one person could hold.

defensive stock Shares in companies that are not affected by economic cycles because they produce necessities (such as food).

deferral Spreading the befits accruing from an asset over the whole life of the asset, rather than accounting for them in the financial year of its acquisition.

deferred charges Outgoings that are not regarded as an expense in the accounting period in which they occur but which are carried forward (as an asset) and written off in a later accounting period. They are also known as a deferred costs.

deferred coupon note Bond on which interest is not paid until after a specified date. It is known in the USA as a deferred interest bond or extended bond.

deferred futures Futures contracts that are farthest away from maturity.

deferred interest bond US term for a ***deferred coupon note***.

deferred shares Shares with special dividend rights, often allocated all company profits remaining after a given percentage has been paid on other kinds of shares. Such shares are usually issued to the founders of a company.

deferred taxation Tax for which a company or person is liable, but which has not yet been considered or demanded by the Inland Revenue.

deficit Excess of expenditure over income, or liabilities over assets; it is therefore a loss.

deflation Persistent decrease in prices, generally caused by a fall in the level of economic activity within a country; the opposite of inflation. It should not be confused with ***disinflation***.

deflationary gap Difference between the actual level of investment and the level necessary to restore full employment.

defunct company Company that is no longer active (and has been removed from the register of companies).

***del credere* agent** Person who accepts goods on consignment from exporters, agreeing (in return for a commission) to pay for them in the event that the original purchaser defaults.

delagatus non potest delegare Latin for a "delegate cannot delegate", a principle that prevents a contractor from subcontracting part of the work.

delivered at docks Applied to goods shipped by sea, acknowledgement that an exporter has fulfilled his or her obligations when the goods have arrived at the docks and been unloaded (but without having passed through customs).

delivered at frontier Applied principally to goods shipped by land transport, acknowledgement that an exporter has fulfilled his or her obligations when the goods have arrived at the frontier, (but without having passed through customs).

delivery Handing over of property or monetary assets. In the City of London the term has two more specific meanings: it describes the transfer of securities, or the receipt of the financial instrument or cash payment specified in a financial futures contract.

delivery note Document that advises a recipient of the intended delivery of goods or that accompanies goods on delivery.

delivery verification certificate (DVC) Document used in the USA to record the movement of imported goods from an importer to a manufacturer, used to substantiate any claim for manufacturing ***drawback***.

delta Stock exchange classification of shares that are traded on the ***Alternative Investment Market***. They are generally relatively inactive and stable shares in small companies. *See also* ***alpha; beta; gamma***.

demand Desire for possession of a particular good or service at a specified price expressed by those able and willing to purchase it; or a request, such as a request for payment of a debt.

demand bill ***Bill of exchange*** that has to be paid on demand, also called a demand draft.

demand curve Relationship between demand and price, in the form of a graph that plots the likely demand for a product at various prices.

demand deposit Money, deposited with a financial institution, that may be withdrawn at a moment's notice (on demand).

demand-pull inflation Overall price rises resulting from excess demand in an economy (i.e. there are not enough goods and services to meet the demand for them).

demarcation Dividing line that separates the activities of one group of workers in a company (such as maintenance engineers) from another group (such as maintenance electricians).

dematerialize To convert into electronic form information that was once recorded on paper.

demerger Splitting of a company into two or more independent parts, either by floating them separately on the stock exchange or by selling them off.

demurrage Damages claimed by a shipowner from a charterer when loading or unloading of cargo takes longer than contracted for.

demutualization *See mutual.*

denationalization Privatization of a previously nationalized industry by floating the company concerned on the stock exchange and selling shares to members of the public or to institutions. In the UK, denationalized industries include British Telecom, British Gas and British Airways.

Department of Trade and Industry (DTI) UK government department that advises and controls business, finance and overseas trade, according to the government's policies.

department store Large retail outlet where separate types of goods are sold in their own departments.

deposit Initial payment made on an item to reserve it, or an initial payment for something bought on credit or by hire purchase. The term is also used for goods or money placed with a bank or other financial institution.

depository Secure place where money, valuables or other goods are stored (deposited). Depositories are different from banks because they do not transact other business and do not necessarily offer ready access to the assets stored in them.

Depository Institutions Deregulation and Monetary Decontrol Act 1980 (DIDMCA) US legislation that removed the limit on interest rates for passbook savings accounts (which thereafter followed market trends).

depository receipt Also termed a warehouse receipt, a document recording the delivery of goods to a warehouse.

Depository Trust Company (DTC) In the USA, the central depository for stock exchange securities.

depot Warehouse or storage area, usually to hold stocks of goods for distribution locally to retailers.

depreciated cost Also called depreciated value or net book value (NBV), the value of an asset on a company's books minus any depreciation since purchase or revaluation.

depreciation Positive decline in the real value of a tangible asset because of consumption, wear or obsolescence. The concept of depreciation is widely used for the purpose of writing off the cost of an asset against profit over an extended period (its depreciable life), irrespective of the real value of the asset. Depreciation is charged against income or the profit and loss account, and there are various ways of calculating it.

depression Major and persistent downswing of a trade cycle, characterized by high unemployment and the underutilization of other factors of production. A less severe downswing is known as a slump or recession.

deregulation Removal of controls and abandonment of state supervision of private enterprise. One of the most notable recent deregulations was that of the ***London Stock Exchange***.

derivative Transferrable, often high-risk security, such as a future or an option.

dernier cours French for ***closing prices***.

designated investment exchange (DIE) Foreign investment exchange that has equivalent operating standards to home exchanges, as acknowledged by the ***Securities and Investment Board (SIB)***.

designated market maker Market maker who undertakes to be present on the trading floor of the stock exchange and to maintain up-to-date two-way prices in return for certain concessions.

Desk, The Colloquial name for the Securities Department of the New York Federal Reserve Bank.

destocking Deliberate reduction in the stock (inventory) held by a company, achieved by cutting production or by buying less stock. It reduces the amount of capital locked up in stock (or the need for borrowing to pay for it).

detention Similar to demurrage, an extra charge levied by a transport company for holding goods beyond the time when they should have been delivered.

detinue Legal term for an action to recover something that has been detained.

Deutsche Aktienindex (DAX) German share price index, calculated every minute, for 30 leading shares on the Frankfurt stock exchange.

Deutsche Terminborse (DTB) German futures and options exchange, opened in 1990 in Frankfurt.

devaluation Reduction in the relative value of currency. The devaluation may be relative to an absolute value (e.g. the gold standard) or to other may be relative to an absolute value (e.g. the gold standard) or to relative values (e.g. other currencies).

development capital Funds made available (to venture capital companies and other specialists) through investment in equities and loan capital.

development cost Expense incurred by a company in order to improve a process or product. It is usually written off immediately to the profit and loss account, unless the process or product will probably create future income (when the cost can be written off against that income when it accrues).

development expenditure Money spent by a company on research and development (R & D), which may be tax deductible.

Devisen German for foreign exchange.

devises French for foreign exchange.

DIDMCA Abbreviation of ***Depository Institutions Deregulation and Monetary Decontrol Act 1980***.

DIE Abbreviation of ***designated investment exchange***.

dies non Latin for "day that is not...", describing a day that is not counted for some purpose. For example, Saturday and Sunday are not counted as days of the working week.

differential Difference between two values, e.g. of prices or salaries.

differential piece rate Higher payment per unit of production (piece rate) that is paid once a target number of units have been produced.

dilapidations At the end of the term of a lease, cost (charged to the lessee) of restoring leasehold property to the state it was in at the beginning of the lease.

dilution Reduction in the skill of a workforce overall as comparatively unskilled workers are recruited in response to a rise in demand for a given product or service.

dilution of control Result of deliberately increasing the number of a company's shares on the market, effectively reducing the price of each individual share and reducing the power of each existing shareholder to influence corporate affairs.

dilution of earnings Result of deliberately increasing the number of a company's shares on the market, effectively reducing the earnings per share.

diminishing returns Concept that suggests that as additional units of one factor of production are added, the relative increase in output will eventually begin to decline. For example, a factory can increase its output by employing more labour, but unless other factors of production (e.g. machinery) are also increased each additional employee will be working with a smaller proportion of the other, fixed, resources available.

direct action Attempt to take control of a company by purchasing a controlling interest of shares, rather than by negotiation with the company itself.

direct arbitrage Foreign exchange dealings that are restricted to one centre.

direct cost Also called variable cost, the cost of materials, items or activities (including labour) that are directly involved in the production of goods, and without which those goods could not be produced in the short term. The prime cost is the total of direct expenses, direct labour and direct materials.

direct expenses Expenses that may be attributed to one or another factor of production. They are included in ***direct costs***.

direct exporting Transaction between an exporter and an importer that does not involve a third party (such as an agent).

directive *European Union (EU)* legislation that states what has to be done within a given timescale, without defining how it is to be done.

direct labour Members of a company's workforce who are directly involved in the production of goods or services. For example, a welder is a member of the direct labour force whereas an estimator is not.

direct mail Form of advertising and selling. Individual potential customers receive promotional material and information through the post, and order goods that are delivered by post or courier. It is also known as mail order.

direct marketing Selling activity aimed directly at potential customers, such as door-to-door selling and direct mail.

direct materials Materials that directly become part of a company's product or cost unit.

director One of the principals of a company, in a public liability company (plc) appointed by its shareholders. Most companies have a group of directors (the board of directors) who act collectively as the senior management of the company, being responsible to the shareholders for its efficient running and future development. The duties and legal responsibilities of a director are defined in the Companies Acts. They include the compilation of an ***annual report*** and the recommendation of an annual dividend on shares.

directors' interests Interests in a company's debentures, shares and share options held by its directors, which must in law be disclosed.

directors' remuneration Also sometimes known as directors' emoluments, money received by directors by virtue of their office, including fees, salaries, perquisites and other profit. Certain benefits and expenses paid by the company may also be deemed to be remuneration. The total (although not necessarily individual) directors' remuneration appears in the company's annual financial report.

directors' report Report by a company's directors to its shareholders, which is published with the annual accounts and filed with the Register of Companies at Companies House.

directors' valuation Right of a company's board of directors to estimate the value of its shareholding in an unquoted company. It is called for only if the value of the shares concerned has changed since they were purchased.

direct placement Selling of shares directly to the public without using an underwriter.

direct quotation Quotation of a currency exchange rate in terms of one unit of the home currency (for example, 1£ = 3.35 DM).

direct response marketing Method of marketing that aims to get customers to contact a suppler (often the manufacturer) directly.

direct sale Sale made directly to the end-user (usually by a manufacturer or wholesaler), without the intervention of a retail outlet.

direct taxation System of taxation whereby companies and individuals pay tax on income directly the authorities (Inland Revenue in the UK, Internal Revenue Service in the USA) or through an employer, as opposed to indirect taxation, in which tax is added to the prices of goods and services.

dirty cargo Unclean cargo shipped in bulk or in containers with a disposable lining, possibly posing a fire or health risk.

dirty float Partly-managed floating exchange rate in which the central bank continues to intervene in the market for its own currency.

dirty money Money obtained illegally, generally through unlawful international business activities.

dirty price Price of a gilt-edged security including any interest that may have accrued since the last payment of a dividend.

discharge To pay a debt, such as a bill of exchange.

discharged bill *Bill of exchange* that has been paid by the drawer or drawee, or is being held by an acceptor. If a holder denounces rights to the debt against an acceptor, the bill is also deemed to be discharged.

discharge of contract End of a contract, either because it has been fulfilled or because it is impossible to fulfil.

disciplinary procedure Formal procedure laid down to take to task an employee who does not fulfil his or her contract of employment. The usual stages are verbal warning, written warning, final written warning and dismissal.

disclaimer Clause in a contract that states that one of the parties does not take responsibility for some occurrence. For example, the owners of many car parks advertise to motorists that they disclaim any responsibility for loss or damage to cars or anything contained in them.

disclosure Revealing of relevant information. The term has two major uses:

1. It is the requirement that a limited company in the UK must disclose its financial dealings and position by the publication of annual accounts, and deposit at Companies House lists of directors and shareholders in the company.
2. It is the requirement that the parties to any contract should disclose relevant information, for example a person holding a life assurance policy must notify the assurers of his or her medical history.

discount To make a reduction in the face value of an article (or the list price), generally in order to make the purchase more attractive to a customer or perhaps for paying by cash. Bulk discounts and trade discounts are also sometimes available. Discounts are shown as expenses in a company's profit and loss account. The term has several other meanings.

discount broker Broker who acts as an intermediary between those who want to buy and sell ***bills of exchange***.

discounted cash flow (DCF) Method of assessing a company's investments according to when they are due to yield their expected returns, in order to indicate cash flows and the present worth of the future sum. In this way it is possible to determine preferences for one of a number of alternative investments.

discount factor Also called present-value factor, factor that, when applied to a predicted annual cash flow, converts it to a present value. It is equal to $1/(1 + r)^t$, where r is the hurdle rate and t is the duration of the project concerned.

discount house Organization whose main activity is discounting ***bills of exchange***.

discounting back Method of estimating the present value of a future sum, carried out by finding what sum earning x per cent ***compound interest*** over the time in question will equal the future sum. The interest rate x is the one in use when the calculation is made.

discount market That part of a money market that involves the buying and selling of short-term debt between the commercial banks, the discount houses and the central bank.

discount rate Interest rate applied to future earnings to convert them to present values. It is the capital rate of interest or hurdle rate used with a discount factor in calculating a discounted cash flow.

discount store Retail outlet that sells goods (usually consumer durables) at a discount on normal prices. It is generally able to do so by having low overheads and high turnover (to offset small margins).

discretionary account (DA) Account into which ***discretionary funds*** are placed.

discretionary funds Money left with a stockbroker, to be invested at his or her discretion.

discretionary income Income that remains after meeting the cost of taxes and such necessities as food and accommodation, to be spent at the owner's discretion.

dishonour To refuse to accept or discharge a ***bill of exchange*** when it falls due for payment.

disinflation Curbing of inflation by the adoption of mild economic measures such as the restriction of expenditure. Other measures include increasing interest rates and the deliberate creation of a budget surplus. Disinflation is a mild form of ***deflation***, which by contrast indicates an uncontrollable fall in prices.

disintermediation Withdrawal of a financial intermediary from a negotiation. The term may also be applied to the flow of funds from lenders to borrowers "off the balance sheet" without the intervention of an intermediary (such as a mortgage broker).

dismissal Being dismissed from employment because of a breach of discipline or for incompetence. It is not the same as ***redundancy***. *See also* ***summary dismissal***.

disposable income That part of a person's income that he or she may dispose of in any way, i.e., what is left after taxes have been paid.

disposables Non-durable goods; those that are consumed during their use. Food, drink and fuel are all disposables.

disputes procedure Formal procedure for dealing with disputes between management and employees (generally through their ***trade union***).

dissolution Winding up of a company, usually by the legal process of liquidation. In the case of a partnership, dissolution may be occasioned by the death or retirement of one or more partners, by ***bankruptcy*** or by the expiry of a specified time period, without recourse to law.

distraint Legally-authorized seizure of assets to compel a debtor to pay a debt. If the debt remains outstanding, goods obtained by distraint may be sold in order that the creditor may obtain satisfaction.

distress merchandise Goods or assets made available for sale by a company facing or already consigned to ***liquidation***. Most distress merchandise is placed on the market on the orders of an official receiver in order to provide liquid sums for the payment of creditors.

distributable reserves Retained profits that a company can distribute to its shareholders.

distribution Transport, allocation and placement of raw materials or goods to and from a factory to warehouses and shops; or payments made by a company from its profits (i.e. dividends); or the apportioning of a ***scrip issue*** or ***rights issue*** of shares.

distribution channel Route followed by a product from its producer to its ultimate purchaser.

distributive trade Part of industry that sells goods and services direct to the consumer. Retailers are the main contributors to the distributive trade.

distributor Wholesaler; a person or company that acts as an agent in the distribution of goods to retail outlets.

diversification Extension of the range of goods and services offered into new areas, either material or geographical. By extension the term may also be applied to attempts by local authorities or central government to attract a variety of industries to an area heavily dependent upon a single industry, particularly one in decline.

divestment Sale or liquidation of parts of a company, generally in an attempt to improve efficiency by cutting loss-making business and/or concentrating on one product or industry. Divestment is therefore the opposite process to merger.

dividend A share in the profits of a limited company, usually paid annually. Dividends are usually expressed as a percentage of the nominal value of a single ordinary share. Thus a payment of 10p on each £1 share (or 10c on each $1 share) would be termed a dividend of 10%. They may also be expressed in terms of the dividend yield, which is the dividend expressed as a percentage of the share value. Dividends are determined by the directors of a company and are announced at the end of the ***annual general meeting (AGM)*** of the company.

dividend cover Degree to which a dividend payment on ordinary shares is covered by profits earned. Thus a company that declares after-tax profits of $10m and makes a total dividend payment of $2m on ordinary shares is said to be "covered five times". An uncovered dividend, on the other hand, is a payment made at least partly from reserves rather than current profits.

dividend mandate Mandate signed by a shareholder and delivered to a company, instructing it to pay dividends directly to a third party (generally into a bank account).

dividend per share (DPS) Expression of a ***dividend*** in cents, pence etc. per share rather than as a percentage of the total value of the share. Thus a 10% dividend on a share worth £1 would be termed a "10p per share dividend".

dividend stripping Method of tax avoidance that makes it unnecessary for a person or company to receive dividend payments (on which tax is payable). Also called ***bond washing***, the technique involves buying gilt-edged securities ***ex dividend*** and selling them ***cum dividend*** before the next dividend falls due.

dividend warrant Order to a company's bankers to pay a specified dividend or interest to a shareholder or other investor.

dividend yield Yield calculated in relation to the current market price of the investment; the dividend divided by the share price. *See* ***dividend***.

division Separate main operational section of a company.

division of labour Splitting of a job or other task into small repeating parts that can each be done by one person.

dock dues Charge levied on vessels entering or leaving dock.

dock receipt Document that acknowledges that export goods have been transported (by a home carrier) to the port of departure and placed in the care of an international carrier.

dock warrant Document that establishes the ownership of goods stored in a warehouse at the docks.

document against acceptance (D/A) In the export of goods, a document of title passed by the master of the ship carrying the goods to the importer when he or she signs a ***bill of exchange*** (and on acceptance of the bill, the goods are released).

document against payment In the export of goods, a ***bill of sight*** passed by the master of the ship carrying the goods to the importer (or his agent), which the importer must pay before taking possession of them.

documentary credit In the export of goods, credit facilities made available at a home bank by a foreign importer. An exporter can then use this credit to discount bills drawn upon the importer.

dog US colloquial term for a financial product that has a low share of a slowly growing or stagnant market.

dollar cost averaging *See* ***pound cost averaging***.

dollar glut Overabundance of US dollars on international finance markets, leading to a fall in the value of the dollar.

dollar premium Extra charge, above the official exchange rate, sometimes demanded for the purchase of US dollars.

dolphin Informal term for somebody who buys shares in new issues and then sells for a high profit as soon as trading opens.

domestic content requirements (DCR) Condition imposed by some countries that imported goods should contain a certain amount of components made within that country using domestic labour and materials.

dormant company Company that does not operate or require accounts to be kept (except for the initial issue of shares).

dot com stocks Colloquial description of a company that relies in some way on the ***Internet*** to market its products or services.

douane French for ***customs*** or customs duty.

double auction Normal type of outcry for trading in commodity markets, in which both bids and offers are made in competition with each other.

double bottom In the analysis of share market trends, describing a price that hits a low point equal to the last low point. The prediction is that once two similar low points have been reached, the price will tend to go up.

double option ***Option*** to either buy or sell.

double-taxation agreement Agreement between two countries that the income of non-residents should not be taxed both in their country of origin and in the country in which they live.

double time Twice the normal hourly rate of pay, sometimes paid to employees who work unsociable hours or for working on public holidays and at weekends.

double top In the analysis of share market trends, describing a price that rises twice to similar high points. The prediction is that after the double top, the price will tend to fall.

doubtful debts Money that is owed but thought unlikely to be paid. Provision can be made for such sums in a company's accounts until they become ***bad debts***.

Dow Jones Index Formal name the Dow Jones Industrial Average, often called simply the Dow Jones, a security price index used on the ***New York Stock Exchange*** and issued by the US firm of Dow Jones & Co. (publishers of the *Wall Street Journal*). It is based on the average closing prices of a selection of 30 quoted companies.

down and dirty Colloquial term for the practice of arranging, for a company in financial difficulties, a refinancing package that would severely dilute the holdings of minor shareholders were they not to participate.

down-and-in call/put option Option that becomes valid only when the price of the underlying security falls below a pre-set price.

down-and-out call/put option Option that becomes invalid when the price of the underlying security falls below a pre-set price.

downgrade To reduce the status of somebody or something. For example, a person downgrades his or her shareholding by selling part of it.

down-market Describing something that is of poor quality and often low-priced.

downside The amount a person stands to lose when taking a risk.

downsize To reduce the size of a company's workforce (i.e. making employees redundant), usually to make financial savings. The term also means to move applications from (large) mainframe computers to (small) personal computers (PCs).

downstream Describing the movement of funds from a parent company to one of its subsidiaries.

downstream dumping Sale by a foreign producer to another producer in the home market at below cost price. The second producer then further processes the goods and exports them.

downstream pricing Control of the price of a particular commodity by a large producer who purchases most of it.

downtick Describing a transaction concluded at a lower price than a similar previous transaction. It is also a term for a small and temporary fall in the price of a share.

downtime Time during which a machine, although wanted, cannot be used (perhaps because of breakdown, repair or maintenance). It has the effect of adding to fixed costs.

DPS Abbreviation of ***dividend per share***.

dr Abbreviation of ***debtor***.

draft Written order from a customer to a financial institution, requesting that money is paid from the customer's account to a third party (such as a ***banker's draft***). In the USA, it is the usual term for a bill of exchange. To draft (verb) is to draw up any document, especially a contract draft.

dragon bond Colloquial term for a bond issued in the markets of a far Eastern country (usually Hong Kong or Singapore).

draw To write a ***bill of exchange***, cheque or ***promissory note***. The person who does so is the drawer, and the person or institution it is addressed to is the drawee.

drawback Repayment of customs and excise duty on certain goods to an exporter who has already paid duty on imported raw materials to make them.

drawdown Sum of money borrowed, usually referring to the staged drawing of funds from a credit facility.

drawee *See* ***draw***.

drawer *See* ***draw***.

drawing rights Method by means of which members of the ***International Monetary Fund (IMF)*** that have balance of payments difficulties get financial help. Each member has a quota, up to 25% of which can be drawn on demand. *See also* ***special drawing rights***.

drawings Payments (or goods in kind) made to a partner or sole proprietor.

drip Method of re-investment in which a company uses a planned dividend to buy its own shares on the stock exchange (instead of making a bonus issue).

drip-feed Steady payment of money at regular intervals. It is usually a pejorative term implying that the recipient is dependent on the payments. It is often applied to foreign aid to underdeveloped countries. The term is also used by venture capitalists for ***venture capital*** payments made to a start-up company in stages.

drop-dead date Date on which it is expected that a troubled company will run out of funds.

drop-dead fee Payment offered to a bidder by the target of a (usually take-over) bid in an effort to induce the bidder to withdraw the bid.

drop-dead rate Amount demanded by a would-be corporate raider to withdraw the bid.

drop lock Loan stock issued when a specific interest rate is reached. The purpose is to convert short-term borrowings into long-term loans.

drop ship Specification that the price of a shipment by an exporter directly to an importer includes all shipping expenses.

DTB Abbreviation of ***Deutsche Terminborse***.

DTC Abbreviation of ***Depository Trust Company***.

DTI Abbreviation of ***Department of Trade and Industry***.

dual capacity Stock exchange system that makes no distinction between the functions of stockbrokers and ***jobbers***. One person (called a ***market-maker***) may therefore both buy and sell stocks and shares on the exchange.

dual pricing Method of costing transfers (of goods or services) between divisions of a single organization in order to encourage interdivisional transactions. The buying division may be charged only the marginal cost while crediting the full cost to the selling division.

due date Date on which a ***bill of exchange*** is due to be paid. In the UK, instruments not payable on demand, on sight or on presentation are allowed three ***days of grace***.

dumping Sale of surplus goods overseas at extremely low prices (less than cost price). It may be done to get rid of excess production, to earn foreign exchange or to harm foreign industry. It is frowned upon and countries may take retaliatory action (such as the imposition of antidumping duty)

duopoly Market in which there are only two competing companies. Because competition between duopolists is particularly fierce and destructive, there tends to be some form of implicit or even explicit agreement to share the market (e.g. on a regional basis).

duopsony Market in which there are only two purchasers of a type of goods or services, but a number of competing suppliers.

durable goods Goods that are not consumed by their use but which endure for a reasonable period of time. Some manufacturers of durables incorporate some form of ***obsolescence*** to ensure a continuity of demand.

Dutch auction Type of auction in which the seller begins by proposing a high price and gradually lowers it until somebody agrees to buy.

dutiable Describing items that are liable to ***duty***.

duty Broadly, any tax levied by a public authority, particularly that imposed on imports, exports and manufactured goods. *See also* ***excise duty***.

duty-free Describing goods on which no ***duty*** has to be paid. The practice of allowing people entering or leaving a country to purchase duty-free goods at ports and airports ended in the EU in June 1999.

duty-paid Authenticated statement attached to goods on which duty has been paid, to facilitate their passage through customs.

duty-paid contract Type of ***ex ship*** contract in which import duty is paid by the seller.

duty-paid foreign goods Imported goods on which all duty and taxes have been paid and which have been cleared by customs.

DVC Abbreviation of ***delivery verification certificate***.

E

E & OE Abbreviation of ***errors and omissions excepted***.

early bargain Deal struck on the stock exchange after the exchange has closed and considered to be among the first transactions of the following day. Early bargains are also known as after-hours dealings or trading.

early stage investment Funds, usually provided by a ***venture capital*** company, that finance the start-up of a new business.

early withdrawal penalty Penalty charged for withdrawal of funds from a fixed-term investment before the maturity date.

earned income Income received in exchange for labour, rather than derived from investments (for UK tax purposes, the definition does, however, include some pension payments and state benefits).

earnest money Part payment (a deposit) made on goods or services, showing that the buyer is serious about buying; or the margin on a futures market.

earning capacity Value of an employee's services to a company. For example, the earning capacity of an advertising sales executive is equivalent to the revenue he or she brings in. The term is also applied more colloquially to describe the maximum wage that can be earned in a specific job.

earning power Value of a person's services at a specified time in a free market. It is indicated by the salary that could be commanded if the person were to change jobs.

earnings per share (EPS) Method of expressing the income of a company, arrived at by dividing the net annual income attributable to the shareholders by the number of shares. Earnings per share can then be used to calculate the ***price-earnings ratio*** of the company.

earnings yield Hypothetical figure that provides a reliable measurement of the worth of an investment. It is reached by relating a company's divisible net earnings to the market price of the investment (earnings per share divided by market price, expressed as a percentage). Sometimes, with reference to fixed-interest securities, the term is used interchangeably with ***flat yield***.

earn-out Employee incentive scheme whereby the employee is offered share options that give him or her an interest in the company for which he or she works. The term also describes an agreement to buy a company where the buyer pays a lump sum and promises to pay more if specified earnings levels are achieved. The latter is also known as a contingent agreement.

EAS Abbreviation of ***Enterprise Allowance Scheme***.

EASDAQ Abbreviation of ***European Association of Securities Dealers Automated Quotation System***.

easy market Market in which there are few buyers; prices are therefore low.

easy money Money borrowed at a low rate of interest, usually consisting of funds made available by authorities wishing to encourage economic activity. It is also known as cheap money.

EC Abbreviation of ***European Commission*** and of European Community, now replaced by the ***European Union (EU)***.

ECGD Abbreviation of ***Export Credit Guarantee Department***.

ECHO Abbreviation of ***Exchange Clearing House***.

eco-label Mark applied to goods by EU producers to indicate that they are environmentally friendly.

e-commerce Commerce carried out electronically, particularly over the ***Internet***.

Economic and Monetary Union (EMU) Plan to bring together the currencies and monetary policies of the EU member states, as laid down by the Maastricht Treaty. There would thus be a single currency (the ***euro***) and a single central bank. The plan was implemented in January 1999, but not all member states (including the UK) initially took part.

economic exposure Foreign exchange risk of a company in such areas as overseas investment and raw material costs.

economic sanction Alternative term for an embargo on trade with another country, almost always for political reasons.

economic union Agreement between two or more countries to do away with trade barriers with each other and to apply common tariffs on imports from non-union members.

economic value added (EVA) Amount by which a company's rate of return on investment exceeds its cost of capital.

economies of scale Reduction in the average cost of production with increase in production, generally made possible by the large size of a company or industry. Internal economies of scale are defined as those enjoyed by a large single company or operation and are, broadly, made possible by the distribution of indirect costs and improvements in technology, which increase the optimum level of output. External economies of scale are those associated with an industry or location. For example, a concentration of ship-building companies on a river leads to the creation of a large pool of skilled labour which can be drawn on if one company wishes to expand.

ECP Abbreviation of *euro-commercial paper*.

ECU Abbreviation of *European Currency Unit*.

EDF Abbreviation of *European Development Fund*.

EEA Abbreviation of *European Economic Area*.

EEC Abbreviation of *European Economic Community*.

effective demand Desire for goods or services (demand) that is backed by the ability to pay.

effective exchange rate Weighted average of a country's exchange rate and that of its significant trading partners.

EFTA Abbreviation of *European Free Trade Association*.

EGM Abbreviation of *extraordinary general meeting*.

eighty/twenty rule Rule of thumb that states that 80% of benefits (or disbenefits) come from 20% of items or objects. It is also known as the Pareto analysis.

EIS Abbreviation of *Enterprise Investment Scheme*.

elastic currency US principle that home currency should meet the needs of trade and commerce, with the expansion of credit keeping pace with the expansion of business.

elephant Colloquial term for a large corporate entity that is slow but dominant and displays a tendency towards the creation of monopolies.

eligible bank UK bank that is entitled to discount acceptances at the *Bank of England*.

eligible bill In the UK, a bank bill that is issued by a bank entitled to discount acceptances at the Bank of England (an eligible bank); it may be rediscounted at the Bank of England. In the USA, another term for *eligible paper*.

eligible paper In the USA, a banker's acceptance that may be rediscounted at a ***federal reserve bank***.

EMA Abbreviation of ***European Monetary Agreement***.

embargo Prohibition on the export or import of specified goods to or from a particular country or bloc, generally for political reasons.

emerging market Security market in a newly industrialized country (such as those in eastern Europe and eastern Asia).

Emerging Markets Traders Association (EMTA) Organization established in New York in the late 1980s for overseeing trade in bank loans to emerging nations. ***Brady bonds*** and ***eurobonds*** were included in its remit in 1990.

EMI Abbreviation of ***European Monetary Institute***.

emolument Salary and other benefits, particularly those paid to the holder of high office.

employee buy-out Take-over of a company by employees who have purchased the majority of its voting shares.

employee stock ownership plan (ESOP) US plan that lets employees buy shares (stock) in their own company.

Employment Acts UK legislation, passed in 1980, 1982, 1988, 1989 and 1990, that deal with conditions of employment, trade unions and, latterly, the employment of women and young people.

employment agency Also termed an employment bureau, a business that finds employees for potential employers. The employer pays a fee if a person found by the agency is employed; there is no charge to the employee.

employment contract *See* ***contract of employment***.

employment legislation *See* ***Employment Acts***.

EMS Abbreviation of ***European Monetary System***.

EMTA Abbreviation of ***Emerging Markets Traders Association***.

EMU Abbreviation of ***Economic and Monetary Union***.

endorsement Signature or explanatory statement on a document. For example, an open cheque cashed at a bank or transferred by the payee to a third party must bear the payee's endorsement on the reverse. The person making the endorsement is the endorser; the recipient is the endorsee. The term is sometimes spelled indorsement.

enforcement agency Government agency or ***self-regulating organization (SRO)*** that can investigate and if necessary discipline companies or individuals for breaches of agreed codes of practice.

enforcement order UK court order that deals with default on a loan subject to the ***Consumer Credit Act 1974***.

enroute expenses US term for travelling expenses incurred in the course of doing business overseas.

enterprise Any undertaking, but particularly a bold or remarkable one; or the quality of boldness and imagination in an undertaking.

enterprise allowance Regular funding from the UK government for people starting up in business, payable for the first year.

Enterprise Allowance Scheme (EAS) UK government scheme set up to encourage the establishment of new businesses by the unemployed by offering, among other incentives, grants and tax concessions.

Enterprise Investment Scheme (EIS) UK government scheme established in 1994 that allows relief when shares in a company (not quoted on the Stock Exchange) are issued on subscription. It superseded the former ***Business Expansion Scheme***.

enterprise zone Geographical area in which economic activity is promoted by the UK government. Small businesses are encouraged, and the relocation of companies and industries to enterprise zones is helped by the provision of various incentives.

entrepôt trade Trade based on the re-export of imported goods. The exporter may be entitled to a refund of any customs duty paid (drawback), unless the goods are exported directly from a bonded warehouse.

entertainment allowance Amount the executive of a company is allowed to spend on entertaining clients or potential clients during the course of his or her business.

entertainment expenses Expense of entertaining business associates (for example, the cost of meals in restaurants or seats in a theatre).

entrepreneur Person who controls a commercial enterprise – the risk-taker or profit-maker – the person who assembled the factors of production and supervises their combination. The term also has the connotation of somebody who has an idea and then finds the money to back it.

entry and exit Appearance of companies in an industry and the disappearance of other companies, as new companies are stablished and other ones diversify, go into liquidation, or merely cease to trade.

entry documents Documents that an importer needs when goods are being cleared through customs.

entry summary documentation Documents prepared by customs after inspecting imported goods and estimating the duty to be paid.

environmental audit Also known as a green audit, an audit that reveals the impact of a company's activities on the environment.

EPS Abbreviation of ***earnings per share***.

equalization Return of capital invested in a unit trust. All investors in a trust receive an equal sum per unit held, although some may only have invested in the period since the last distribution. The distribution paid on the latter's stock therefore comprises the dividend and an equalization that brings the returns up to par.

equal opportunity Policy that ensures that employees or potential employees have equal chances of promotion or employment, irrespective of colour, disability, race, religion or sex. In the UK this policy is actively pursued by the Equal Opportunities Commission, set up by the ***Sex Discrimination Act 1975***.

Equal Pay Act 1970 UK legislation that requires employers to provide equal pay and conditions to employees who do the same jobs.

equilibrium Theoretical situation in a market where ***supply and demand*** are equal.

equity In general terms, the concept of fairness, of central importance to a branch of law distinct from common law, and as such having a significant effect on all kinds of contracts, dealings and trusts. The term also has various specific meanings. It is the ordinary share capital (risk capital) of a company, or a company's net assets, or the residual value of common stock over the debit balance of a margin account, or the difference between the market value of a property and the outstanding mortgage on it. In the last definition, if the amount still owing is greater than the present market value of the property, the mortgagor (borrower) has negative equity in the property.

equity capital Capital of a company that belongs to its owners (in many cases, holders of ordinary shares), rather than capital provided by owners of fixed-interest securities.

equity carve out Sale, using an initial public offering on the stock market, by a parent company of a minority holding in a subsidiary.

equity dilution Reduction in the unit value of ordinary shares as a result of a bonus issue.

equity gearing Ratio of a company's borrowing to its equity.

ERM Abbreviation of ***Exchange Rate Mechanism***.

errors and omissions excepted (E & OE) Denial of responsibility for clerical errors and omissions, often included on invoices as a safeguard.

escalation clause Also called an escalator clause, a condition in a long-term contract that sets out the agreement concerning rising costs (of, e.g., raw materials or labour).

escape clause Clause in a contract that allows one or other party to withdraw from the contract should certain events take place. For example, in a lease, it is possible to have a clause that allows the lessee to withdraw should the lessor increase the rent.

escrow account Bank account for holding foreign earnings from export sales, for use in making purchases abroad. The term is also used for an account whose accumulated funds are used for paying insurance premiums, taxes, and so on.

ESOP Abbreviation of ***employee stock ownership plan***.

establishment charge Also called establishment fee, the overheads of a department store or shopping centre which are divided up and paid by the individual departments or shops. Establishment charges include rent, rates, taxes and the costs of heating and lighting.

estate duty Alternative term for ***death duty***.

ethical investment Investment made in a company that is not active in anything that the investor thinks is antisocial or unethical in its dealings. Thus some investors would not put money into companies that deal in or manufacture animal furs, armaments, cigarettes, and so on.

EU *Abbreviation of* ***European Union***.

euro Standard currency unit of the ***European Monetary Union***, introduced at the beginning of 1999 (but not adopted then by Denmark, Greece, Sweden and the UK). Until January 2002, only non-cash payments may be made in euros. *See also* ***European Currency Unit (ECU)***.

eurobond Medium- or long-term bearer bond denominated in a ***eurocurrency***. Eurobonds are issued by governments or multinational companies. The eurobond market developed in the 1960s and is independent of the stock market.

euro-commercial paper (ECP) Commercial paper issued in a eurocurrency, in a market (chiefly centred on London) that was established in 1985.

eurocurrency Currency of any nation held offshore in a European country. The eurocurrency markets deal in very large-scale loans and deposits rather than the purchase or sale of foreign exchange. *See also* ***euro***.

eurodollars US dollars held outside the USA, particularly those circulating in Europe. The postwar economic ascendancy of the USA has made the eurodollar an international currency medium. *See also* ***eurocurrency***.

Euroland Theoretical political association comprising EU countries that adopted the ***euro*** in 1999.

euromarket Market in which eurocurrency is traded.

EURO.NM Alliance of European stock markets, established in 1996 mainly for smaller companies. Its members include the Amsterdam Stock Exchange, ***Brussels Stock Exchange***, ***German Stock Exchange*** and Le Société du Nouveau Marché.

euronote Negotiable, short-term, bearer-form note (usually in US dollars) issued through a syndicate of European banks.

European Association of Securities Dealers Automated Quotation System (EASDAQ) Europe-wide stock market, established in Brussels in 1966, based on the US ***National Association of Security Dealers Automated Quotation System (NASDAQ)*** and catering mainly for high-growth companies.

European Commission (EC) Major institution of the EU, established in 1967, responsible for implementing the Treaty of Rome. It introduces EU legislation and reconciles disagreements between members.

European Community (EC) Short form of the European Economic Community (EEC), now called the ***European Union (EU)***.

European company Planned status of all companies in the EU countries, when some standard form is agreed. This will take time, particularly because of the present wide variation in regulations regarding limited liability companies.

European Currency Unit (ECU) Unit of account dating in use by the European Economic Community (EEC) from 1979 and now by the ***European Union (EU)***. The value of the ECU is calculated by taking a weighted average of the current value of EU member-states' own currencies. It exists on paper, but is used to settle intra-Union debts and in the calculation of Union budgets. Because it is an inherently stable currency, the ECU is increasingly favoured in the international money markets as a medium for international trade. *See also* ***euro***.

European Development Fund (EDF) Fund established in 1976 by the European Community (now EU) to provide financial aid on advantageous terms to certain developing countries.

European Economic Area (EEA) European free trade area, established in 1994 by agreement between the ***European Union (EU)*** and the ***European Free Trade Association (EFTA)***.

European Economic Community (EEC) Association of some twelve European nations that were joined by a customs union and committed to the promotion of free trade within the boundaries of the community, now renamed the ***European Union (EU)***. It was often abbreviated to European Community (EC) and was originally known as the Common Market.

European Free Trade Association (EFTA) Trade association, established in 1960 between several west European countries, some of whom left when they joined the ***European Union (EU)***.

European Monetary Agreement (EMA) Agreement that allows currencies of European member states to be traded without restriction. It was made in 1958 by the then ***Organization for European Economic Cooperation (OEEC)*** (now the ***Organization for Economic Cooperation and Development, OECD***).

European Monetary Institute (EMI) Institute created in 1991 under the Maastricht Treaty to manage currency reserves of EU central banks, with a view towards a single monetary policy and the use of the European Currency Unit (ECU).

European Monetary System (EMS) System established in 1979 for stabilizing exchange rates between EU member states. It was seen as a step towards a European Central Bank and a single currency as part of European Monetary Union.

European Monetary Union (EMU) One of the aims of the Maastricht Treaty that would result in all EU member states having a common currency (the ***European currency unit, ECU***).

European Union (EU) Association of European nations formerly known as the ***European Economic Community (EEC)*** or European Community (EC), and before that the Common Market. It is intended that in the long run all the factors of production may be moved within the community at will, and remaining customs barriers are expected to be removed in the near future. The EU operates a protectionist policy by maintaining common tariffs on imports, and generates a substantial part of its income from import duties and value-added tax. In finance, its committed aims include a ***European Monetary System (EMS)***, and all that it entails.

EVA Abbreviation of ***economic value added***.

event of default Clause in a loan agreement that, if breached, requires repayment of the loan immediately.

evergreen clause In a letter of credit, a clause that specifies a regular expiry date with automatic extension.

ex *ante* Latin for "from before" or "before the event": what is expected to be the position after some future event. *See also* ***ex post***.

excess capacity Capacity to produce goods over and above the current rate. Excess capacity is more strictly used to denote the increase in production necessary to bring the average production cost to a minimum.

Exchange Clearing House (ECHO) Clearing house for foreign exchange derivatives, founded by an association of Barclays Bank (UK), Banque National de Paris (France), Commerzbank (Germany) and Rabobank.

exchange control Control of foreign exchange dealings by the government, either by restrictions on trade or by direct intervention in the market. Exchange controls help a government to exert some influence over the international value of its own currency. They were abolished in the UK in 1979.

exchange exposure Extent of the risk that results from quoting assets or liabilities in a foreign currency, because variations in the exchange rate can affect the values.

exchange gain Profit made by an importer if there is a favourable change in the exchange rate.

exchange loss Loss made by an importer if there is an unfavourable change in the exchange rate.

exchange rate Price at which one currency may be exchanged for another. Such transactions may be carried out on either the spot or forward markets, and are usually conducted either to permit investment abroad or to pay for imports. There is, in addition, considerable speculation on the exchange rates.

Exchange Rate Mechanism (ERM) EU regulation that restricts variations in the exchange rates of its member states to within closely defined limits. It is a vital feature of the ***European Monetary System (EMS)***. Britain and Italy left the ERM in 1992.

exchange risk guarantee scheme UK government scheme to cover any exchange risk (for an annual service charge) on loans in foreign currencies from the European Coal and Steel Community or the European Investment Bank.

excise duty Duty levied on home-produced goods, either to control consumption and thus influence spending, or to raise revenue. Goods that currently attract excise duty in the UK include alcohol, betting, petrol and tobacco. In the USA, a similar levy is known as excise tax.

excise tax *See* ***excise duty***.

ex coupon Describing stock that does not give the purchaser the right to the next interest payment due to be paid on it.

ex dividend Often shortened to ex div, describing stock that does not give the purchaser the right to the next dividend payment, or to any dividend payment due within a specified period, generally the next calendar month. However, he or she does have the right to receive subsequent dividends.

executive Person charged with decision-making, specifically a member of the senior management of a company.

executive director Also called a working director, a company director who is an employee of the company and therefore involved in its day-to-day management.

executive share option Allocation of shares to a company's executives or rights to buy shares at less than market value, used as an incentive or reward for senior employees. It is effectively a profit-sharing scheme.

exemption clause Clause in a sales contract that excludes the seller from liability for breach of a condition or warranty.

exercice French for financial year.

exercise To make use of a right or option.

exercise notice Formal notification that a call option is to be taken up. The price paid is known as the ***exercise price*** or striking price.

exercise notice Notice issued when the holder of an option wishes to take up his or her right to buy or sell the security for which the option has been agreed.

exercise price Also known as striking price, the price at which an option for purchase or sale of a security is exercised.

ex-factory Describing goods that are collected from the manufacturer's factory (rather than a warehouse). The manufacturer therefore pays no storage costs.

ex *gratia* Describing a payment made in thanks, e.g. a tip or a golden handshake paid to a retiring worker.

Eximbank Short form of ***Export-Import Bank of the United States***.

exit To leave a market by selling all relevant stocks and shares, or to cease production.

ex new Alternative term for ***ex rights***.

expenditure Money spent on attaining (or trying to attain) some objective.

expense account Sum of money that an employee can spend on out-of-pocket expenses (such as travel and entertainment) in order to do his or her job. In company accounting, the term also describes a ledger account in which the organization's costs are detailed under various expenditure headings. At the end of an accounting period, they are summed and transferred to the profit and loss account.

expenses Costs incurred by a company or individual in the course of normal activities, such as the value of assets consumed by a process (to produce goods or services).

expiry date Known in the USA also as expiration date, the date by which a bill of sale or documents needed in a letter of credit must be presented to the advising bank. It is also a general term for any date on which an agreement lapses.

export To sell goods or services outside their country of origin; or the goods or services themselves.

export broker Person or company that brings together buyers and sellers (for a commission) but does not take part in sales transactions.

export controls Government restrictions on goods leaving the country (exports).

export credit Financial facilities or delayed payment terms made available to foreign buyers.

Export Credits Guarantee Department (ECGD) UK government department, part of the ***Department of Trade and Industry (DTI)***, established in 1991 and partly privatized that makes available export credit insurance and guarantees to repay banks that give credit (over two years or more) to exporters.

export declaration Statement provided to the ***Customs and Excise*** detailing the cost, price, destination and nature of goods leaving the country.

export duty Tax levied on exports. Export duties tend to discourage exports and adversely affect the balance of payments, and for these reasons they are seldom used.

export house Company that assists other companies involved in the export trade, either by providing short- or medium-term credit (e.g. an export finance house) or by acting as an overseas agent for companies that do not maintain their own representatives in the countries to which they export.

Export-Import Bank of the United States (Eximbank) Bank established by the US government in 1934 to provide loans to foreign importers of US goods and services. It also refinances and guarantees export credit provided by US banks.

export incentives Government incentives designed to encourage exports. They include direct-tax incentives, subsidies, favourable terms for insurance and the provision of cheap credit.

export leasing Practice of selling goods for export to a leasing company in the country of origin, which ships them overseas and leases then to foreign customers.

export licence Government document required by exporters of certain goods or to certain destinations.

ex post Abbreviation of *ex post facto*, Latin for "after the event". It describes the position that arises after a certain event has taken place. *See also* ***ex ante***.

exposure Extend of financial risk.

ex quay Describing goods that are sold for collection after they have been unloaded from a ship. The seller therefore pays for freightage and the cost of unloading.

ex rights Also known as ex new, a stock exchange term for shares that are sold minus the right to take up bonus issues.

ex ship Describing goods sold to a purchaser who must pay the cost of unloading. The seller therefore pays only the cost of freightage.

extended bond US term for a ***deferred coupon note***.

extended credit Credit that is to be repaid over a very long period of time.

extension strategy Plan for lengthening the marketable life of a product or brand, either by postponing obsolescence (perhaps by adding "extras") or by re-promoting it into a different market.

external finance Finance made available to a company from outside the company (from borrowing, grants or issue of bonds or shares).

external growth Growth that originates outside a company (as through an acquisition or merger).

extraordinary general meeting (EGM) Company shareholders' meeting other than the ***annual general meeting (AGM)***.

extraordinary item Non-recurrent material item listed below the line on a company's balance sheet, such as the sale or purchase of premises or a loss resulting from a major natural disaster, which would distort the profit and loss figures if not accounted for separately.

ex warehouse Describing goods that are priced exclusive of all delivery costs. The purchaser must arrange (and pay) for the collection, loading and delivery of the goods concerned from the seller's warehouse.

ex works Describing goods that are priced exclusive of all delivery costs except those of loading. The purchaser must arrange (and pay) for the collection and delivery of the goods concerned.

F

face value Also called nominal value, the price or value written on something, such as the par value of stocks or shares or the denomination of a banknote.

facilitating intermediary US term for any person or organization that arranges for shipments to be sent to overseas destinations.

facility General term for any kind of loan, usually from a bank.

factor Person or company that undertakes ***factoring.***

factoring Method of managing the trade debts of another organization. Commonly, a company sells due debts to a factor at a discount. The factor then makes a profit by recovering the debts at a price nearer the face value. Factoring relives companies of the burden of administering debts and gives them access to cash before payment is due.

factoring house Company that buys export receivables at a discount (of about 2-4% of face value). Invoices to foreign buyers may be discounted in this way by a factoring house.

factors of production Collective term for those things necessary for production to take place. They are usually divided into the following categories: capital, labour and land, to which may be added organizational ability (i.e., management).

factory door cost Cost of a product with no allowance for cost of sales or administration costs.

factory farming Also called intensive farming, the use of mass production techniques to rear or use livestock.

factory inspector Employee of the UK ***Health and Safety Executive*** who checks that companies comply with the various pieces of legislation that apply to safety in the workplace.

faculative endorsement Endorsement to a ***bill of exchange*** that absolves the endorser of certain duties (such as waiving the need for a notice of dishonour).

failure investment Practice of buying shares in companies that are doing badly, in the hope that their performance will improve.

fair price provisions Termed fair price amendments in the USA, a clause in a corporate charter whereby a buyer of the company's shares must pay the same amount or make the same consideration for all the shares purchased. It is used as a defensive tactic against bootstrapping (*see* ***bootstrap***). In another context fair price provisions are also price controls, generally instituted by a government, that guarantee fair prices to the consumer by ensuring that manufacturers and retailers make reasonable rather than excessive profits.

Fair Trading Act 1973 UK legislation that established the ***Office of Fair Trading (OFT)***, which provides government ministers with advice about mergers, monopolies and restrictive practices in trade and industry.

fair value Value of an asset that could be obtained in an arm's-length transaction between a willing seller and a willing buyer, each acting in his or her own self-interest.

fallen angel Colloquial term for a company, or shares in a company, whose rating has recently fallen significantly.

fan club Group of investors who buy shares or use their holdings to back one side in a take-over bid, without collusion (*see* ***concert party***).

Fannie Mae US nickname for the ***Federal National Mortgage Association (FNMA)***.

FAS Abbreviation of ***free alongside ship***.

FASB Abbreviation of ***Financial Accounting Standards Board***.

fate Decision whether or not to pay a cheque or other negotiable instrument when it is presented for payment.

FDI Abbreviation of ***foreign direct investment***.

FECDBA Abbreviation of ***Foreign Exchange and Currency Deposit Brokers' Association***.

Fed Common abbreviation of ***Federal Reserve System***.

Federal Agency Securities US market that can be divided into federally-sponsored agency securities and the federally related institution securities market. Federally-sponsored agencies or government-sponsored entities are privately-owned, publicly-chartered entities created by Congress to reduce the cost of capital for certain borrowing sectors of the economy deemed worthy of assistance, including homeowners, farmers and students.

Federal Credit Union In the USA, a credit union is a financial cooperative that aids its members by encouraging thrift and by providing members with a source of credit for provident purposes at reasonable rates of interest. Federal credit unions serve occupational, associational and residential groups.

federal funds Deposits held by US federal reserve banks that bear no interest.

federal funds rate US interest rate at which one federal reserve bank borrows funds from another such bank. It is regulated by the federal reserve.

federal home loan bank Type of US bank that provides secured loans to their savings and loan customers, who must hold stock in the regional bank.

Federal Home Loan Bank Board (FHLBB) In the USA, a regulatory body established in 1933 for savings and loan associations, and which has credit reserves for various mortgage lending institutions.

Federal Home Loan Mortgage Corporation (FHLMC) Nicknamed Freddie Mac, a US organization established in 1970 that purchases mortgages from savings and loans associations to sell them in the secondary market. Its stock is held by the Federal Home Loan Bank System.

Federal National Mortgage Association (FNMA) Nicknamed Fannie Mae, a US government sponsored organization that provides funding for mortgages to people buying their own homes.

Federal Open Market Committee (FOMC) Committee that determines the monetary policy of the US Federal Reserve System, particularly with regard to its open market operations.

federal reserve bank Any of the USA's central banks, each of which is controlled by a state government.

Federal Reserve Board Board that controls the growth of US bank reserves and the money supply.

Federal Reserve System (Fed) US central bank system, under which 12 regional federal reserve banks are governed by the ***Federal Reserve Board*** in Washington, appointed by the President. Like the Bank of England in the UK, it sets banking policy and controls the money supply.

fellow subsidiary One of several companies that are all subsidiaries of the same holding company.

Festverzinslich German for fixed interest.

FHLBB Abbreviation of ***Federal Home Loan Bank Board***.

fictitious value Imaginary or assumed value of goods, which cannot be used for customs purposes in the USA.

fidelity guarantee Guarantee by one person for the fidelity or integrity of another, usually for employment purposes.

fiduciary Person or body acting in trust. Anybody holding, say, cash in trust for another is said to be acting in a fiduciary capacity.

fiduciary deposit Bank deposit that the bank lends to somebody else at the depositor's risk (although the depositor earns a fairly high rate of interest). It is a system used by some Swiss banks.

fiduciary issue Money issued by the ***Bank of England*** backed by securities, mainly in the form of the government's debt to the Bank. It is termed fiduciary because of the public's trust that the government will repay the debts backing the issue.

field trial Test of a new or revamped product on consumers in a particular target market.

FIFO Abbreviation of ***first in first out***.

fight to the tape Practice of selling while prices are rising and buying when prices are falling. The tape is the ticker tape that once relayed prices to brokers.

fill or kill On a futures market, an order to trade that must be either fulfilled immediately or cancelled.

FIMBRA Abbreviation of ***Financial Intermediaries, Managers and Brokers Regulatory Association***.

final accounts Usually, a company's annual accounts. But the term may also refer to the final report submitted by a liquidator at the end of ***liquidation***.

final dividend Last share dividend paid by a company during a trading year.

Finance Act Annual UK legislation that enforces the measures set out in the government's budget.

Finance Corporation for Industry Limited Company established in 1945 by the ***Bank of England*** and various UK financial institutions with the purpose of making loans to rehabilitate industries of national interest (initially after World War II).

finance house Company that provides funding (credit), e.g. for hire-purchase agreements. The finance house pays a trader in full, and charges interest to the purchaser of goods provided by the trader.

finance house base rate Rate of interest charged to borrowers by UK finance houses. It is set monthly by averaging the three-weekly average of the three-month LIBOR (London interbank offered rate), rounded up to the nearest ½%.

finance house deposit Deposit placed with a finance house by a large lender such as a bank.

Finance Houses Association Organization established in 1945, originally by six large UK finance houses. It ensures that the houses have a consistent policy on deposits, interest rates and ***hire-purchase*** finance.

Financial Accounting Standards Board (FASB) Private regulatory body, established in 1973, that sets the accounting standards for US public companies.

financial adviser Person (or institution) who gives advice on raising, lending or managing money, or on particular transactions, usually for a fee or commission. *See also* ***independent financial adviser (IFA)***.

Financial Analysts Federation International non-profit making professional organization, established in 1947, whose members are all financial analyst societies located in major cities in Canada and the USA.

financial centre Any city (or other place) in which large amounts of financial business are transacted.

financial future Contract for the delivery of a financial instrument (i.e. a currency) on a future date. Financial futures are used to hedge against the rise and fall of interest and exchange rates.

financial instrument Any method of financing, such as a bond, certificate of deposit (CD) or treasury bill.

Financial Intermediaries, Managers and Brokers Regulatory Association (FIMBRA) Former UK self-regulating organization that regulated financial advisers and a firms selling and managing securities and unit trusts. In 1994 its functions were taken over by the ***Personal Investment Authority (PIA)***.

Financial Reporting Council UK organization established in 1990 in response to the Dearing Committee's report (on accounting standards).

Financial Reporting Review Panel Subsidiary body of the UK Financial Reporting Council which supervises the use of accounting standards.

Financial Services Act 1986 (FSAct) Act of Parliament in the UK, in force since April 1988, introduced to prevent abuse of the de-regulated stock exchange system, principally by placing all people and institutions involved in financial services under the authority of a ***self-regulating organization (SRO)***. It implemented many of the recommendations of the Gower Report.

Financial Services Authority (FSA) A UK organization established in 1997 by the combination of four former self-regulatory organizations (SROs); the Investment Managers Regulatory Organization, the Personal Investment Authority, the Securities and Futures Authority and the Security and Investment Authority. It also regulates building societies, credit unions, friendly societies and the insurance industry. Banking was also planned to come under its remit.

***Financial Times* Stock Exchange 100 Index (FTSE, FTSE 100** or **Footsie)** Index of shares of the 100 largest UK companies, a weighted average of which is updated every minute during the working day. The index value of 1000 was set on the base date of 3 January 1984.

Financial Times* Ordinary Share Index (FT Index)** Also known as the *Financial Times* 30 Index, an index of changes in prices of 30 major industrial and commercial ordinary shares on the ***London Stock Exchange, updated hourly during the working day. The index value of 100 was set on the base date of 1 July 1935.

financial year Twelve-month period, beginning anywhere in the calendar year, that is covered by a company's accounts. In the UK the national financial year runs from 6 April to 5 April and is sued for calculating income tax and corporation tax. It is also known as the fiscal year.

fine bank bill Bill of exchange accepted by or drawn on an eligible bank. It is also termed a prime bank bill.

fine bill Bill of exchange for which the backer is extremely creditworthy and so there is little or no risk.

fine price Price of a security on a market in which the difference between the buying and selling prices is very small.

fine rate Best rate of interest that can be obtained in a given situation.

fine trade bill Trade bill with reputable drawer and drawee, which commands a fine rate of discount.

F.I.O. Abbreviation of ***free in and out***.

firm Commonly, any company or business. Strictly, under UK law a firm is a partnership of professionally qualified people, such as accountants, civil engineers, lawyers or surveyors. In this case, the firms are legally distinct from companies and do not, for instance, issue shares. Also the liability of individual partners is not (and legally cannot be) limited. *See also* ***partnership***.

firm bid Also called a firm offer, a bid (or offer) that has no conditions.

firm market Market in which prices are steady.

firm order Order to buy or sell a security that can be carried out without further confirmation.

firm price Guaranteed price, usually offered if the cost of providing goods and services can be assessed extremely accurately.

first-class paper Bills issued by financial institutions of high standing (such as the ***Treasury***).

first in first out (FIFO) Accountancy principle whereby stock-in-trade is assumed to be issued to customers in the order that it is received. Thus, stock currently held may be valued at current prices. *See also* ***last in first out (LIFO)***.

first notice day On a futures contract, the first day on which notice can be given of intended (or expected) actual delivery.

fiscal agent In the USA, the role of the Federal Reserve when it processes payments from and to the government.

fiscal drag Effect during times of inflation in which pay increases push employees into higher tax brackets (giving the government a higher proportion of incomes).

fiscal year Period of twelve months for the purposes of tax calculation. In the UK the fiscal year runs from 6 April to the following 5 April. In the USA, the term can be synonymous with ***financial year***.

fitness for purpose Test of the quality of a product or service by assessing how well it matches up to a consumer's requirements.

fix To settle a price in the commodity markets by trading.

fixed asset Also known as a capital asset, an asset that is used in furtherance of a company's business, such as machinery or property.

fixed charge Part of the charge, usually made for a service, that is unchanged no matter how much a service is used. Examples of utilities that levy fixed charges are electricity, gas and some telephone companies. A fixed charge (also called a specific charge) is also a charge that gives a creditor the right to have an asset sold and the receipts put towards repayment of a debt that is outstanding. A legal mortgage is an example of such a fixed charge.

fixed cost Also called a fixed expense, a cost that does not vary with short-term changes in the level of output or sales (such as heating costs, business rates, and certain other overheads).

fixed costs per unit The ratio of total fixed costs to the number of units produced, also known as average fixed costs. They can be reduced by increasing output.

fixed exchange rate Exchange rate that a government attempts to control and fix in the short term by instructing the central bank to buy or sell foreign exchange reserves, or by introducing tariffs.

fixed-interest security Security for which the income is fixed and does not vary. Such securities include bonds, debentures and gilt-edged securities.

fixed overhead Overhead that does not vary in the short term, such as heating, lighting, rent and salaries.

fixed price Price that is not negotiable or subject to variation.

fixed rate Charge or interest that does not change.

fixed-rate loan Loan with an interest rate fixed at the beginning of the loan period (irrespective of subsequent changes in the cost of borrowing).

fixing Setting of the London gold price by several large dealers (twice-daily at 10.30 a.m. and again about 3 p.m.).

fixtures and fittings Immovable assets, fixed to land or property but not themselves part of the property, such as shelves and light fittings screwed to a wall.

flag of convenience Flag flown by a merchant vessel registered in a country whose manning, taxation and safety requirements are less stringent than elsewhere, to the advantage of the shipowner.

flatline Colloquial expression describing something or a situation that is beyond recovery or redemption. The term comes from its medical use to mean dead, referring to the ECG trace of a patient who has died.

flat yield Also known as running yield, the interest rate expressed as a percentage of the price paid for a fixed-interest security.

flexible trust Unit trust in which investors' money is not invested in a set portfolio, but moved from one investment to another in order to obtains the best rates of growth.

flexitime Method of working that allows employees to complete their agreed hours of work at times that suit them.

flight capital Capital that is hurredly removed from one country that seems to be politically (or economically) unstable, and taken to a more stable environment.

flip Practice of buying then selling shares (usually in the manner of a stag) at high speed in order to make a quick profit.

flip-flop bond Bond that an investor can easily convert into another kind of debt instrument, and then just as easily convert back.

float Cash or funds used either to give change to customers or to pay for expenses (*see also* ***petty cash***). In the USA, cheques credited to someone's bank account but not yet debited to the drawer's account are also term float. To float (verb) is to start a new company; or to sell shares in order to raise share capital and obtain a listing on the stock exchange.

floater Security owned by the bearer, the person who holds it. More formally it is termed a bearer security.

floating assets Alternative name for ***circulating assets***.

floating capital Capital invested in wages paid, work in progress and anything other than fixed assets.

floating charge Charge over a company's assets that comes into effect only if a specified event occurs (such as liquidation of the company).

floating currency Currency whose value varies up and down according to its supply and demand.

floating debt Short-term government borrowing.

floating exchange rate Also known as a free exchange rate, an exchange rate that is not in any way manipulated by the central bank, but which moves according to supply and demand.

floating interest rate Interest rate for a loan that rises and falls in response to an appropriate index (such as ***LIBOR***).

floating money Money for which no profitable investment can be found quickly, usually at a time of high liquidity.

floating rate *See* ***floating exchange rate; floating interest rate***.

floating-rate note Also called a floating-rate bond, a security issued by a borrower on the Eurobonds market that has a variable rate of interest.

floating rate certificate of deposit (FRCD) Certificate of deposit (CD), originating in US finance, on which the issuing bank pays variable interest (or coupon).

floating warranty Guarantee given by one party that induces a second party to enter into a contract with a third party.

floor Fixed minimum interest for a loan; *see* ***collar***. The trading area of an exchange is also referred to as the floor.

floor broker Member of a commodity market who is authorized to deal on the trading floor. In the USA, a floor broker is a member of an exchange who deals in securities, on behalf of clients, on the trading floor. *See also* ***floor trader***.

floor trader Member an exchange who deals in securities on the trading floor on his or her own behalf. *See also* ***floor broker***.

flotation Act of selling shares in a company to raise capital and be listed on the stock exchange.

flotsam Goods or part of a shipwreck found floating on the surface of the sea.

flow chart Graphical way of illustrating the various activities of a project against a timescale. It can also track the flow of money or materials through a business.

Flow of Funds Accounts US national statistical system developed by the ***Federal Reserve Board*** and published regularly since 1947. It is constructed to show the financial activities of the US economy in a manner that enables financial activities to be related to the non-financial activities of economic functions that turn out income, savings, goods and services.

fluctuation Movement of prices up or down on a market. Downward fluctuation is also known as slippage.

FMV Abbreviation of *foreign market value*.

FO Abbreviation of *free out*.

FOB Abbreviation of *free on board*.

focus group US term for a group discussion, which uses a small group of consumers to research in depth their attitudes and buying habits.

FOMC Abbreviation of *Federal Open Market Committee*.

fonds d'état French for government stocks.

fonds publics French for public bonds.

Food Act 1984 UK legislation that dealt with consumer protection in the food sector, later incorporated into the Food Safety Act 1990.

Food Safety Act 1990 UK legislation that widened and strengthened the provisions of the Food Act 1984, emphasizing the responsibilities of farmers and growers and of food retailers with regard to quality and staff training.

Footsie Abbreviation of *Financial Times Stock Exchange 100 Index.*

forced savings Savings that do not involve a conscious decision to save but which nevertheless accumulate. Examples include government taxes that contribute to retirement pensions.

force majeure Standard clause in a contract that absolves either of the parties of blame for non-fulfilment of obligations caused by events beyond their control (such as earthquakes, floods or acts of war).

foreclosure If a property has been mortgaged, that is it stands as security against a loan, the lender may take possession and ownership of the property of the borrower fails to pay off the loan. Such an act of possession is known as foreclosure (and requires a foreclosure order issued by the court).

foreign bank From the point of view of somebody in the UK, a bank with headquarters abroad that is authorized to open offices in the UK. Substitute any other country for "UK" and the definition still stands.

foreign bill *Bill of exchange* drawn in a foreign country, i.e. that is not an *inland bill* (in the UK an inland bill is designated by the Bills of Exchange Act 1882 as a bill drawn and payable in Britain or drawn in Britain on a British resident).

foreign bond Bond denominated in a currency other than that of the issuer and sold in the domestic market of that currency (such as a Japanese yen bond issued by a German company and sold in Japan). Such bonds are known as bulldog bonds in the UK and yankee bonds in the USA.

foreign currency account Also called a nostro account, an account held by a home bank in a foreign country. The term may also describe a home bank account whose funds are in a foreign currency.

foreign currency swap Deal in which currency of one country is traded for the currency of another on the understanding that the deal will be reversed at a later date.

foreign direct investment (FDI) Investment in assets overseas or in the overseas operations of a company.

foreign draft *Bill of exchange* that is payable abroad; or a bank draft drawn on a foreign branch, usually in the foreign currency.

foreign exchange (F/X) Currency (or credit instruments) of a foreign country, and the buying and selling of such currencies.

Foreign Exchange and Currency Deposit Brokers' Association (FECDBA) UK professional organization for brokers who deal in foreign exchange or deposits in foreign currencies.

foreign exchange broker Broker who deals in foreign exchange, usually on the foreign exchange market (FOREX).

foreign exchange dealer Bank employee who deals in foreign exchange on the foreign exchange market on behalf of the bank's customers, who pay a commission for such services.

foreign exchange market (FOREX) Market where foreign currencies are traded by foreign exchange brokers (intermediaries) and foreign exchange dealers (bank employees). Options and futures on forward exchange rates are also traded.

foreign exchange risk Risk taken in buying or selling foreign currency (because the exchange rate could change unfavourably between buying and selling).

foreign market value (FMV) Price at which goods are sold (or offered for sale) in the main markets of the exporting country.

FOREX Abbreviation of *foreign exchange market*.

forfaiting Specialist banking service by which the bank buys foreign debts at a discount without recourse, thus removing the risk to the seller of non-payment.

forfeiture Loss of property for failure to comply with a contract or with the law.

forged share transfer If a bank accepts a share certificate with a forged stock transfer form, the bank is liable to the company that issued the shares.

forged signature Any ***bill of exchange*** carrying a forged signature is invalid and inoperative.

Form 10-K In the USA, the ***Securities and Exchange Commission's (SEC's)*** annual report form, which a US public company must file with the SEC within 90 days of its fiscal year-end.

Form 10-Q In the USA, the ***Securities and Exchange Commission's (SEC's)*** quarterly report form, on which a US public company must detail interim financial statements (with comparative figures for the same period in the previous year).

Form 20-F In the USA, the ***Securities and Exchange Commission's (SEC's)*** annual report form which must be completed annually by non-USA companies.

for the account Describing stock exchange dealings that have to be settled on the next account day.

forward To send something on to somebody (e.g. to a new address); or describing something (e.g. a futures contact) to be completed some time in the future.

forwardation Situation in which spot goods are bought by a dealer (usually on a commodities market) and carried forward to deliver against a forward contract (because the spot goods are cheaper than goods for forward delivery). *See also* ***backwardation***.

forward buying Contracting to purchase goods or foreign currency at a price agreed today (spot price) for delivery at a specified future date.

forward contract *See* ***forward buying***.

forward cover Method of covering future payments or receipts by buying now the currency needed for payment (using the ***futures market***) or selling now a receipt due for settlement in the future.

forward dating Dating a document (such as a cheque or invoice) in advance. Such a document is termed post-dated.

forward dealing Making a deal to buy or sell goods (commodities) or currencies at a stated price at some stated future date. Futures are such contracts that are set up primarily for buying and selling of the contracts themselves.

forward exchange contract Agreement to buy foreign exchange at some future date at an agreed rate of exchange.

forward integration Taking on by a company of activities at a subsequent stage of production or distribution (which could be carried out by another company). For example, an oil production company undertakes forward integration when it invests in refineries, tankers and petrol stations.

forwardizing agent Agent who arranges for (and often owns) transport of goods from a factory, warehouse or port of entry to their intended destination.

forward market Market in (contracts or options for) goods that are to be delivered at some future date.

forward price Price quoted for goods not immediately available or not yet manufactured. The forward price is usually lower than the eventual retail price because it takes into account only the estimated costs of manufacture at some future date. More specifically, it is the price quoted on a futures deal.

forward purchase Buying of securities or commodities in advance of delivery.

forward rate Exchange rate quoted on a ***forward exchange contract***.

foul bill of lading Also known as a dirty bill of lading, a carrier's receipt for goods (bill of lading) that states that the goods were damaged when received.

founders' shares Alternative term for ***deferred shares***.

Fourth Directive EU directive aimed at harmonizing company law among member states, particularly with regard to the way in which company accounts are drawn up. It was incorporated into the UK Companies Act 1981.

franchise Licence bought by a retailer of goods or supplier of services (the franchisee) that entitles him or her to sell the products of a particular manufacturer (the franchisor) under a particular trading name. This system enables the manufacturer to have direct control over who sells the goods, and often gives the seller exclusive rights to sell those products in his or her area.

franchisee *See franchise.*

franchisor *See franchise.*

franco Alternative term for ***rendu***.

franked investment income Company's investment income that has already been taxed at source.

fraud Illegal practice of obtaining money from people under false pretences. For example, fraud is committed if facts pertaining to a contract are purposefully misrepresented. Fraudulently diverting one's company's or employer's money for one's own use is embezzlement.

FRCD Abbreviation of ***floating rate certificate of deposit***.

Freddie Mac US nickname for the *Federal Home Loan Mortgage Corporation (FHMLC)*.

free alongside ship (FAS) Describing goods whose price includes the cost of carriage up to the point when they are standing on the dockside ready to be loaded onto the ship.

free capital That part of a company's equity that is available for trading on the stock market; ***working capital***.

free competition Situation in which rival companies are allowed to compete freely with each other for a share of the market. In a free competition or free market economy, the laws of ***supply and demand*** regulate prices.

free contract Alternative term for ***rendu***.

free depreciation Depreciation of a company's asset over any time period it thinks fit.

free enterprise Economic system in which individuals or groups may own the factors of production and exploit them for their own benefit within the limits of the law.

free exchange rate Exchange rate in a foreign market that is determined only by supply and demand, with no government intervention (as opposed to a fixed exchange rate).

free float US term for ***free capital***.

freehold Describing land or buildings that are owned absolutely by the freeholder.

free in Describing goods whose price includes the costs of loading.

free in and out (F.I.O.) Describing goods whose price includes the costs of loading and unloading.

freelance Employment status of a self-employed person who earns a living providing a service, usually to several clients and on an irregular basis.

free market Market that operates essentially by the laws of ***supply and demand***. Or, on the stock market, a situation in which a particular security is freely available and in reasonably large quantities.

free on board (FOB) Describing goods whose price includes the cost of carriage up to the point when they are loaded onto the ship.

free out (FO) Describing goods whose price includes the cost of unloading from the vessel.

free-port Type of free trade zone that encompasses the area around a port.

free stocks Stocks (inventories) of commodities held by commercial organizations, as opposed to those held by producers.

free trade Concept of international trading where there are no tariff barriers between countries.

Free Trade Agreement Agreement between Canada and the USA, signed in 1988 and ratified a year later, that abolished all tariffs between the two countries.

free trade agreement (FTA) Agreement between nations to abolish all tariffs between the two countries.

free trade area (FTA) Region in which the countries concerned have signed a ***free trade agreement***.

freeze Broadly, the act of stopping something (e.g. wages or prices) from moving or being available (as in a credit squeeze).

freeze-out Situation in which a company successfully out-competes its competitors, effectively freezing them out of the market.

freight Goods being carried (cargo); or money paid to a carrier for carrying goods or by a charterer to a shipowner for the use of cargo space on a vessel. The latter is also called freightage.

freight note Document from a shipowner to a shipper specifying the amount of freight (i.e. freight charge) due.

French companies *See* ***Société Anonyme*** *and* ***Société à Responsibilité Limitée***.

frictional unemployment Unemployment that results from the movement of people between jobs. Thus although there may be enough jobs to go round, some people may experience periods of unemployment between the finish date of one job and the start date of the next.

friendly society Organization (first coming to existence in the UK in the 17th century, to help to provide working people with some form of security) that provides mutual benefits to its members, such as life assurance and pensions, in return for yearly subscriptions.

friendly take-over Purchase of control of a company that is welcomed by the target company's board of directors and shareholders.

fringe benefit Item that is given to an employee as part of his or her payment but apart from wages or salary (such as a company car, health insurance, or goods at a discount). Fringe benefits are usually taxable. *See also* ***perks***.

fringes Colloquial US abbreviation of ***fringe benefits***.

front company Company established to conceal its true ownership or the true activities of its owners.

front door Popular term for the Bank of England's practice of lending money to discount houses in order to inject cash into the money market.

front end The marketing (rather than the manufacturing) side of a company.

front-end finance UK bank loan to a foreign buyer for paying the UK exporter, usually covered by the ***Exports Credits Guarantee Department***.

front-end loading Including charges such as administrative costs and commission with the first repayment of a loan or the first payment of an insurance premium, with the result that the first payment is larger than the remainder. *See also* ***packing***.

front money Also termed seed money, money lent as ***venture capital*** to a company that is setting up or very young.

front month Also termed the nearby month, the first month that is available for trading in a derivative.

front running Illegal private trading by a broker or market-maker who has prior knowledge of a forthcoming large movement in prices.

frozen assets Assets that may not be converted into ready money without incurring a loss of some kind, or which may not be converted because someone has claim on them or there is an order that they may not be transferred. The latter is also called a frozen fund. *See also* ***liquid assets***.

frustration of contract Failure to carry out a contract through no fault of the contracted parties.

FSA Abbreviation of ***Financial Services Authority***.

FSAct Abbreviation of ***Financial Services Act 1986***.

FTA Abbreviation of ***free trade agreement*** *and* ***free trade area***.

FT Index Abbreviated form of ***Financial Times Ordinary Share Index***.

FTSE 100 or **FTSE** Abbreviation of ***Financial Times Stock Exchange 100 Index***.

full costing Alternative US term for ***absorption costing***. In the UK it is usually taken to mean a costing method in which all of a company's costs (direct and overhead) are charged to a product or service (i.e., total absorption costing).

full line forcing Action of a supplier who insists that a retailer must stock the full range of that supplier's products (and cannot choose just one or a few).

full listing Inclusion of a company's name on the official list of the ***London Stock Exchange***.

functional currency Currency of the main economic area in which a company operates (and the one in which it may have to prepare its financial statements).

functional discount Special discount given to intermediaries during the launch of a new product (to compensate them from the extra work involved).

fund Money set aside for a specific purpose (e.g. from which to pay pensions or insurance claims); or money lent to an institution or government. As a verb, fund means to make finance available.

fundamental analysis Detailed analysis of a quoted company's annual report and accounts to check on the market value of its shares.

fundamentalist Also called a fundamental market analyst, somebody who takes the performance of a company as the basis for predicting its share-price movements.

fundamental terms Contractual terms that are so basic that breach of them is equated with non-performance (as opposed to conditions and warranties).

funded debt Generally, any short-term debt that has been converted into a long-term debt.

funding Substituting long-term debt for short-term liabilities.

fund management Management of the investment fund of an institution such as an insurance company or a pension scheme. It is sometimes known as investment management.

fund-raising Any method used by an existing company to raise money from shareholders, such as rights issues, open offers and placings.

fund of funds Unit trust that is organized and managed by an institution to invest in other of its own unit trusts.

funds General term for ***working capital*** (i.e., current assets less current liabilities). Sometimes the term is limited to mean cash or cash and liquid assets. Somebody who is out of funds has no ready money.

funds broker In the USA, a broker who negotiates short-term loans between US banks.

fungible Stock market term describing securities that are in hand, i.e. that have not yet been settled.

futures Contracts that are made for the delivery of e.g. currencies or commodities on a future date. Futures markets provide an opportunity for speculation, in that contracts may be bought and sold (with no intention on the part of the traders to take delivery of the goods) before the delivery date arrives and their prices may rise and fall during that time.

Futures and Options Exchange *See* ***London Futures and Options Exchange***.

Futures Industry Association Organization that represents dealers in the US futures market.

futures market Market that deals in futures and options on bonds, commodities, foreign currencies are shares.

F/X Abbreviation of ***foreign exchange***.

G

G-5 *See* ***Group of Five***.

G-7 *See* ***Group of Seven***.

G-10 *See* ***Group of Ten***.

GAB Abbreviation of ***General Arrangements to Borrow***.

gadfly Colloquial term for a shareholder who turns up at shareholders' meetings and asks awkward questions.

gain Alternative term for profit.

gain to redemption Difference between the amount realized by selling stock now and keeping it until maturity.

galloping inflation Alternative term for ***hyperinflation***.

gamma Describing a share that is traded infrequently and then in only small quantities.

G & A Abbreviation of ***general and administrative expenses***.

gap Market opportunity (a gap in the market) that nobody else has yet exploited.

gap analysis Method of investigating the difference between a company's expected market potential and the sales actually achieved.

garnishee order Court order made on somebody who owes money to somebody else who has been judged to be a debtor, instructing him or her not to pay the debtor until that debtor has repaid others. If it is issued by the County Court, it is called a garnishee summons.

Garn-St Germain Act 1982 US legislation concerning savings and loan associations that allowed them access to the commercial lending market.

GATT Abbreviation of ***General Agreement on Tariffs and Trade***.

gazetted Describing items published in the *London Gazette* (in Scotland, the *Edinburgh Gazette*), a weekly publication that includes details of company appointments, bankruptcy orders, notices of winding up, changes in company constitutions, and so on. If information is gazetted, it is assumed that everybody in the country has been notified, even if they have never seen or heard of the publication.

gazumping Raising the asking price for a property after an offer has been agreed verbally or in writing but before the exchange of contracts, in order to take advantage of a better offer or a rising market in property values.

GDP Abbreviation of ***gross domestic product***.

gearing Proportion of long-term debt to equity finance on the balance sheet of a company. More specifically, it is the ratio of borrowed capital to total capital employed, expressed as a percentage (gearing ratio). It is sometimes known by the equivalent US term leverage.

GEMMS Abbreviation of ***gilt-edged market-makers***.

GEMU Abbreviation of ***German Economic Monetary Union***.

general agent Agent with the authority to represent the principle in all matters concerning a particular activity.

General Agreement on Tariffs and Trade (GATT) International organization, established in 1947 with headquarters in Geneva, Switzerland, and now with more than 100 member countries, whose object is to negotiate on matters of trade policy, notably the reduction of tariffs and other barriers to free trade.

general and administrative expenses (G & A) Administrative expenses plus operating costs.

General Arrangements to Borrow (GAB) Agreement established in 1962 under which the ***International Monetary Fund (IMF)*** may call upon the major industrialized nations to borrow money if required.

general expenses Non-specific expenses incurred in the day-to-day running of a company or business. More specifically, they are operating costs other than ones that are assignable to such areas as administration, cost of sales, and so on.

general offer Offer that is made to the public at large, with no restriction.

general partner Partner whose liability for the debts of the partnership is unlimited.

general partnership Partnership in which each partner shares equally in the running of the firm.

general reserves Profits not distributed to a company's shareholder, also known as revenue reserves.

general tariff In international trade, a tariff that applies to nations that do not have most favoured nation status or other preferential treatment.

general undertaking Document signed by a company's directors that acknowledges their obligation to notify the stock exchange about share issues on the unlisted securities market.

gentleman's agreement Verbal agreement between two parties who trust each other and have a strong sense of honour.

German Economic Monetary Union (GEMU) Following the reunification of the former East and West Germany in 1990, the process of bringing together their monetary and economic policies.

German stock exchanges Various stock exchanges in Germany (Frankfurt is the largest) are grouped under Deutsche Börse AG, which uses an electronic order-driven system. Frankfurt also has computerized futures and options exchanges although a plan to merge with the *London Stock Exchange* in 2000 did not come off.

Gesellschaft German equivalent of a UK *limited company (Ltd)*.

***Gesellschaft mit beschrankte Haftung* (GmbH)** German equivalent of a UK *private limited company (plc)*.

generic brand Brand name (such as Hoover or Thermos) that has come to stand for the product, no matter who produces it.

ghost worker Person who appears on the payroll of a company but does not work.

gift tax In the USA, a tax on the value of property given to somebody else. It is paid by the giver. In the UK, gifts made within seven years of the giver's death may qualify for capital transfer (inheritance) tax.

gilt-edged market In general in the UK, the market in gilt-edged securities.

gilt-edged market-makers (GEMMS) UK market-makers who trade in government securities on their own account.

gilt-edged security Security that carries little or no risk, in particular government-issued stocks, which are known as gilts for short. In the USA, the term gilt-edged refers to bonds issued by companies with a good reputation for dividend payment and with a good profit record.

gilt repos Introduced by the ***Bank of England*** in 1996, a market in (agreed sales and repurchases of) gilt-edged securities.

gilts Shortened term for ***gilt-edged securities***.

gilt strip Type of gilt-edged stock issued from late 1997 by the ***Bank of England***. It is issued at a discount to compensate for the fact that no interest is paid (until maturity).

gilt switching Process of selling one gilt-edged security and investing the entire proceeds in another. This may be to take advantage of changes in interest rates, when a long-dated gilt may be switched for a short-dated gilt, or vice versa.

Glass-Steagall Act 1933 US Act of Congress that separated the activities of commercial and investment bankers.

global bond Fixed-interest security issued simultaneously in Asia, Europe and the USA.

global brand Market brand (such as Coca-Cola and McDonald's) that has successfully been marketed worldwide.

global custody Service, usually for fund managers, for settling cross-border transactions, offered by major investment banks.

global equities market Worldwide market in equities, involving principally the stock exchanges in London, New York and Tokyo.

globalization Increasing internationalization of all markets, industries and commerce.

GmbH Abbreviation of ***Gesellschaft mit beschrankte Haftung***.

GNP Abbreviation of ***gross national product***.

godfather offer Offer that cannot be refused. In a take-over situation, a godfather offer for the company's shares is made at such a good price that the management of the target company can only accept it.

godown Far-eastern term for a warehouse.

gogo fund Colloquial term for an investment fund that is being actively traded, producing high capital gains and high market prices.

going concern It is an assumption in company accounting that an organization will continue trading for current plans to be completed. It is also known as the continuity convention.

going private Removing a company from stock exchange listing, a process achieved by the company purchasing its own shares. Going private is usually a decision by the principal shareholders that they require more direct control of the company. Its primary purpose is to reduce interference by outside investors and to render the company considerably less vulnerable to take-over bids.

going public To offer shares in a company to financial institutions and the general public, and thereby receive a listing on the ***stock exchange***.

going rate Rate that is currently applicable in most instances. For example, there may be a going rate that is charged or paid for certain kinds of work (the going rate for the job).

gold and dollar reserves Stock of gold and US national currency held by the US government or central banks.

gold and foreign exchange reserves Same as ***gold and dollar reserves***, but with national currencies other than the US dollar included in the stock.

gold bug Investor who uses gold reserves as a cushion against inflation.

golden handcuffs Contractual arrangement between a company and its employee whereby the employee has a strong financial incentive (other than the loss of normal salary) to remain with the company, such as a low-interest mortgage or share options that expire if the employee resigns.

golden handshake Gratuitous payment made by a company to an employee who is leaving, or has recently left. Such payment may be made out of goodwill, or to maintain good relations with an ex-employee, or to induce an employee to resign where there are no grounds, or dubious grounds, for statutory ***dismissal*** or ***redundancy***.

golden hello Payment other than normal salary paid to an employee on joining a company in order to induce him or her to do so.

golden parachute Term in a contract of employment whereby the employer is bound to pay the employee a substantial sum of money in the event of ***dismissal*** or ***redundancy***.

gold fixing Activity that takes place twice a day when the five dealers of gold bullion on the London exchange meet to determine the price of gold.

Goldilocks economy Economy where there is strong economic growth combined with rising share prices and low inflation.

gold pool *Group of Ten (G-10)* agreement to maintain a reserve of gold for the London market, to prevent the official price rising above a certain price (US$35 per troy ounce).

gold reserves Funds held by a nation in the form of gold. They fluctuate with the balance of payments and are used for international transactions.

gold share Also called a golden share, a company share that has special voting rights such that it can outvote all other shares in certain circumstances.

gold warrant Similar to a call and put option, a financial instrument that allows the holder to buy or sell gold at a pre-set price and time (which has to be over a year).

good faith *See **bona fide**.*

goods Physical items manufactured, sold or exchanged, from raw materials to finished products (as opposed to services, for which no physical items are transferred).

goods on approval Goods delivered to a customer for which payment is not required unless the customer is satisfied. If the customer is not satisfied in a stated period of time the goods are returned to the supplier. A retailer may hold goods on approval, and return them if they are not sold.

goods on consignment Method of trading in goods whereby they are sent to an agent on consignment. Although the agent has no title to the goods, he or she may sell them on to a buyer. If the goods are not sold, they are returned to the owner.

good-till-cancelled (GTC) Describing an order that remains in force unless it is expressly cancelled. Cancellation is usually dependent upon a satisfactory profit level being reached. It is also known as a resting order or open order.

goodwill Value of a business over and above the book value of its identifiable or physical assets. Or it is the amount paid on acquisition of a business over and above its current market valuation (including any stock). It can refer, for example, to the literal good will of the established customers of a retail business (shop or restaurant) whose benevolent habit (or custom) of using it can be quantified. It may be identified as an intangible fixed asset and amortized (to the profit and loss account) during its economic life, or written off to reserves.

go-slow Type of industrial action in which workers decrease their rate of production as a protest.

government bond Fixed-interest security issued by a government agent such as the ***Treasury***. It is also known as a Treasury bond.

government broker Firm formerly nominated by the ***Bank of England*** for dealing with new issues of gilt-edged securities, now replaced by a number of market-makers in gilts.

government securities Treasury bills, gilt-edged securities and any other government fixed-interest paper. They are sold as a means of borrowing, often to offset a budget deficit.

government stock Any bond issued by a government, most often central government stock (gilt-edged securities in the UK).

grace period Time that elapses between the granting of a loan and when the first repayment is made. *See also* ***days of grace***.

grading Setting of standards for type and quality for commodities (and checking them).

graft Informal term for money made in illegal dealings undertaken by somebody in public office.

grant Funds provided by national or local government, or some other institution (such as the Leverhume Trust or the Nuffield Foundation in the UK).

grant price In instances where US employees have a preferred option on their company's stock, the price at which that option may be exercised.

gratuity Payment made voluntarily in excess of statutory or contractual obligations, such as a tip in a restaurant or a bonus payment on retirement. Regular gratuities are often regarded as earnings for tax purposes.

greenback Informal name for the US dollar.

green baize door Alternative term for a ***Chinese wall***.

Green Book Informal name for the *Unlisted Securities Market*, published by the London Stock Exchange, setting out requirements for entry into the ***Unlisted Securities Market (USM)*** and associated regulations.

green currency Currency of an EU country (based on the ***European Currency Unit, ECU***) that uses an artificial rate of exchange to protect farm prices from fluctuations in the real rates of exchange.

greenmail Procedure by which a person with a sufficient shareholding in a company seeks a sum of money, or the repurchase by the company of his or her shares at an unreasonably high price, in order to induce him or her to refrain from making a take-over bid.

green pound Notional unit of currency used in the administration of the ***Common Agricultural Policy*** of the EU to determine the relative prices (and hence subsidies) of farm produce from the different member countries.

green shoe When a company goes public it may grant its underwriting firm an option on extra numbers of shares. This prevents the underwriter from making a loss if the issue is undersubscribed and the underwriter having to buy shares on the open market to cover a short position.

grey knight In a take-over situation, a third party, acting as a counterbidder, whose intentions towards the target company are not at all clear. Grey knights are normally unwelcome to both the target and the original raider. *See also* ***white knight***.

grey market Any semi-legal market, usually for goods that are in short supply; it is one that keeps within the letter if not the spirit of the law. The term is most usually applied to the market dealing in any stock or share whose issue has been announced but which has not yet taken place. Traders therefore gamble on the eventual selling price of the issue when it comes onto the market. *See also* ***black market***.

grey pound Colloquial term for the purchasing power of retired and elderly people, who are becoming an increasingly large sector of the population in Western countries.

grey wave Term normally used by venture capitalists to describe a company or new industry that shows potential but whose realization is, however, a long way in the future.

gross Amount calculated before the deduction of certain items, the items generally being specified according to context. For example, a salary or interest paid "gross of tax" is paid before deduction of income tax, in contrast to "net of tax", where tax is deducted before payment.

gross domestic product (GDP) Measure of the value of goods and services produced within a country, normally in one year. GDP does not take into account the value of goods and services generated overseas. It is sometimes also known as gross value added. *See also* ***gross national product (GNP)***.

grossing up Calculation of a gross amount from the net amount by adding back the amount deducted.

gross interest Interest on a deposit or investment before deduction of income tax (*see* ***gross***).

gross margin (GM) Also called gross profit or gross profit margin, the price at which goods are sold minus what they cost, usually expressed as a percentage of the selling price. More formally it is the difference between a company's sales revenue and the cost of the goods sold, ignoring costs of administration, distribution or finance.

gross mark-up Amount by which a trader increases the purchase price of an item in order to sell it at a profit, usually expressed as a percentage of its purchase price.

gross national product (GNP) Measure of the value of all goods and services produced by a country, including those produced overseas, usually in one year. *See also* ***gross domestic product (GDP)***.

gross profit Alternative term for ***gross margin***.

gross weight Total weight of a cargo or other item, including its packing.

ground rent Payment made, normally annually, by the occupier of a building to the owner of the land on which the building stands (the freeholder). Ground rent is paid only if the building is occupied leasehold. If the lessee fails to pay, the property owner has the right to terminate the lease.

group Another name for a ***conglomerate***.

Group of Five (G-5) Five leading industrial nations (France, Germany, Japan, the UK and the USA), which meet from time to time to discuss common economic problems.

Group of Seven (G-7) Seven leading non-communist nations consisting of the Group of Five countries with the addition of Canada and Italy.

Group of Ten (G-10) Also known colloquially as the Paris Club, the ten countries Belgium, Canada, France, Germany, Italy, Japan, the Netherlands, Sweden, the UK and the USA. These countries signed an agreement in 1962 to increase the funds available to the ***International Monetary Fund (IMF)*** and to aid those member countries with balance of payments difficulties.

growth funds Long-term investments that concentrate on capital growth.

growth stocks Stocks or shares that are expected to provide the investor with a larger proportion of capital growth (i.e., growth in the value of the stock or share) to income (in the form of dividends) than other shares.

growth recession Situation in which the gross national product (GNP) and unemployment are both increasing slowly.

GTC Abbreviation of ***good till cancelled***.

guarantee Promise to pay the debt of somebody else in the event that the debtor defaults (compare with ***indemnity***). Guarantee is also the name given to a document stating that goods or services are of good (merchandizable) quality.

guesstimate Colloqual term for an estimate that is based largely on intuition or guesswork.

guest worker Foreign worker that a government brings in for certain jobs, usually for a specified time.

H

haircut Usually a discount on the market value of a bond. It may also be any discount or deduction from the normal value, or the cutting of the budget for a particular project or operation without harming the budget itself.

half a bar Slang for £0.5 million.

half-commission man Person whose business is to introduce new clients to a stockbroking firm, receiving in return a share of the commission received from those clients.

hammering In the UK, former stock exchange term that refers to the announcement of the inability of a member to pay his or her debts. In the USA, it is intense selling pressure, when investors perceive that market prices are too high.

Hang Seng index Index of share prices on the Hong Kong Stock Exchange.

hard arbitrage Borrowing of a (considerable) sum of money from a bank and re-lending it profitably on a secondary market, a device disliked by central banks.

hard currency Currency, widely used in international trade, from a country with a stable and prosperous economy. It is thus in high demand and preferred to less stable or legally restricted currencies.

hard dollars Dollars traded on the foreign exchange markets, for which demand is persistently high because of a US trade surplus. The value of hard dollars tends to rise.

hard goods Consumer durables, such as furniture and household appliances.

hard numbers Financial projection that can be relied upon.

harmonized system (HS) Method used in international trade for classifying goods, each being given an HS number.

haulage Cost of road transport. There may be additional charges for loading and unloading.

headage Per capita payment for livestock.

head and shoulders Pattern that may emerge in a graph of share prices plotted against time. Some analysts believe that it predicts a significant downturn in prices.

headhunter Person or agency that actively finds suitable (usually high-grade) staff for posts that companies have vacant, taking a commission from the company involved in relation to the "head's" salary.

Health and Safety at Work Act 1974 UK Act of Parliament that requires employers to protect employees against preventable hazards at work. Factory inspectors working for the ***Health and Safety Executive*** check that the Act is implemented.

Health and Safety Commission UK government organization, a statutory authority, set up under the terms of the ***Health and Safety at Work Act 1974*** to determine and recommend safety policy.

Health and Safety Executive UK government-financed organization that, through its factory inspectors, checks on the implementation of the *Health and Safety at Work Act 1974*.

heavy industry Vague term for manufacturing industries that produce large or heavy products, such as steel, ships, cars and lorries.

heavy shares Shares that command a relatively high price on the stock market.

hedge fund Investment fund that seeks high returns, usually by taking high risks (such as investing in new financial instruments).

hedging Method of protecting against price fluctuations, commonly on the commodities futures market. The term is also used to describe the practice of protecting against fluctuations in exchange rates (by buying forward) to minimize risks and possible losses.

hell or high water contract Informal US term for a guarantee that a municipal bond will be paid ("come hell or high water").

Her Majesty's Customs and Excise Full name of the UK ***Customs and Excise*** department.

Herstatt risk Risk of making a loss on a currency transaction when one side of the deal has been completed but completion of the other side is delayed. It is named after a German bank which made such a loss in 1974.

hidden damage Damage incurred by goods in transit that cannot be seen by a simple external examination, especially if the goods are in crates or packages.

hidden reserve Also called secret reserve, a reserve that is not declared on a company's balance sheet.

hidden tax Tax included in the price of goods or services so that it is not obvious to the purchaser. It includes most forms of indirect taxation, such as duty on alcohol, petrol and tobacco.

high-beta Describing shares that are volatile.

high-end Description of goods that are produced for the top of the market and are consequently very expensive.

high seas Waters that are not part of the territorial waters of any particular country.

high-yield bond Bond, especially common in the USA, issued by a company with a low credit rating. It is often used to raise funds for a leveraged buyout, secured against the assets of the target company. It is also called a junk bond.

hire purchase (HP) Form of credit, normally extended on consumer goods, in which the customer takes and uses the goods and pays for them in instalments (with interest) over an agreed period of time. The seller can in theory repossess the goods at any time if the hirer defaults on payment (unlike with a ***credit sale***). The finance for such business usually comes from a ***finance house***. The equivalent US term is instalment plan.

Hire Purchase Act 1965 UK Act of Parliament that formerly defined regulations that apply to ***hire purchase*** agreements. It was superseded by the ***Consumer Credit Act 1974***.

historical cost Cost of an asset at the time it was acquired, rather than the current cost of its replacement. It is also called acquisition cost or original cost; some US accountants prefer the term sunk cost.

historical dividend Total dividend paid on a company's shares in the last financial year.

hit bid Bargain in which a dealer sells immediately at a price a buyer is willing to pay, instead of waiting for a possibly better price.

hive off To split off an operating arm of a company to make it into a subsidiary company. It is said to have hived off that part of its operation.

hoekmen Members (market-makers) of the Amsterdam Stock Exchange.

holder for value Person who holds a ***bill of exchange*** for which a value has at one time been given.

holder in due course Person who has taken up a ***bill for value*** before payment is due, and who has no good reason to suspect the title of the previous holder.

holding company Company that exists to hold shares in other companies, which are (depending on the level of shareholding) its subsidiaries. An immediate holding company is one that holds a controlling interest in another company but, in turn, the immediate holding company itself may be owned by a holding company. It is also known as a parent.

holding out Continuing liability of an ex-member of a partnership who does not ensure his name is deleted from the firm's name after he leaves. *See* ***partnership***.

hold over To defer settlement of a deal on the Stock Exchange until the next settlement day.

home country Country that houses the headquarters of a company that engages in international trade or investment.

Hong Kong stock exchanges *See* ***Stock Exchange of Hong Kong***.

honararium Money paid to a professional such as an accountant or a solicitor when he or she does not request a fee.

horizontal diversification Diversification into industries or businesses at the same stage of production as the diversifying company. For example, a suit manufacturer might diversify into leisurewear, or a yacht builder into the construction of motor boats. *See also* ***vertical diversification***.

horizontal integration Amalgamation of companies in the same stage of production, and which are therefore likely to possess similar skills and benefit from ***economies of scale***.

horizontal promotion Transferring to a different department at the same level of seniority, but with better career prospects, salary and status, seen as a real promotion in Japanese business.

horizontal spread Combination of a long-call option and a short-call option with different expiry dates.

host country Country other than its ***home country*** in which an international company operates.

hostile take-over bid Attempt to purchase control of a company that is unwelcome to some of the target company's shareholders and directors.

hot money In business, money that is moved rapidly and at short notice from one country to another to take advantage of changes in short-term interest rates or to avoid imminent devaluation of a currency. It is also an informal term for money obtained illegally (e.g., by fraud or theft).

HP Abbreviation of ***hire purchase***.

HS Abbreviation of ***harmonized system***.

human capital Value of a company's employees.

hurdle rate In capital budgeting, the rate of interest that a proposal must exceed before it is given consideration; i.e., the required rate of return. It is usually related to the cost of capital, taking into account any risk factors.

hyperinflation Inflation (a general increase in price levels) that is running extremely high, also known as galloping inflation.

I

IBEX Abbreviation of ***International Bank for Economic Cooperation***.

IBOR Abbreviation of ***interbank offered rate***.

IBRD Abbreviation of ***International Bank for Reconstruction and Development*** (World Bank).

ICCH Abbreviation of ***International Commodities Clearing House***.

ICON Abbreviation of ***indexed currency option note***.

IDB Abbreviation of ***inter-dealer broker***.

IDR Abbreviation of ***international depository receipt***.

IFA Abbreviation of ***independent financial adviser***.

IFAA Abbreviation for ***Independent Financial Advisers Association***.

IFC Abbreviation of ***International Finance Corporation***.

IFS Abbreviation of ***Institute for Fiscal Studies***.

idle time Time for which a production process cannot operate, measured in labour hours or machine hours. It usually requires wages to be paid to workers who are idle through no fault of their own.

ignoratia juris neminem excusat Latin for "ignorance of the law is no defence". It is a doctrine that warns that people who break the law will be punished, regardless of whether or not they are aware that they are committing a crime.

IHT Abbreviation of ***inheritance tax***.

illiquidity Situation in which an asset is not easily converted into cash, or in which a person is not able to raise cash quickly and/or easily.

IM Abbreviation of ***Institute of Management***.

IMF Abbreviation of ***International Monetary Fund***.

immediate holding company Company that holds the controlling interest in another company, even though it may itself be controlled by a third company.

impact day Day on which a company is scheduled to publish details of a new issue.

Imperial system System of measurement used day-to-day in the UK and its former colonies and possessions, often called the customary system or standard units in the USA. It contrasts with the metric system used in Continental Europe and science (which uses the version known as SI units).

implied terms Terms of a contract that are not expressly stated, but that the law considers to be necessary to the sense of the contract and therefore implicit.

import Goods and services brought into a country for sale, from abroad.

import ban Also called an embargo, a ban on specified imports, often for political rather than economic reasons.

import controls Quotas (specifying quantities of goods) or tariffs (taxes) designed to limit the amount of imports, usually to protect the home market.

import duty Government tax levied on imports.

import licence Government document that authorizes the importation of (specified) goods.

import penetration Measure of the home market share taken by importers.

import quota Amount of a particular good that a government allows to be imported.

import restrictions Government controls on the amount of goods that can be imported, usually because there is an adverse trade balance.

import specie point Point in the variation of exchange rates at which it becomes cheaper for a nation on the gold standard to import gold than buy foreign currency.

import tariff *See **import controls**.*

imprest Sum of money made available for petty expenses; ***petty cash***.

impulse purchase Purchase that is unplanned, but made on the spur of the moment. Products usually bought in this way, such as snacks and sweets, are often displayed near the exits or checkouts of shops.

imputation system UK taxation system, established in 1973, that partly governs the payment of ***corporation tax***. Under this system, a shareholder's dividends are taxed at source, and he or she is issued with a credit for the tax imputed.

IMRO Abbreviation of ***Investment Management Regulatory Organization***.

in-and-out trader Stock-market trader who buys and rapidly sells a security on the same day.

in case of need Endorsement on a ***bill of exchange*** that identifies somebody who the holder can apply to if the bill is not honoured.

incentive bonus Extra money offered or paid to an employee to encourage harder work (and therefore greater productivity). It is also called a productivity bonus.

incestuous share dealing Dealing in the shares of associated companies in order to win tax concessions. It is often illegal, although not necessarily so.

inchoate instrument Bill of exchange, cheque or promissory note that is incomplete in some way. Completion of the details may be authorized by the drawer of the financial instrument (for example, the name of the drawee on a bill of exchange may be filled in by a third party).

income Money, goods or services received from an activity. Income may be a return on one of the factors of production – a salary, rent, interest or profit – or it may be a transfer payment made for other reasons, such as (in the UK) unemployment benefit. The definition also includes non-monetary income, such as the benefit a company or individual derives from the possession of assets. For a company it is therefore the amount by which revenue and gains exceed expenses and liabilities (debts).

income gearing Number of times by which profits exceed interest payments on a debt, a measure of the borrower's ability to repay. It is also termed times covered.

income statement Alternative term for a company's profit and loss account.

income tax Direct annual tax levied on ***income***, such as on fees, salaries and wages. In accounting terms it is regarded as an expense or, if not yet paid, a liability.

inconvertible Describing money that cannot be exchanged for gold of equal value. UK currency has been inconvertible since the country came off the gold standard in 1931.

incorporation Process of setting up a business as a legal entity.

incremental cost Extra cost incurred when a company agrees to take on a new project.

indebtedness day When a company issues a prospectus, it must make known the day on which its statement of debt (the extent of its indebtedness) was made. It is assumed that the indebtedness figure was correct at the time, called the indebtedness day or date.

indemnity Undertaking that gives protection against loss or damage. It may be in the form of replacement or repair of property lost or damaged, or the provision of cash to the value of the property.

indent To order goods, either through a company's ordering system or from its own stores, or from abroad through an agent.

indenture Deed or instrument to which there is more than one party. It is so called because such deeds were often cut or torn (indented) into portions, one for each party, to prevent forgery and to provide proof of each person's involvement in the transaction. Indentures were formerly widely used to bind an apprentice to his master for the period of his apprenticeship.

independent company Company that operates entirely under its own authority, and is not owned or controlled (in part or in whole) by any other company.

independent financial adviser (IFA) Financial adviser who can give advice about the products of any company (i.e., he or she is not tied to only one company as its employee or agent). He or she must offer best advice based on all the products available.

Independent Financial Advisers Association (IFAA) UK organization established in 1994 to represent the interests of independent financial advisers (IFAs) to official bodies and to promote high standards within the profession.

index Form of measurement or comparison; a listing giving an indication of change.

index arbitrage Process of selling stocks at the same time as buying stock-index futures, or vice versa. It is a form of programme trading.

indexation Form of index-linking that ties, say, income to the ***retail price index*** and therefore prevents a fall in real wages during a period of inflation. Annuities, pensions or taxes may also be index-linked. The term also describes an adjustment (the indexation allowance) to the value of an asset to take into account a change in the retail price index.

This prevents the owner of the asset from having to pay capital gains tax on a gain that was due entirely to inflation.

indexed currency option note (ICON) Document that records a debt whose value depends on the effective exchange rates between the currencies concerned. A pre-arranged rate is set between defined limits for interest payments, but changes if the limits are exceeded.

indexed portfolio Portfolio of securities linked to a stock index, such as the ***Financial Times Stock Exchange 100 Index (Footsie)***.

index fund Investment fund that is linked directly to a share index, in that it has investments in shares in that index.

index futures Futures contracts that are based on figures provided by indices.

indexing *See* ***index number***.

index-linked *See* ***indexation***.

indexed-linked gilts Gilt-edged securities that have a variable rate of interest adjusted to take account of inflation (using index-linking to the retail price index).

index-linking System of linking costs, prices or wages to the price fluctuations of an economy in order to allow for inflation and to maintain value in real terms. *See also* ***index number***.

index number Weighted average that permits the comparison of prices or production over a number of years. The components elected for comparison are weighted according to their importance and then averaged. Figures are compared to those for a base year, selected for its typicality and given the index number 100 or 1000.

index of members Alphabetical index of the names of members of a company (i.e. the shareholders) required of every company with more than 50 members. It is not required if the register of members is already in alphabetical order.

index tracking Method of measuring the success of an investment portfolio by comparing its performance with the movements of a relevant stock-market index.

indication-only price Price quoted by a market-maker that indicates what he or she thinks a security is worth although he or she is not prepared to deal in it.

indirect costs Also called indirect expenses, costs of items or activities, such as maintenance of buildings or machinery, that are not used in the production of goods, nor are they immediately necessary for their production. They are generally regarded as overheads, although in some methods of costing they may be allocated to cost centres.

indirect expenses Alternative term for ***indirect costs***.

indirect labour Workers who are not directly involved in a production process (such as cleaners, maintenance staff and supervisors). In other words, all labour that is not ***direct labour***.

indirect production Production of goods for sale by employing labour and machinery and using a system of divided labour in order to make a profit (as opposed to direct production, in which everyone merely makes the things that he or she requires and none is sold).

indirect sales Sales made through agents, distributors, retailers, wholesalers and other intermediaries (as opposed to, say, door-to-door selling and other forms of direct sales).

indirect taxation Tax paid to one person or organization (often a retailer), who then pays it to the ***Inland Revenue*** or ***Treasury***. Duty and value added tax are forms of indirect taxation.

individually validated license (IVL) Written US government approval for the export of a specified amount of items to a single (specified) customer.

individual savings account (ISA) Method of long-term tax-free saving introduced by the UK government in 1999 to replace ***personal equity plans (PEPs)*** and ***tax exempt special savings accounts (TESSAs)***. Sums can be invested as cash, life products (insurance) or stocks and shares (equity) or any combinaton of these. Tax relief is lost if funds are withdrawn prematurely.

indivisibility Inability of a machine or production process to produce fewer than a certain large number of units (without working inefficiently at less than optimum capacity).

industrial action Action such as a go-slow, overtime ban, strike or work-to-rule taken by workers to focus the attention of management on their grievances.

industrial dispute Disagreement between managers and workers or their trade union, which may lead to ***industrial action***.

industrial espionage Attempt by one company or group to gain access to confidential information about another, generally to acquire commercial advantage and improve efficiency by imitation. It may or may not be illegal.

industrials Shares in an industrial company, usually manufacturing.

industrial sabotage Unfair competition between rival companies. The term applies to any dubious acts, not merely physical sabotage.

inelastic demand Situation in which a price increase (for goods or services) does not produce a proportionate decrease in demand. It usually occurs with necessities or goods with a very strong brand image.

inertia selling Method of selling in which unsolicited goods are mailed to a "customer" and then followed by an invoice. The practice is illegal in many countries. *See* ***Unsolicited Goods and Services Act 1971***.

infant industry Newly-established national industry in the early stages of growth.

inferior goods Products, such as a supermarket's "own brand" range, that sell better when general purchasing power decreases (because they are perceived as cheaper alternatives to more desirable goods).

inflation Persistent general increase in the level of prices. Strictly defined, it includes neither one-off increases in price (occasioned by, for example, a sudden scarcity of one product) nor any other increases caused by real factors. Its causes include an excess of demand over supply and increases in the money supply, perhaps brought about by increased government expenditure, which causes a decline in the real value of money.

inflation-adjusted Describing wages that have been modified to maintain real income by increasing pay in line with inflation. The term may also be applied to the economist's technique of discounting price changes to obtain a truer picture of quantitative changes in output.

infopreneur Person who makes a living by collecting, assessing and selling information to interested parties.

information technology (IT) Area of microelectronics that combines computing and telecommunications technology to organize, store, retrieve and transfer information.

Inhaberobligation German for bearer bond.

inherent vice Property of goods that is not obvious but makes them an exceptional risk, so absolving the carrier for liability for their loss or damage.

inheritance tax (IHT) Tax paid on inheritances by heirs, often calculated in relation to the closeness of the relationship between the heir and the deceased person. In the UK, ***capital gains tax*** covers income from inheritances.

initial allowance Amount deducted from a company's profits for the purpose of calculating tax in the first year after acquisition.

initial public offering (IPO) First share offer made by a company going public.

inland bill ***Bill of exchange*** that is drawn and payable within the same country.

inland bill of lading ***Bill of lading*** used when carrying goods overland to the international carrier to be used by an exporter (usually a shipping company at a port).

Inland Revenue UK government department whose major responsibility is the collection of various taxes, such as income tax, capital gains tax and corporation tax. Its full name is the Board of the Inland Revenue.

in play Describing a quoted company for which a take-over bid is expected in the very near future.

input Capital, components, raw materials, labour or any other elements that go into producing goods or services.

input tax In the UK's value added tax system, the tax that is collected from the seller of goods by the Customs and Excise. *See also* ***output tax***.

inscribed stock Also termed registered stock, a now discontinued method of registering the name of a stockholder, in which the holder was issued with a slip indicating that the holder's name had been registered. The slip did not have the status of a certificate. *See also* ***registered bond***.

insider dealing Also called insider trading, illegal profitable transactions made on the basis of privileged information available as a result of working inside an organization. Most insider dealing concerns trading in stocks and shares whose value is likely to be affected by the release of news that only a few people are aware of.

insolvency State in which total liabilities (excluding equity capital) exceed total assets; it is therefore the inability to pay debts when called to do so. If insolvency is chronic, bankruptcy or liquidation generally follow.

Insolvency Act 1986 UK Act of Parliament that details how an insolvent company can be dealt with. Among the choices are winding up (if there is no way of saving the company) using an administrator or receiver; appointing an administrator to reorganize the company (to the best interests of creditors and shareholders); or recapitalization through a voluntary agreement between the company and its creditors.

instalment Part payment of a debt, such as one undertaken as part of a ***credit sale*** or ***hire purchase*** agreement. Instalment payments fall due at fixed and specified intervals and when totalled equal the original debt, usually with the addition of interest.

instalment credit *See* ***credit sale***.

instalment plan US term for ***hire purchase***.

Instinet Reuters-owned electronic equity brokering service linked directly to the stock exchanges at Frankfurt, London, Paris and Stockholm.

Institute for Fiscal Studies (IFS) UK organization established in 1969 to research taxation and associated subjects. Its annual forecast of the UK budget is published as the *Green Budget*.

Institute of Directors (IOD) Organization established in 1903, and given a Royal Charter in 1906, which promotes its members' interests and the concept of free enterprise, especially for smaller businesses.

Institute of Management (IM) Professional organization of managers, formerly (before 1992) the British Institute of Management.

Institute of Marketing Organization established in 1911 (as the Institute of Marketing and Sales Management) to provide training and qualifications in marketing.

Institute of Office Management Organization established soon after the turn of the 20th century to provide training and qualification in office management.

Institute of Practitioners in Advertising Organization that acts as a trade association for UK advertising agencies.

institutional investor Corporate rather than individual investor; a company that invests funds on behalf of clients, generally intending to reap profits only in the long term. Institutional investors include banks, insurance companies, pension funds and unit trusts. In the UK, institutional investors hold from 50% to 70% of all negotiable securities.

instrument Broadly, any legally binding document (such as a ***financial instrument***).

intangible asset Non-monetary asset that is neither physical nor current. The many examples include brand names, copyright, franchises, goodwill, leases, licences, mailing lists, patents and trademarks. It is sometimes known as an invisible asset.

in-store concession In order to diversify and maintain their own profits, some large stores allow smaller retail operations to set up and staff areas of the store for the sale of their own goods. The store then receives a percentage of the in-store concession's takings in payment.

integration Amalgamation of two or more companies to improve efficiency. Also, an industry is said to be integrated if profits from different partaking companies are compatible.

intellectual property Expression of the theory that ideas as well as tangible inventions are unique to one person or a group and should be patentable. Currently intellectual property has no clear legal standing in many countries, other than in copyright.

interbank offered rate (IBOR) Rate of interest that banks charge to lend to other prime banks. *See also* ***London Inter Bank Offered Rate (LIBOR)***.

interbank sterling market Money market that involves all UK banks, allowing speedy informal trading to best use or obtain funds. Transactions are carried out through brokers.

inter-dealer broker (IDB) Person who matches deals between anonymous buyers and sellers on behalf of two market-makers.

interest Charge made by a lender to a borrower in exchange for the service of lending funds. It is usually expressed as a percentage of the sum borrowed for a specific period (normally a year), termed the interest rate, but it may be paid in kind. Interest is also payment made by a bank or building society to customers who deposit money with them. *See* ***compound interest; simple interest***.

interest cover Ratio of earnings to the fixed-interest payments necessary to service loan capital. It is an indication of how vulnerable a company is to fluctuations in profit or interest rates.

interest holiday Period during which a lender (usually a bank) postpones the requirement to pay interest on a loan (usually made to a start-up business or one in financial difficulties).

interest-only loan Type of loan for which regular interest payments are made until the loan matures, when the whole of the principal also falls due.

interest rate Interest charged to a borrower or paid to an investor, usually expressed as a percentage per annum (*see* ***interest***).

interest rate futures Financial futures purchased as a hedge against an adverse change in interest rates. If interest changes on the hedger's financial instruments produce a loss, the futures contract offsets it.

interest rate margin Also called spread, the difference between a base rate of interest (usually the ***London Inter-Bank Offered Rate, LIBOR***) and the rate paid on a debt security, as used for ***floating rate notes*** on the Euromarket.

interest rate swap Exchange of two interest rate payments in a transaction, in which a borrower of lower creditworthiness benefits from the higher interest rate available to a borrower of higher creditworthiness (who makes a profit on the deal).

interest warrant Government cheque issued by the ***Bank of England*** for paying interest due on a loan. A company may also issue an interest warrant.

interim accounts Also called interim financial statements, short financial statements produced by a company (often unaudited) in the middle of the financial year halfway between publications of annual accounts. It is a requirement that listed companies produce such a half-yearly report.

interim dividend Any dividend other than the final dividend declared by a company at the conclusion of each trading year. Interim dividends may be made as a reward for a particularly good economic performance or simply as an effective advance on the final dividend, which will be correspondingly reduced in value. Many UK companies quoted on the stock market make interim dividend payments per annum; it is unusual for a firm to exceed this frequency of interim payments.

interim note Means of advising an investor that he or she has been allotted shares and will eventually receive a share certificate.

interim report Short statement published at the end of the first half of a public company's financial year, detailing results for the previous six months and declaring any ***interim dividend***.

intermediary Someone who acts between and deals with two parties who themselves make no direct contact with each other.

internal cost Spending, such as that on materials and wages, that affect a company's own accounts.

internal financing Cash generated within a company's own accounts (such as retained profits) or from its own resources (such as assets or working capital).

internalization Cost-saving resulting from a company's desire to control its overseas operations, rather than use another company for that purpose.

internal rate of return (IRR) Discount rate at which, applied to the expected pattern of cash expenditure and income of a capital project, would give a net present value of zero. It may be compared with the return on alternative investments, or on some target rate of return.

internal repurchase agreement pool Derived from repurchase agreements, the sum of all short-term investment balances held by the US Federal Reserve in the names of international organizations and overseas central banks.

Internal Revenue Service (IRS) US equivalent of the UK's ***Inland Revenue***.

International Agreement for Guidelines on Officially Supported Export Credit Commonly known as Consensus, an agreement between members of the ***Organization for Economic Cooperation and Development (OECD)*** on how much they will subsidize the interest rate on loans to purchaser's of their own country's exports.

International Bank for Economic Cooperation (IBEX) Financial organization established in 1949 that acts as the central bank for the Communist-based ***Council of Mutual Economic Assistance (CMEA)***, later (1991) superseded by the ***Organization for International Economic Cooperation*** (OIEC).

International Bank for Reconstruction and Development (IBRD) Part of the World Bank, established in 1945 with headquarters in Washington D.C., to help economic reconstruction in countries after World War II. It makes loans to developing nations or guarantees loans from other sources. The bank's capital comes from the member nations of the ***International Monetary Fund (IMF)***.

International Commodities Clearing House (ICCH) Major clearing house for the London commodity market's futures dealings, established

I

in 1888 (as the London Produce Clearing House). It adopted its present name in 1973, and today deals mainly in soft commodities (with the exception of barley and wheat) and metals. It is also a market for options in most soft commodities.

international depository receipt (IDR) Negotiable certificate issued by a bank that proves the ownership of securities by someone outside the country of origin.

International Finance Corporation (IFC) Organization established in 1956 by the ***International Bank for Reconstruction and Development (IBRD)*** to raise capital to instigate growth in a developing country's private sector.

International Monetary Fund (IMF) International organization established in 1944 after the Bretton Woods conference, to organize and administer the international monetary system. It was designed to help countries in financial difficulties, especially with their balance of payments. It makes loans and provides financial advisers.

International Securities Market Association (ISMA) Organization established in Zurich in 1969 as the Association of International Bond Dealers (AIBD). It adopted its present name in 1991, and today deals in and underwrites international bonds. There are more than 800 members from over 40 countries.

International Swaps and Derivatives Association (ISDA) Worldwide trade association established in 1985 to represent the privately-negotiated derivatives industry. There are more than 200 members.

Internet Message-forwarding system that interlinks computers worldwide. Its applications grow daily, and include e-mail, banking, shopping, and entertainment, as well as other types of information access and transmission. It is funded largely by the sites that receive or relay messages (not the senders), although access may not be free. Any statement about the number of users is out of date immediately, because of the rate of current growth, but at the beginning of the year 2000 there were an estimated 26 million users.

intervention Action of a central bank in the foreign currency markets when it buys or sells currency in an attempt to control its exchange rate.

intervention mechanism Type of ***intervention*** employed by the ***European Monetary System (EMS)*** to stabilize exchange rate relationships as agreed between members. It provides short-term (75-day) finance to the central bank of a country whose exchange rate is under pressure, or grants ***short-term monetary support (STMS)*** or ***medium-term financial assistance (MTFA)***.

intervention price Price slightly below the ***threshold price*** at which the European Commission intervenes to purchase agricultural surpluses, thus supporting home markets and helping to achieve the average or ***target price***.

intestacy Situation in which a person dies without making a valid will, leaving the estate without a designated heir. If a person dies intestate, the Crown divides the estate between the surviving relatives, making provision first for the spouse, and then for any children. If neither spouse nor children are living, other relatives are entitled to share in the estate. If no relatives can be traced, the estate goes to the Crown.

in-the-money option Option to buy shares (a call option) for which the price on the open market has risen above the price fixed (the option's exercise price). Or it is an option to sell (a put option) for which the market price has fallen in relation to the exercise price. An in-the-money option is said to carry ***intrinsic value***.

in the window Describing anything obviously for sale. For example, a company may put an unquoted subsidiary in the window by discreetly inviting potential purchasers to make themselves known. The term is also a virtual synonym for ***in play***.

intranet Internal links between a company's computers that provide similar function to the ***Internet*** but in house.

intrapreneur Member of the staff of a company who is given relative autonomy in order that he or she may make use of entrepreneurial skills to the advantage of the company.

intrinsic value Value of the materials from which an object is made, rather than its market or face value. For example, a coin may be said to be worth so much and is exchanged on the basis of that stated value, but the metal used in minting it may be worth much less.

introduction Means of offering a new share issue to the public, through the medium of a stock exchange but without the publication of a prospectus and the provision of an application form. Introductions are possible only if there is a large number of potential shareholders and no large bargains have been struck to market the stock.

inventory List of the stock of raw materials, goods in production or finished goods owned and stored by a company, usually giving details of their cost, value and price. In the USA, the term inventory is synonymous with ***stock***.

inventory control Stock control. Most efficient businesses are managed, using inventories, in such a way that minimum levels of stock-in-trade sufficient to meet any likely demand are always maintained.

inventory turnover Also termed stock turnover, the number of times items of stock are used each accounting period (usually per year). For this period it equals the number of units used each year divided by the number of units in stock. Units in stock may be those at the beginning of the year, those at the end, or an average of the two.

inverse yield curve Describing a plot of interest rate against maturity that slopes downwards left to right (i.e., the longer the maturity, the lower the rate). It happens during times of high inflation that is expected soon to fall rapidly. *See also* ***yield curve***.

investment Expenditure on real or financial assets rather than on funding of consumption. In this sense, expenditure consists of the purchase of any asset which is expected to increase in value. To an economist, however, investment covers spending that results in economic growth (such as money spent on the purchase of machinery or the building of plant that will produce goods and services for sale). In this sense, it extends to funds applied to the improvement of the infrastructure, and the term may also be applied to expenditure on human resources.

investment allowance Alternative term for ***capital allowance***.

investment analyst Person who studies financial securities and company results with a view to advising about buying and selling shares.

investment bank US bank that acts mainly as an intermediary between investors and companies that want to issue shares. It also carries out many of the functions performed by a UK ***merchant bank***.

investment credit Former tax credit in the USA, abolished in 1986, that equalled 10% of the price a business paid for investment goods (such as fixed assets). It was similar to the UK ***capital allowances***.

investment club Voluntary group of private investors who pool their resources and manage their own fund (thus saving the cost of a professional fund manager).

investment company Company that employs its funds to buy securities or shares, as opposed to conducting business on its own account. It is run by a board of directors and so is not the same as an ***investment trust***.

Investment Company Act 1940 US legislation designed to control many of the abuses associated with investment companies and investment advisers.

investment grade Describing a US bond that has been given a higher rating than a defined minimum by a credit-rating agency such as Standard and Poor. Bonds of lower than the required minimum are termed ***junk bonds***.

investment grant UK government grant formerly available (from 1966 until 1970) for industrial companies to buy machinery and so on. Initially worth 20% of the purchase price (40% in development areas), it rose to 25% (and 45%) in 1967 and 1968.

investment income Company's income from outside investments (as opposed to revenue from normal business activities).

investment instrument Any medium of investment, including stocks, shares and securities of all kinds, unit trusts and funds, grouped investment media, and so on.

Investment Management Regulatory Organization (IMRO) Self-regulating UK organization set up under the ***Financial Services Act 1986*** to regulate the activities of people or firms that give investment advice.

investment portfolio Collection of bonds, stocks, shares and other securities held by an individual or an institution that invests on behalf of other people.

Investment Services Directive (ISD) Directive of the EU, issued in 1966, that deals with cross-border transactions by investment banks and dealers in securities.

investment trust Investment scheme, similar to a ***unit trust***, in which a small investor is able to invest in a range of securities through the agency of the scheme's managers.

Investors' Compensation Scheme Scheme established in 1988 by the UK ***Securities and Investments Board*** to help people who lose money because of default by an investment company authorized under the Financial Services Act. It pays the full loss up to £30,000 and 90% of any further loss up to a total of £50,000 (i.e. a maximum of £48,000 may be paid out).

Investors in Industry (3i) Large UK ***venture capital*** organization that is a holding company of the Finance Corporation for Industry, the

Industrial and Commercial Finance Corporation and the Technical Development Council. It provides a mixture of loan capital and equity.

invisible asset *See **intangible asset**.*

invisible earnings Income earned from payment for services rather than goods, on a national scale. Invisible earnings include profits from tourism, shipping, and the provision of insurance, banking and other financial services. They are also called invisibles.

invisible export Sale of a service, such as banking, shipping or insurance, to an overseas buyer. Revenue from tourism (e.g. from foreign tourists in the UK) is also regarded as an invisible export.

invisible import Purchase of a service from an overseas supplier.

invisible trade Trade in services rather than in tangible goods.

invitation to treat Suggestion, made from one person to another, that he or she enter into negotiations that may result in a formal offer to trade. The difference between an invitation to treat and an offer proper is that an invitation does not bind the parties concerned to the conditions of the invitation, whereas the terms of an offer are legally binding.

invoice Document that summarizes a business transaction and often doubles as a request for payment. An invoice lists and describes the goods (or services) ordered and details their price, and usually records the dates and times of dispatch and delivery.

invoice discounting Practice of offering a discount on unpaid invoices sold to a ***factoring*** company, which then tries to claim the money owed on its own account. The size of the discounting reflects the likely difficulty of securing payment.

inward investment Alternative term for foreign investment.

IOD Abbreviation of ***Institute of Directors***.

IOU Abbreviation of "I owe you", a non-negotiable written note recording a debt.

IPO Abbreviation of ***initial public offering***.

IRR Abbreviation of ***internal rate of return***.

irrevocable and confirmed credit Credit facilities that are confirmed by a bank in London on an account held by a non-UK resident.

irrevocable documentary acceptance credit Credit facilities arranged by an overseas customer with a bank in London, who is then presented with a letter of credit to facilitate foreign trade.

irrevocable letter of credit *Letter of credit* that an issuing bank is obliged to pay to an exporter, when all conditions and terms (which cannot be changed except by agreement of all parties) have been met.

IRS Abbreviation of *Internal Revenue Service*.

ISA Abbreviation of *individual savings account*.

ISDA Abbreviation of *International Swaps and Derivatives Association*.

ISE/Nikkei 50 Index Share index based on the prices of shares in 50 Japanese companese that are traded on the Tokyo Stock Exchange and on the International Stock Exchange (ISE) in London.

ISMA Abbreviation of *International Securities Market Association*.

issuancc Procedure of issuing securities, carried out by a company or an issuing house.

issue Quantity of a particular stock or share offered to the public.

issue by tender Stocks and shares may be issued by the process of inviting tenders above a certain stated minimum price and then selling to the highest bidder.

issue date Date from which accrued interest is calculated (e.g. on a security).

issue price Price, including commission, of any issue of securities (i.e. the price at which it is offered).

issued share capital Amount of a company's authorized share capital that has actually been taken up (i.e. sold to investors).

issuing bank Financial institution that administers a new issue of shares.

issuing house Connecting link between those who need capital and those willing to lend it. Often, an issuing house also operates as a share issue underwriter or merchant bank.

Issuing Houses Association Organization established in 1945 to represent the interests of issuing houses, especially with regard to other financial institutions.

IT Abbreviation of *information technology*.

IVL Abbreviation of *individually validated license*.

J

jajo Abbreviation of January, April, July, October, the months in which some stock opotions expire.

Jenkins Report Report published in the UK in 1962 concerning the law as it related to companies. Many of its recommendations were incorporated in subsequent Companies Acts.

jetsam Goods deliberately thrown overboard from a ship, in an emergency, to make it lighter.

jettison To deliberately throw goods overboard from a ship to lighten it in an emergency.

JIT Abbreviation of ***just in time***.

job analysis Analysis of what is involved in doing a particular job, and determining how it should be done and by what type of employee.

jobber Also known as a stockjobber, a member of the ***London Stock Exchange*** who deals in securities with stockbrokers and other jobbers, but not directly with the public. Formerly, the activities of jobbers and stockbrokers were kept separate on the London exchange. Now jobbers have been replaced by market-makers. In the USA, a jobber is any middleman between a wholesaler and a retailer, or a person on a stock exchange who deals in securities that are worthless (e.g. ***junk bonds***). The US synonym for a jobber in the UK sense is dealer.

jobber's turn Profit made in a deal by a jobber.

job description Formal document that sets out the duties and responsibilities of a particular job. Sometimes, the job description forms part of a contract of employment.

job evaluation Evaluation of the skills and qualities necessary for a person to be able to perform a particular job, or of the ability of a person to do a specific job.

job lot Collection of stocks or goods sold together, perhaps to somebody who wants only some of them.

job production Producing items one at a time to meet a particular specification, usually by a small company that cannot enjoy economies of scale. The next stage up is batch production, and the next mass production.

job-share Also known as time-share, employment that is held by two people, each working part-time.

job specification Often shortened to job spec, a description (sometimes informal) of what a particular position or job entails.

joint and several Concept by which joint debtors (e.g. two or more partners in a partnership) are responsible for the debt, both jointly and as individuals. Joint and several liability gives the lender the recourse to each of the partners in the debt in the event of default.

joint holders If two or more people hold shares jointly, they may have them registered as such but only the first person named receives notices from the company. The holding can, however, be split and registered separately in individual names.

joint-stock company Alternative name for a ***limited company***.

joint tenants Two or more people who have equal rights to the tenancy of a property. If a joint tenant dies, the property reverts to the other tenants, and so on until one tenant remains, with sole tenancy rights. *See also* ***tenancy in common***.

joint tenure Partnership that is made for a specific limited period, often without there being a written agreement.

joint venture Situtation in which one (reporting) entity has a long-term contractual interest in another which is controlled jointly by the reporting entity and some other venture. The reporting entity details in its accounts its share of assets, cash flows and liabilities of the joint venture.

jour de règlement French for settlement day.

journal Book in which daily transactions are recorded before being transferred to the books of account; the book of prime entry.

judgement debt Debt that has come before the courts and which is confirmed by the court as being repayable. The judgement creditor can then apply for repayment remedies through the court.

junior debt Debt that ranks after another (is subordinated), termed the senior debt, when it comes to payment in the event of default.

junk bond Also sometimes called a ***high-yield bond***, a bond issued by a company with a low credit rating.

junior capital Company shares that represent the company's equity.

junior stock Shares offered to a company's executives at below the market price. Junior stock has a low dividend rate, but may be converted to ordinary shares to provide a capital gain.

just in case Maintaining buffer stocks for a production and distribution process, just in case supplies become hard to get or there is a sudden increase in demand. Because of the amount of capital this ties up, it is not favoured as much as ***just in time (JIT)***.

just in time (JIT) Method of minimizing the costs of holding stocks (of raw materials, work in progress and finished goods). It requires careful planning and scheduling, and reliable sources of supply. *See also* ***just in case***.

K

kaffir Racist stock exchange nickname for shares in South African mining companies.

kamikaze pricing Granting of loans by a financial institution at very low interest rates to increase its share of the banking market.

kangaroo Stock exchange nickname for shares in Australian companies, especially those dealing in tobacco, property or mining.

Kapitaalvennootschap Dutch for corporation.

Kapitalanlag German for investment.

keiretsu Group of Japanese companies, often including a bank, that have interlocking shareholdings.

Kennedy Round Large-scale renegotiation of international tariff agreements, within the limits of the ***General Agreement on Tariffs and Trade (GATT)***, initiated by President Kennedy in 1963.

kerb market Trading in securities that takes place outside an official exchange.

kerb trading Closing a deal on a financial futures market after hours. It is so called because originally traders would emerge from the exchange after official trading stopped for the day and remain outside (on the kerb) to close any unfinished business.

kerb weight *See* ***net weight***.

kickback Form of bribery of a customer who is offered a discount price then charged the original (full) price, for accounting purposes, and later reimbursed the difference.

kick-up Chance offered to holders of bonds to convert them into shares at a profit.

kick upstairs To promote a senior executive to a position in which he or she has relatively little influence and can therefore do no (more) harm.

kite Another name for an ***accommodation bill***. It is also UK slang for a cheque.

kite flying Raising money by way of an ***accommodation bill***.

kiting Fraudulently issuing a cheque that is not backed by funds in the account.

knight Third party who appears at the scene of a take-over battle. *See* ***grey knight; white knight***.

knock-out Financial option that terminates automatically if the underlying asset's price reaches a predefined level.

know your customer rules (KYC rules) US regulations, principally to prevent money laundering, established in the late 1990s to ensure that a financial institution knows who is the true beneficiary of any newly-opened account.

Konzern Large German company grouping consisting of a holding company and several subsidiaries.

Konzernrechnungslegung German for ***corporation***.

Kursmakler Official broker who deals and fixes prices on the German stock exchange, acting as an intermediary between banks but not for the general public.

KYC rules Abbreviation of ***know your customer rules***.

L

labour-intensive Describing an industry or process in which labour is the most important and costly factor of production, such as one in which the major cost is the payment of salaries, incentives and bonuses. Service industries or those operating job production or batch production tend to be labour intensive.

labour market Supply and demand for labour, which is the main determiner of wages and salaries.

labour turnover Rate at which employees leave a company or other organization, equal to the ratio of the number of people who leave in a year and the average number of employees (usually expressed as a percentage).

laches Legal term for negligence in performing a duty, asserting a right or claiming a privilege.

ladder option Also known as a step-lock option, a type of ***option*** that enables the holder to add in gains in the underlying price of the security.

laesio enormis Latin for extraordinary injury. It is a doctrine (derived from Roman law) which states that a contract price must be fair and reasonable. An unfair or unreasonable price is grounds for terminating the contract.

LAFTA Abbreviation of ***Latin American Free Trade Association***.

LAIA Abbreviation of ***Latin American Integration Association***.

laggard Share that does not keep up with the average price of comparable shares.

lame duck Weak individual or company; one ripe for take-over or unable to provide effective competition.

Landesbank Financial institution in Germany that acts as a minor central bank for the region's (i.e. the *Land*'s) savings banks.

landmail Practice in the USA of buying the shareholding of an actual or potential corporate raider in return for land as opposed to cash. *See also* ***greenmail***.

larceny Obtaining goods by trickery (from somebody who did not want to part with them). If the person did intend to part with the goods but was defrauded, the offence is obtaining goods under false pretences.

LASH Abbreviation of ***lighter aboard ship***.

last in first out (LIFO) Term with two meanings:

1. It describes the method by which some companies make employees redundant, on the basis of length of service. Thus, the last people to be employed are the first to be laid off.
2. It is an accounting term for a system of stock-keeping whereby the latest items manufactured or bought are used or sold before old stock is cleared. In a period of deflation this has the effect of maximizing profit, because new goods or materials have cost less to manufacture or buy.

last trading day In trading in financial futures, the last day on which trading can take place before delivery.

late-kerb Trading in metals that goes on after hours, usually over the telephone. *See* ***kerb trading***.

latent need In marketing, an existing need that the customer is unaware of – a good need for a seller to satisfy.

Latin American Free Trade Association (LAFTA) Organization established in 1960 to coordinate the economic activities of major South American countries (and Mexico). It was superseded by the ***Latin American Integration Association (LAIA)*** in 1981.

Latin American Integration Association (LAIA) Organization established in 1981 with headquarters in Montevideo, which superseded the ***Latin American Free Trade Association (LAFTA)***. It is an economic grouping of Argentina, Bolivia, Brazil, Chile, Colombia, Ecuador, Mexico, Paraguay, Peru, Uruguay and Venezuela.

laundering Method of disguising the origin of money by moving it rapidly from one country to another. It thus becomes a complicated business to trace its origins, movements and eventual destination. Counterfeit or stolen money may be laundered, although more usually the money represents the proceeds of other types of crime.

LAUTRO Abbreviation of ***Life Assurance and Unit Trust Regulatory Authority***.

lay days Days on which a vessel may unload cargo without incurring port charges.

laying-off Making an employee redundant, either temporarily or permanently, usually because there are insufficient orders for the whole workforce to remain employed.

LBMA Abbreviation of ***London Bullion Market Association***.

LBO Abbreviation of ***leveraged buy-out***.

L/C Abbreviation of ***letter of credit***.

LCH Abbreviation of ***London Clearing House***.

LDT Abbreviation of ***licensed deposit taker***.

lead manager In a syndicate, the company that does the administration. For this service, the lead manager usually receives a higher commission than the other members of the syndicate.

lead time Time that elapses between a company's receiving an order and delivering the product or service.

leaning into the wind Colloquial US term for the Federal Reserve's policy (particularly in the 1950s and 1960s) of reducing interest rates when there is little economic demand and then increasing them when demand becomes high.

lease Contract that gives temporary possession of property, sometimes in areas where prices are appreciating so rapidly that it is not in the owner's best interest to sell. Buildings are the most common subjects of a lease, although it is also possible to lease land and other possessions, such as vehicles and machinery. Long-term leases are often mortgaged, bought and sold.

lease-back Arrangement by which a property is sold on condition that it is immediately leased back to the original owner. Capital tied up in the property is thereby released for other uses.

lease financing Type of off-balance sheet financing in which goods (for example, machinery) are leased rather than being purchased outright. Lease financing is therefore generally thought of as a form of disguised borrowing.

leasehold Describing property held on a lease. On leasehold land, the lessee pays ground rent to the person who holds the freehold.

leasing *See* ***lease***.

Leeman's Act 1867 UK legislation that requires the number of shares given in a company's share register to be stated in any contract for the sale of shares. If this is not done the sale is void.

lender of last resort Central bank that is prepared to lend to the banking system as a whole, including to commercial banks. In the UK the lender of last resort is the ***Bank of England***. It must be prepared to advance money to discount houses that have insufficient funds to balance their books, preventing their bankruptcy. It therefore gives confidence to the markets and helps to prevent a damaging run on the banks. By acting as a lender of the last resort, the Bank of England is able to influence the money supply and interest rates.

lessee Person who is granted a lease.

lessee deposit Deposit that is paid by the lessee on a rented property, intended to cover the lessor against damage or loss and returnable on termination of the lease. *See also* ***dilapidations***.

lessor Person who grants a lease.

letter of allotment Means by which shares are allotted. A letter of allotment may be used as proof of ownership and entitles the holder to a certificate for the number of shares stated in the letter. It should not be confused with an ***allotment note***.

letter of administration Letter granted by the Court to a person appointed to settle a deceased person's affairs, in accordance with a will when there is no executor or in cases of ***intestacy***.

letter of comfort Letter from a parent company to a bank at which a subsidiary has applied for a loan which, while not offering to guarantee the loan, expresses an awareness of the situation and an intention of keeping the subsidiary in business.

letter of credit (L/C) Letter from a bank authorizing another bank to pay the sum specified to the person named in the letter. It is also referred to as a documentary credit.

letter of identification Alternative term for a ***letter of indication***.

letter of indemnity Letter from an exporter agreeing to make good any loss arising from faulty or underweight packing, thus ensuring a clean ***bill of lading***.

letter of indication Also called a letter of identification, a letter from a bank to a depositor who has been issued with a ***letter of credit***. It is used with the letter of credit as proof of the bearer's signature and identity.

letter of regret Letter that informs an applicant that he or she has been unsuccessful in applying for a new share issue.

letter of renunciation Letter from an existing shareholder who does not wish to take advantage of a rights issue, either absolutely or in favour of somebody else.

leverage Alternative, and mainly US, term for ***gearing***.

leveraged company Company that is seriously in debt.

leveraged buy-out (LBO) Buy-out of a large company by a smaller one, the capital for which has been borrowed from a friendly source, secured on the assets of the company being bought.

levy Duty applied by EU countries to imports of agricultural products from countries outside the Union (thus bringing their prices in line with inter-EU prices).

LGS Abbreviation of ***Loan Guarantee Scheme***.

liabilities Company's or person's debts. Long-term (or deferred) liabilities are usually distinguished from current liabilities, as are secured debts from unsecured debts.

LIBBR Abbreviation of ***London Inter-Bank Bid Rate***.

LIBID Abbreviation of ***London Inter-Bank Bid Rate***.

LIBOR Abbreviation of ***London Inter-Bank Offered Rate***.

licensed deposit taker (LDT) Organization authorized by the Bank of England to accept deposits (but not allowed to call itself a bank).

licensing Practice of allowing a person or company to use a copyright or patent in return for a royalty, usually calculated as a percentage of value or a price per unit sold.

lien Right to possession of property until such time that an outstanding liability has been paid. A banker's lien gives a bank the right to retain or sell the property of a debtor in lieu of payment.

Life Assurance and Unit Trust Regulatory Authority (LAUTRO) Former UK ***self-regulating organization (SRO)*** that governed the trading and operation of unit trusts, replaced by the ***Personal Investment Authority (PIA)*** in 1994.

LIFFE Abbreviation of ***London International Financial Futures Exchange***.

LIFO Abbreviation of ***last in first out***.

light dues Sums levied on shipowners to help to pay for beacons, buoys, lights and other navigational aids in channels and rivers. In the UK they are paid through ***Customs and Excise*** to Trinity House.

lighter aboard ship (LASH) Shallow-draught vessel that carries cargo between a ship and the shore, usually in a harbour or inland waterway. Generally unpowered, it is towed by another vessel.

light industry Manufacturing sector that produces most goods, except those produced by large-scale heavy industry.

LIMEAN Abbreviation of ***London Inter-Bank Mean Rate***.

limited Short form of ***limited company (Ltd)***.

limited company (Ltd) Also called a limited liability company, a company formed from a group of people whose liability is limited to the extent of the investment they have made (usually to purchase shares in the company), although occasionally limited liability is limited by guarantee to a certain amount as specified in the company's memorandum. *See also* ***public company***.

limited liability *See* ***limited company***.

limited partner Partner whose liability for the debts of the partnership is limited in law to the sum he or she invested in it. A limited partner does not generally share in the management of the firm. He or she may, however, offer advice and examine the books of account. *See* ***limited partnership***.

limited partnership Partnership in which one or more of the partners has only limited liability for the firm's debts. In each limited partnership there must be one general partner with unlimited liability. A limited partnership is therefore unpopular and a public limited company is preferred, because all shareholders in such a company have only limited liability.

limit order On a stock exchange commodity exchange, an instruction given by a client to his or her stockbroker which specifies the maximum price the broker is authorized to pay to buy a shareholding, or the minimum price at which it can be sold. It is also the US term for a stop loss order.

limit up/down The maximum and minimum limits within which the price of some commodity futures and financial futures are permitted to fluctuate in one day's trading.

line extension In marketing, the addition of a new feature to an existing product line.

line of credit Facility for a loan made available by a creditor on condition that he or she uses the money to buy goods or services from the creditor. A bank may establish a line of credit for a customer to draw down money in stages, in which case it is similar to an overdraft facility.

liquid assets Assets that consist of cash or can readily be converted into cash. They are also known by various other names, such as liquid capital, quick assets and realizable assets.

liquid assets ratio Ratio of the total assets held by a company to the value of assets that may be converted to cash without loss.

liquidate Closing out or cancelling a futures contract where the contract's owner has assets available for sale on the prescribed date, usually achieved by selling the assets.

liquidation Winding-up of a copmany, so-called because the company's assets are liquidated – converted into cash money – in order that outstanding creditors may be paid (in whole or, more usually, in part). In the USA the term is also used to denote payment of a debt.

liquidator Person who officially oversees the winding up of a company, acting as a receiver and manager. *See* ***liquidation***, ***receivership***.

liquidity Ease with which an asset can be converted into cash. Cash deposits in current bank accounts may be quickly withdrawn and are said to be highly liquid; money in most deposit accounts is slightly less liquid because notice must usually be given before withdrawal. Of a company, liquidity is the availability of cash (or near cash) to meet its debts and take advantage of investment opportunities.

liquidity index Method of measuring a company's liquidity in terms of the number of days it would take to convert current assets into cash.

liquidity risk In lending, the risk that an investment cannot, without substantial cost, be liquidated during its lifetime.

liquid ratio Alternative term for ***acid-test ratio***.

listed company Company whose shares are listed on a stock exchange.

listed security Security recognized for quotation and trading on a stock exchange.

listing Flotation of a company on a stock exchange; the sum of the actions that permits securities to be traded on a stock market. The issued shares are then listed in the exchange records and their price fluctuations recorded and published.

list price Published or quoted price for goods or services. *See also* ***discount***.

Little Neddie *See* ***National Economic Development Council (NEDC*** or ***Neddie)***.

Lloyd's Short form of ***Lloyd's of London***.

Lloyd's agents Agents appointed by ***Lloyd's of London*** throughout the world to report about shipping and aviation, and survey any damage or loss.

Lloyd's of London Incorporated association of insurers that specializes in marine insurance. Formally established by Act of Parliament in 1871, the Corporation developed from a group of 17th century underwriters who met at Edward Lloyd's coffee house in London. Lloyd's supervises about 20,000 individual insurers ("names") grouped into syndicates, each of which has unlimited liability and accepts a fraction of the risk of business brought to them by one of more than 200 registered brokers. Lloyd's involvement in marine insurance currently comprises less than half the total business transacted by Lloyd's underwriters. Following disastrous losses between 1988-1994, limited liability companies are now allowed to become "corporate names".

LME Abbreviation of ***London Metal Exchange***.

loading broker Person who acts for a shipowner, obtaining cargoes for the vessel to transport.

loan Sum of money borrowed by one person or organization from another on condition that it is repaid, generally for a specified time and often at an agreed rate of interest.

loan capital Another name for ***borrowed capital***.

loan creditor Person or organization from which a business has borrowed money.

loan rate Rate of interest charged for a loan, often expressed as a certain percentage above base rate.

Loan Guarantee Scheme (LGS) UK government scheme introduced in 1981 to promote the establishment and development of small businesses. The government agrees to underwrite 70% of approved loans made to such firms in return for a 2.5% annual premium on this portion, and on condition that the lending institution underwrites the balance of 30%.

Loan Guarantee Repayment guarantee made to banks and financial institutions by the Canadian Export Development Corporation (EDC) for loans to foreign purchasers of Canadian goods and services.

loan selling Sale (usually at a discount) of outstanding loans by a lending bank to another financial institution, often involving underdeveloped countries with payment difficulties. The term also means the issue of debt instruments (such as Euronotes and floating rate notes) in facilities for note issuance.

loan stock Unsecured security issued in respect of loan funds made available to company by investors. It is similar to a ***debenture*** (which is, however, secured).

local authority bond Bond issued by a local government authority, also known as a ***municipal bond***.

local currency Currency of a foreign country with which an exporter or trader is dealing.

local taxation Tax levied on people, businesses or their property in a particular area. The chief local taxes in the UK are business rates and council tax.

lock-out Employer's version of a strike, in which the employer refuses to allow workers into their workplace, unless they accept certain terms.

lock-up On financial markets, an investment expected to yield profit only in the long term, and in which the capital will therefore be "locked up" for some time.

locus poenitentiae Latin for "opportunity to repent". It is an option open to the parties of an illegal contract, who may save it by deciding not to carry out that part which is against the law.

Lombard rate Interest rate used by the German central bank (the *Bundesbank*).

London acceptance credit Credit of an exporter with a London bank or accepting house, on which bills of exchange may be drawn (within specified limits of amount and timing). The lender may requite security for such an arrangement.

London bank export credit Similar arrangement to *London acceptance* *credit*, although any bills of exchange are drawn on the foreign buyer and collected by the bank.

London Bankers' Clearing House Organization established in the 1770s that clears cheques drawn against UK clearing banks.

London Bullion Market Association (LBMA) Organization established in 1987 by members of the gold and silver bullion market, who deal on a forward, options or spot basis. Five of the members are responsible for the daily fixing of the price of gold.

London Clearing House (LCH) Organization established in 1888 that clears futures, options and other forward contracts.

London Derivatives Exchange Financial exchange organizatiion established in 1990 by the merging of the London International Financial Futures Exchange and the Traded Options Market.

London Fox Shortened name of the ***London Futures and Options Exchange***.

London Futures and Options Exchange (London Fox) Commodity market established in 1987 that deals in futures and options. The Baltic International Freight Futures Exchange merged with London Fox in 1991.

London Inter-Bank Bid Rate (LIBID or **LIBBR)** Rate of interest that banks use to buy from and sell funds to each other. See also ***London Inter-Bank Offered Rate (LIBOR)***.

London Inter-Bank Mean Rate (LIMEAN) Average of the ***London Inter-Bank Bid Rate (LIBID*** or ***LIBBR)*** and the ***London Inter-Bank Offered Rate (LIBOR)***.

London Inter-Bank Offered Rate (LIBOR) Rate of interest that commercial banks offer to lend money on the London inter-bank market. Along with the minimum lending rate, it has a significant effect on bank interest rates.

London International Financial Futures and Options Exchange (LIFFE) Financial futures market established in 1982 for dealing in options and futures contracts within the European time zone. Originally the London International Financial Futures Exchange, its name changed in 1992 when it merged with the London Traded Options market (LTOM). A further merger in 1996 with the London Commodity Exchange (LCE) gave it unique status in the financial world.

London International Financial Futures Exchange *See London International Financial Futures and Options Exchange (LIFFE).*

London Metal Exchange (LME) Market established in 1977 to deal in non-ferrous metals, including aluminium, copper, lead, nickel, tin and zinc.

London Stock Exchange (LSE) Organization established in London in 1773. Today it is third in size in the world (after New York and Tokyo) but still the largest in Europe, especially since the large increase in trade in non-UK shares. All trading is done electronically using computer screens and telephones. Plans were announced in spring 2000 to merge the LSE with the German Börse at Frankfurt. Trading in shares of the top 300 companies would be concentrated in London, while business in Internet, hi-tech and telecommunications companies would move to Frankfurt. The merger was not approved by the LSE's members in September 2000.

London Traded Options Market *See London International Financial Futures and Options Exchange (LIFFE).*

long bill *Bill of exchange* with more than 10 years to maturity.

long bond *Bond* with more than 15 years to maturity.

long credit Loan that may be repaid over a long period of time.

long-dated gilt *Gilt-edged security* with a redemption date of more than 15 years.

long-form report Detailed auditor's report on a person's or company's financial statements.

long hedge Hedge against a fall in the interest rate on the futures market.

long liquidation Long-term self-liquidating company.

long position Position taken by a bull speculator, who acquires quantities of stock or commodity in excess of the amount contracted for, in the expectation that the price will rise and permit the surplus to be sold at a profit.

longs Fixed-interest securities with redemtpion dates more than 15 years in the future. It is also a US term for securities that somebody has bought and actually owns.

long tap Long-term government securities issued in unlimited numbers.

long-term Period normally exceeding 15 years, but more loosely applied to stocks issued for an indefinite period of time or in perpetuity. In the City, the phrase "long-term" is loosely applied to any period over one year.

long-term liability Debt that need not be repaid in the next three years.

loss Disadvantage, forfeiture of money or goods, or negative profit (the amount by which expenses of a transaction or project exceed income).

loss leader Product or service offered for sale at a substantial loss in order to attract customers. The hope is that shoppers who buy the loss leader will also purchase other goods in the same store.

LSE Abbreviation of ***London Stock Exchange***.

Ltd Abbreviation of ***limited company***.

lump sum Sum of money paid all at once, as opposed to being paid as a series of separate sums (instalments).

lump sum freight Single freight charge payable, irrespective of the quantity of goods loaded.

lump system System of payment under which workers receive a lump sum for each day's work or for the fulfilment of a daily quota. It is common in the building industry, but frowned upon because it can enable employees to avoid income tax.

luncheon vouchers Vouchers exchangeable for meals (but not cash), issued by employers to their staff. They are thus a tax-free benefit in kind.

M

made bills *Bills of exchange* traded in the UK but drawn and payable overseas.

Madrid Stock Exchange One of four stock exchanges in Spain (the others are at Barcelona, Bilbao and Valencia), which since 1995 have been interlinked by an order-driven computer trading system. Its principal market index is the IBEX-35.

mail entry Method of entry that allows an importer to receive goods in the USA through the postal system. There are restrictions on the value of such goods.

mail order System for buying and selling by post; the customer purchases goods or services directly from the manufacturer or distributor without the intervention of a middleman or retailer.

main market Market in stocks and shares on the London Stock Exchange's official list (and thus excluding unlisted securities).

mainstream corporation tax (MCT) The balance of corporation tax (after *advance corporation tax* based on share dividends has been paid), which is based on a company's undistributed profits.

maintenance Practice of preserving the service potential of an asset (which is different from improvement or repair).

maintenance period Period in which US banks must meet the requirements for reserves specified by the Federal Reserve, usually two weeks from a Thursday to the following second Wednesday.

major US equivalent of a blue chip company; a very large company within its market sector.

majority interest Shareholding that gives the holder control of a company, i.e. one of over 50% of the shares.

major market index (MMI) US futures contract established in 1983 by the Chicago Board of Trade based on the Dow-Jones Industrial Average of the USA's 20 largest companies. It was transferred to the Chicago Metals Exchange in 1993.

making a price Action of a stockbroker or market-maker when he or she quotes a bid price or offer price for a stock or share.

making up day Alternative term for ***settlement day***.

making up price Price at which bargains on the stock exchange are carried over from one period of account to another (usually the market price at mid-day).

Makler German for broker.

mala fide Latin for bad faith; fraudulent.

managed currency Currency whose exchange rate is controlled (via a central bank) by the government. The intervention is called managed floating.

managed float *See* ***dirty float***.

managed floating exchange rate system *See* ***managed currency***.

managed fund Fund that is set up by an intermediary, and invested (using a stockbroker) on behalf of an investor.

managed futures fund Large mutual fund in the USA that deals in derivatives.

managed unit trust UK unit trust invested in other unit trusts owned by the same group. There are restrictions on the number of trusts and the relative amounts (percentages) invested in them.

management Control and supervision of a company, asset or operation; or the group of people who control and administer a company, as distinct from the workforce.

management buy-in Take-over of a company by a group of managers outside it (who purchase shares in order to gain a controlling interest).

management buy-out (MBO) Purchase of a company by its own managers, one of the most common forms of buy-out.

management company Company that practises management consultancy.

management consultant Person or firm that provides independent management advice to companies (with the accent on *independent*).

Management Consultants' Association Organization established in 1956 to establish and maintain standards in management consultancy.

managing agent Overseas intermediary who represents a company in its dealings with a foreign government.

managing director Senior executive director of a company, junior only to the chairman, and charged with implementing decisions made by the board of directors.

M and A Abbreviation of ***mergers and acquisitions***.

mandate Written authority empowering one person to act on behalf of another. Mandates are cancelled when the mandator dies, is declared bankrupt, or certified insane. Mandates are generally used to give access to the mandator's accounts (e.g. a banker's standing order is a mandate).

manifest Document listing a vessel's cargo (by port where loaded or discharged).

Manpower Services Commission (MSC) Former name of the UK *Training Agency*.

manual worker Employee who works mainly with his or her hands, often in a factory or on a farm, usually classified as skilled, semi-skilled or unskilled.

manufacturer's agent Agent who agrees to market a company's products, usually in a specific geographical area, in return for commission.

manufacturer's export agent Type of ***manufacturer's agent*** who seeks overseas customers.

manufacturing industry Aggregate of companies that produce goods rather than providing services.

manufacturing overhead Also called production overhead, production costs that cannot be directly attributed to the product (usually everything but the ***direct costs***). It includes cleansers and lubricants, depreciaton of plant, maintenance costs, and business rent and rates.

marché French for market.

Marché à Reglement Mensuel Prime market of the Paris Bourse.

Marché à Terme des Instruments Financiers (MATIF) French financial futures market (since 1986).

marché de l'argent French for money market.

Marché Libre OTC Unregulated market on the Paris Bourse (formerly the *Marché Hors Cote*).

marché monétaire French for money market.

Mareva injunction Court injunction that prevents the transfer of funds until a case concerning them has been heard in the UK courts.

margin Part of the total cost of a product or service that represents the producer's profit, usually expressed as a percentage of revenue. Or, especially in the USA, a payment on account of a purchase which confers ownership with its attendant risks and privileges upon the buyer, but subjecting him or her to a lien on the purchase to the extent that credit is advanced to finance the full purchase price secured by the purchase.

margin account Account held by a broker on behalf of an investor which allows the investor to purchase securities on credit.

marginal cost Cost incurred in raising the level of output by one unit of production beyond the original target. Marginal cost calculations are used to justify going beyond the target (or, indeed, not doing so).

marginal relief Tax relief granted to a taxpayer whose income only marginally exceeds a specified level or tax bracket. He or she receives a proportion of the relief available to those in the lower bracket. The term is also applied to small companies relief, that is the relief in corporation tax available when a company's profits fall below the upper and lower limits.

margin call Broker's request for more funds from an investor who has not paid the full price for an investment.

margin dealing *See* ***margin***.

margin loan Also known as a top-up loan, a loan generally made on limited security. For example, a group of several lenders may advance money secured on property to 75% of its value. A margin loan would then be secured on the remaining 25%. This would carry a higher risk and therefore attract a slightly higher rate of interest.

margin of safety Amount by which actual or budgeted sales exceed breakeven sales, expressed in cash terms, percentage of capacity or units of production.

margin of safety ratio ***Margin of safety*** expressed as a percentage of a specified level of activity.

margin of solvency Amount by which a company's total assets are greater than its total liabilities (excluding share capital).

margin trading Investing in the stock market using borrowed funds (subscribing only the ***margin***).

mark Price at which a deal is carried out on the stock market.

markdown Reduction in the selling price of goods, either below their marked up price (*see* ***mark-up***) or, in desperate times, below the retailer's purchasing price.

market Term with three meanings:

1. A place where goods and services are bought and sold.
2. Actual or potential demand for those goods or services.
3. Abstract expression denoting any area or condition in which buyers and sellers are in contact and able to do business together.

market access Availablility of a national market to overseas goods and services (allowing unimpeded competition with domestic products).

market-based pricing Also called market-led pricing, the pricing of goods and services in terms of their market (as opposed to their costs).

market capitalization Also termed market valuation, the value of all the securities of a company at current market prices.

market clearing price Price for all goods or services that will find buyers in a given market.

market failure Result if resources are not allocated in the most efficient way to comply with supply and demand. It may lead to idle production facilities and unemployment.

market forces Forces of ***supply and demand***, which together determine the prices of goods and services on the open market.

market if touched (MIT) Instruction to a broker to sell shares as soon as the price reaches a designated level.

marketing Distribution, promotion and presentation of a product (goods or services).

marketing research Alternative term for ***market research***.

market instrument Any short-term debt instrument (for raising a loan).

market leader Company that has the largest share of a particular market. Individual products that have the largest share of a market are called brand leaders.

market-led pricing Alternative term for ***market-based pricing***.

market-maker Market principal who encourages dealing by varying the price of stock to promote its sale or purchase. The term is used especially with reference to the stock market.

market mechanism Operation of ***supply and demand*** (which together determine prices).

market niche Within a particular market, a gap in the range of products and services offered, from which a business could profit by filling.

market order Order to buy or sell securities on the stock market or a financial futures exchange at the best obtainable market price.

market price Also called market value, the price at which something is traded on the open market.

market rate Base interest rate charged for a loan. A spread is added to give the interest rate for a variable-rate loan.

market research Survey that is conducted to assess consumer demand. Companies carry out market research in order to maximize the efficiency of their output and to determine potential markets which may be exploited in the future. In addition, market research often suggests ways in which goods and services may be more attractively presented to the public.

Market Research Society Professional UK organization, established in 1947, for people who conduct market research. It establishes codes of practice and represents its members in discussions with government departments.

market risk Part of the total risk inherent in buying stock, which depends on market movements as a whole rather than on the particular characteristics of the stock itself. For example, during a market crash, the share prices of many sound companies whose earning prospects remain unchanged may fall in line with less sound stock. This illustrates the market risk, rather than the specific risk inherent in stock market dealings.

market saturation Situation in which a market has as much of a product as it can sell.

market share Fraction of all sales in a given market (usually expressed as a percentage) that are held by one company or by one brand.

market-sharing agreement Illegal practice of splitting a market by agreement between a number of companies (who thereby have absolute control over price).

market size Total sales of all producers in a given market, expressed either by value (revenue) or volume (units sold).

market tending Control of a market's stock index, by intervention buying and selling.

market testing Comparison of prices charged for goods or services by a public-sector company and those that would be charged by a private-sector company. In theory and ignoring political considerations, if a private company can charge a lower price, it should be contracted instead of the public-sector company.

market timer US investment manager who operates by moving his or her investments from one instrument to another depending on market prices.

market value Alternative term for ***market price***.

marking up Adjustments of price (say, by a retailer) to allow for a profit margin. The retailer's mark-up is equal to gross profit.

marks of origin Name of the country of origin marked on imported goods, often a customs requirement.

mark to market On a financial futures exchange, the adjustment of a customer's account to allow for profits or losses on his or her open contracts during the previous day's trading.

mark-up *See* ***marking up***.

marzipan layer Broadly, middle management; the group of managers who are perceived, somewhat cynically, as unnecessary and indeed potential harmful to a company's interests. The supposition is that the marzipan layer tends to develop into an overfed bureaucracy. They are alternatively known as marzipan men or marzipan set.

masse monétaire French for money supply.

mass picketing *See* ***picketing***.

mass production Highly mechanized process of producing goods on a continuously moving production line. It works only for large numbers of identical products.

Master of Business Administration (MBA) Post-graduate qualification in management science, based mainly on using case studies by Harvard University.

matched-bargains Deals made by finding clients who wish to sell particular stocks and ones who wish to buy those same stocks.

matched sale-purchase agreement Arrangement, used since 1966, by means of which the US Federal Reserve sells money-market instruments while simultaneously buying the same instruments forward, thus distributing the reserves of the banking system. It gets round the legal restriction of not borrowing from the public.

matched sales technique Method of getting round foreign government-sanctioned price controls by linking the purchase of a price-controlled item with one that is not subject to such controls.

materials handling Transfer of parts and materials through the various stages of production and supply, with the minimum of movement, elapsed time and wastage.

MATIF Abbreviation of ***Marché à Terme des Instruments Financiers***.

maturity Date, specified in advance, on which a financial instrument may be exchanged for its cash value.

maturity balance Mixture of maturities of securities held by the US Federal Reserve for use in operations on the open market.

maturity date *See* ***maturity***.

maximum fluctuation Also known as maximum slippage, the upper limit to which a price may change on any one day's trading. It is fixed in advance as a percentage of the current price, and trading in a contract is halted for the rest of the day if the maximum fluctuation price is reached.

maximum slippage Alternative term for ***maximum fluctuation***.

MBA Abbreviation of ***Master of Business Administration***.

MBO Abbreviation of ***management buy-out***.

MCA Abbreviation of ***monetary compensation amounts***.

MEAL Abbreviation of ***Media Expenditure Analysis Limited***.

mean Also called arithmetic mean, the average. Of a group of numbers it is the sum of all the numbers divided by the number in the group.

mean deviation Measure of statistical dispersion equal, for a group of numbers, the sum of the differences between each number and the arithmetic mean, divided by the number in the group.

mean price Arithmetic mean of two specified prices, such as the highest buying and lowest selling prices of a security. It is also called the middle-market price and is usually the one quoted on the Stock Exchange's daily listing.

Media Expenditure Analysis Limited (MEAL) Publishers of a monthly reference book that lists the expenditures of advertisers in various media.

median Statistical average used as an alternative to the arithmetic mean (when there are a few extreme values in a group of numbers). It is obtained by putting the group of numbers in ascending order and nominating the middle one as the median (or the average of the two middle ones if there is an even number in the group).

mediation Alternative term for ***conciliation***.

medium bond Bond with between 5 and 15 years to maturity.

medium-dated gilt Gilt-edged security with a redemption term of between 5 and 15 years.

medium-dated stock Stock with a redemption term of between 5 and 15 years.

medium-term capital Loan capital lent in the medium term, i.e. for between 5 and 15 years.

medium-term financial assistance (MTFA) Loans for two to five years by one EU member country to another with balance of payments difficulties. There may be economic and financial conditions attached.

medium-term note (MTN) Euro commercial paper with several years' maturity.

megamerger Merger between two very large companies to form a gigantic corporation.

meltdown Sizeable financial crisis; a severe crash. The term is taken from the nuclear power industry, where a meltdown in a reactor would trigger a major disaster.

members of companies Subscribers to a company's memorandum of association or any shareholder.

memorandum of association Document that has to be registered and filed at Companies House in the UK, giving details of a company's particulars and aims. It is accompanied by the articles of association, which sets up the internal regulations of the company's operations, and states, among other things, the powers of the directors.

merchandise Finished goods that are purchased by a wholesaler or retailer for resale.

merchandising Method by which a retailer promotes certain products, using such devices as free samples, discounted prices and point-of-sale displays.

merchandising business Business that purchases finished goods for resale (as opposed to a manufacturing business).

merchantable quality The quality of goods deemed fit for sale; also termed merchandisable quality.

merchant bank Institution that specializes in raising capital, particularly for use in business or industry. *See also* ***venture capital***.

merger Fusion of two or more companies, as distinct from a take-over of one company by another. Mergers may be undertaken for various reasons, notable to improve efficiency of two complementary companies by rationalizing output and taking advantage of ***economies of scale***, and to fight off unwanted take-over bids from other large companies. The companies involved form one new company and their respective shareholders exchange their holdings for shares in the new concern at an agreed rate.

mergermania Fever that is believed to grip sectors of the business world from time to time. It occurs after a well-publicized merger or series of mergers; other companies become concerned that they will become adversely affected by the creation of larger and more powerful rivals and seek to merge themselves with other concerns as a protective measure.

mergers and acquisitions (M and A) Field of arranging mergers between companies or take-overs of companies, or the department within a large organization that is formed to carry out this function.

merit pay Type of bonus paid to employees who have performed to high standards in a year or half year (usually based on a performance appraisal).

merit rating Method of assessing an employee's performance, usually by awarding points for a series of work-related factors.

me-too product In marketing, colloquial term for a new product that largely imitates an existing one.

mezzanine debt Alternative term for ***mezzanine finance***.

mezzanine finance Money lent to a small and growing, but financially viable, company. It is so called because the risk of making the loan falls between that of advancing ***venture capital*** and the safer course of putting the finance into established debt markets. It is also known as quasi-equity.

MFN clause Abbreviation of ***most favoured nation clause***.

middleman Intermediary, usually a wholesaler, retailer or broker, who acts as an agent between a buyer and a seller. Middlemen tend to push up prices by adding their own profit margin to the difference between the buying and selling prices, and it may therefore be in the interests of the buyer and seller to "cut out the middleman" (as, for example, in mail order).

middle market price Price that is midway between the bid price and offer price on the open market. It is the price the Inland Revenue takes into account when calculating capital gains tax on share dealings.

middle price Alternative term for ***middle market price***.

Midwest Stock Exchange Name adopted by the ***Chicago Stock Exchange*** between 1948 and 1993.

Milan Stock Exchange Important Italian exchange administered by the Commissione Nazionale per la Società e la Borsa. All trading has been screen-based since 1996.

milking a product Method of maximizing a brand's profitability in the short term by increasing its price as much as the market will stand (without losing regular customers). It does, however, have the effect of shortening the product's life cycle.

milk round Colloquial term for the annual recruiting campaign for management trainees among undergraduates who have just taken their finals.

minimerger Merger between two small companies.

minimum fluctuation Also known as the basis point, the lower limit to which a price may fall in one day's trading on an exchange. As with the maximum fluctuation, it is fixed in advance and trading is halted for the day if the minimum fluctuation is reached.

minimum lending rate (MLR) Minimum rate at which the Bank of England, acting in its capacity of lender of the last resort, is willing to discount bills of exchange and at which it offers short-term loans. The MLR has a direct effect on bank interest rates.

minimum offing period Minimum period of time for which an offer to the public to purchase shares may be left open. In the UK this period is usually 14 days.

minimum subscription As stated in the prospectus of a new company, the minimum amount the directors consider necessary for a successful launch to take place.

minimum wage Lowest amount a company may pay a worker, often fixed by legislation or trade union agreements.

minority interest Shareholding that does not give the holder control of a company, i.e. less than 50% of the shares. Or it is the interest held by shareholders in a subsidiary company (excluding the holding company's interest).

minority shareholder Person who holds a ***minority interest*** in a company.

Mintel Short for Marketing Intelligence, a UK organization that gathers and analyses secondary marketing information

minutes Record of a meeting, including who attended and what was said (particularly conclusions that lead to action).

minutes book Details of all decisions made by a company's board of directors or at shareholders' meetings.

MIRAS Abbreviation of ***mortgage interest relief at source***.

misfeasance summons Application requesting that a court investigate the actions and conduct of a director of a company in liquidation. The summons may be issued by an interested party, such as the official receiver, a creditor or shareholder, and its requests the court to force the director concerned to compensate them for money misapplied or misappropriated.

misrepresentation Any false statement that encourages a person or company to enter into a contract. It may be either fraudulent, i.e. a deliberate intention to deceive, or innocent, i.e. the result of a genuine mistake. Under UK law the injured party may have the contract dissolved and claim suitable damages.

Misrepresentation Act 1967 UK legislation that deals with innocent ***misrepresentation*** in a contract, making allowances for the award of damages and cancellation of the contract.

mistake Under UK law, any error – short of ***misrepresentation*** – that induces a person or company to enter into a contract. Mistakes may be mutual, i.e. common to both parties, or unilateral. Mutual mistakes include the innocent purchase or exchange of goods that are not in fact for sale; unilateral mistakes include more deliberate deceptions. Either type may invalidate a contract, although they do not necessarily do so.

mission statement Statement that outlines the goals of an organization and the sense of common purpose necessary to achieve them.

MIT Abbreviation of ***market if touched***.

Mitbestimmung German practice of having labour union representatives taking part in company management (as members of the Board).

mixed credit Mixture of trade finance and aid for exporting goods to underdeveloped countries, sometimes known by its French name *crédit mixte*. *See also* ***consensus***.

MLR Abbreviation of ***minimum lending rate***.

MMC Abbreviation of ***Monopolies and Mergers Commission***.

MMI Abbreviation of ***major market index***.

MNC Abbreviation of ***multinational company***.

MNE Abbreviation of multinational enterprise. *See* ***multinational company***.

mobile shop Retail outlet in a van which takes goods (usually food) to customers at their own addresses.

mock auction Auction that is in some way illegal. This may occur in several ways: when goods are sold for a price lower than that of the highest bid; when some goods are given away in order to attract bidders; when those who have not already bought lots are excluded from bidding; and when all or part of the agreed price is returned privately to the bidder.

mode Statistical average equal to the number that occurs most frequently in a group of numbers, a measure of central tendency.

model code Stock Exchange code of conduct that sets out guidelines for share dealings by company directors. It specifies, broadly, that directors should not engage in questionable dealings in their company's stock, and in particular forbids share dealings within two months preceding a company announcement of profit, loss, dividend, a proposed merger, take-over, sale of assets, and so on.

modern portfolio theory Theory of stock valuation developed in the early 1980s. It values stocks by estimating their future earnings discounted back to the present.

momentum In finance, the rate at which a price increases or decreases.

monetary compensation amounts (MCA) Temporary tax or subsidy meant to offset the differentials between the "green" and real exchange rates that arise because of the EU *Common Agricultural Policy*. It is being phased out.

monetary control Method used by a government to control the money supply through its central bank (in the UK the *Bank of England*).

Monetary Control Act US legislation of 1980 that made all US banks members of the *Federal Reserve System*.

monetary inflation Inflation that is caused by an increase in the money supply.

monetary policy Government policy of how to regulate the money supply (and its effects on employment, industrial growth, inflation, and so on).

Monetary Policy Committee Committee of the *Bank of England*, established in 1997, that sets UK interest rates (formerly a function of the Treasury).

monetary system System that controls the exchange rates of a group of countries, or a system that a single country uses to control its own currency exchange while ensuring that there is enough money in circulation for internal use.

monetary union Agreement between countries in an economic union to have a common currency, fixed exchange rates and free movement of capital between countries. It is a short-term aim of the EU.

monetization Method of financing a government's budget deficit by selling Treasury bills to the banking system in the UK, or to the Federal Reserve in the USA.

money Medium of exchange; any generally accepted token (e.g. coins or banknotes) that may be exchanged for – used in payment for – goods or services.

money at call Loans that may be called in at short notice, and which therefore attract only low rates of interest.

money broker Dealer in short-term loans and securities on the money market. On the London Stock Exchange, six firms act as money brokers, channelling borrowed stocks from institutions onto the market, thereby enhancing the liquidity of the gilt-edged securities (gilts) and equity markets in particular.

money-center bank In the large financial centres of the USA, a major bank that acts as a clearing bank for the smaller banks of the area.

money cycle During the fulfilment of an individual order, the flow of cash out of a company (production costs) and then back into it (selling price).

money had and received In law, money in the possession of one person that belongs to another. The term is applied whether or not the possessor obtained the money in good faith.

money income Person's income ignoring inflation and price levels. If a person's income increases by 50% in a year, the money income increases by the same percentage although real income (spending power) may not increase as much if prices have risen during that time.

money laundering See *laundering*.

moneylender Person licensed by the government to lend funds to others. The term is, however, used informally to describe anyone lending money independently of banks and other financial institutions, often at high rates of interest, and as such carries negative connotations.

money market Market operated by banks and other financial institutions to facilitate the short-term (up to one year) borrowing and lending of money, and trading in financial securities; it is also sometimes known as the discount market. In the UK, the ***Bank of England*** is the lender of last resort. A wider money market includes also the markets in bullion and foreign exchange.

money-market fund Fund into which individual small savings are accumulated for investment in the money market, adopted particularly in the USA to get round the controls on interest rates that could be paid by banks. It is also a type of unit trust, sometimes called a money-market unit trust, in which income is invested in high-yield, short-term instruments of credit.

money-market instrument Financial product traded on the money market, including certificates of deposit and other short-term instruments.

money-market unit trust See *money-market fund*.

money remitter Person who transfers money from country to country for people who do not have a bank account, such as immigrants sending money home to their families.

money runner Informal US term for a person who invests in markets throughout the world, probably creating ***hot money*** in the process.

money supply Total amount of money available at short notice in a given country. There are several categories of money supply, designated M0, M1, M2 and M3.

M0 is defined as notes and coins in circulation in bank tills, plus the operational balances that banks place with the Bank of England. M0 is the narrowest category and is sometimes called narrow money.

M1 is defined as notes and coin in circulation and money deposited in bank current accounts. It is the best gauge of money immediately available for exchange.

M2 is an obsolete definition of the money supply. It includes notes and coins in circulation and in bank accounts, together with funds saved in deposit accounts maintained with the clearing banks, National Giro Bank, Bank of England banking department and discount houses.

M3 is defined as M2 plus interest-bearing non-sterling deposit accounts held by British residents, and other certificates of deposit. M3 is the broadest definition of the money supply and may also be known as broad money. A subsidiary measure, £M3, excludes non-sterling deposit accounts.

Monopolies and Mergers Act 1965 UK legislation that established the Monopolies Commission, later (1973) superseded by the ***Monopolies and Mergers Commission (MMC)***.

Monopolies and Mergers Commission (MMC) UK government organization, established by the ***Fair Trading Act 1973***, that monitors takeovers and mergers (in the public and national interest) and acts as a watchdog over monopolies and restrictive trade practices.

monopoly Strictly, an industry with only one supplier. The term is also applied more widely to an industry controlled ("monopolized") by one company, which produces a sufficient proportion of the total output of that industry to effectively control supply and therefore price. In the UK, monopolies, and mergers and takeovers that might lead to monopolies, are subject to the scrutiny of the ***Monopolies and Mergers Commission (MMC)***.

monopsony Industry in which there are many manufacturers but only one customer for the goods produced. By controlling demand the customer can, in theory, set the price. Monopsonies generally evolve to serve nation states; the market for warships, for example, is a virtual monopsony in that the vessels produced are purchased only by the government of the nation concerned, or by other governments that have its approval.

moonlighting Informal term for the practice of having two jobs, one of them generally involving work in the evening or at night.

mopping up Procedure in the UK by which the Bank of England uses Treasury bonds to buy spare funds from discount houses.

moral obligation Obligation, usually to perform some service or complete some transaction, that cannot be enforced in law but which is nevertheless met out of honour.

moratorium Grant of an extended period in which to repay a loan, or a period during which the repayment schedule is suspended. Usually, it refers only to the repayment of capital, and interest payments may still be required.

Morgan Stanley Capital International World Index (MSCI Index) World index of the prices of shares, based on more than 1300 shares from 19 countries. It thereby covers about 60% of the share market value on stock exchanges throughout the world.

mortgage Transfer of the deeds to a property as security for the repayment of a debt. For example, a building society that provides a loan for the purchase of a house takes legal possession of the property until the loan and interest have been repaid. The lender is the mortgagee; the borrower is the mortgagor. A mortgage is also called a legal charge.

mortgage bond Bond that, in the USA, represents a debt secured by a real asset.

mortgagee *See mortgage.*

mortgage interest relief at source (MIRAS) Former income tax relief allowed to a taxpayer on the first £30,000 of a mortgage on his or her main residence. Set at 10% for the year 1999-2000, it was abolished in April 2000.

mortgagor *See mortgage.*

most favoured nation (MFN) clause Clause in a trading agreement between two countries specifying that each will grant the best available tariff and quotas to the other, usually because both are signatories of the ***General Agreement on Tariffs and Trade (GATT)***.

mountain Surplus of EU farm products (such as butter or apples; a surplus of wine is referred to as a lake). Such surpluses result mainly from the application of the ***Common Agricultural Policy (CAP)***, which specifies minimum selling prices for farmers.

MSC Abbreviation of ***Manpower Services Commission***.

MSCI Index *See* ***Morgan Stanley Capital International World Index***.

MTFA Abbreviation of ***medium-term financial assistance***.

MTN Abbreviation of ***medium-term note.***

MTO Abbreviation of ***Multilateral Trade Organization***.

multi-component Euronote facility Facility that allows Euronotes to be issued in a mixture of currencies of the issuer's choice.

multilateralism Indiscriminate multilateral, or international, trade, which involves the use of the proceeds of a sale in one country to fund purchases in another country.

Multilateral Trade Organization (MTO) Organization, established in 1993 as part of the ***General Agreement on Tariffs and Trade (GATT)***, which enforces the agreed rules for international trade.

multinational Concerning more than one nation, particularly with regard to the dealings of large companies.

multinational company (MNC) Also called a multinational enterprise (MNE), a company that has facilities, such as those for production and marketing, in various countries other than its country of origin.

multinational corporation Corporation that has operations and offices in more than one country. *See* ***multinational company (MNC)***.

multi-option facility Facility that allows a borrowing package to be issued in a mixture of short-term financial instruments, such as commercial paper and Euronotes.

multiple Factor by which the cost of producing a unit of goods is multiplied by to arrive at a satisfactory selling price. It is also a term for a multiple store or chain store, a group of shops in various locations that sell the same stock under the same management group.

multiple exchange rate Variable currency exchange rate that some countries quote, often giving a more favourable rate to importers of wanted goods and to tourists.

multiple store *See* ***multiple***.

municipal bond Also called a local authority bond, a bond issued by a UK local authority, generally regarded as being a safe investment.

muster roll Register of the holders of a given security.

mutual Describing a company or organization owned by its depositors or members but which does not issue stocks or shares. In the UK, many insurance companies and (formerly) building societies have this status. The conversion of status of such organizations to incorporation as a limited company (which can issue shares) is termed demutualization.

mutual fund Alternative US term for a ***unit trust***.

mutual organization *See* ***mutual***.

N

naamloze vennootschap (NV) Dutch equivalent of a British public company(PLC).

NAC Abbreviation of ***National Advisory Council on International Monetary and Financial Policies***.

NADBank *See* ***North American Development Bank***.

NAFTA Abbreviation of ***North American Free Trade Agreement***.

naked Describing a security, particularly a derivative, that is not covered or hedged against various risks.

naked debenture Alternative term for simple debenture.

naked option Option to buy shares in which the seller of the option (the option writer) does not already own the shares. In this instance, the option writer hopes to buy back the option before it is exercised and so avoid having to supply the shares. If the option is exercised and the market price of the shares has risen, the option writer makes a loss. An option writer who sells naked options is known as a naked writer.

naked writer *See* ***naked option***.

name day On the London Stock Exchange, the day before ***account day***, on which sellers of securities are supplied with the names of those who have bought from them during the last account.

narcodillars Funds used to buy illegal drugs.

narrow band Describing a currency whose exchange rate is allowed to float within set limits (typically 2.5% above and below the central rate), which if exceeded bring about central bank intervention.

narrow market Market in which there is a shortage of goods or services for sale, particularly of a particular company's shares on a stock market.

NASD Abbreviation of ***National Association of Security Dealers***.

NASDAQ Abbreviation of ***National Association of Security Dealers Automated Quotation System***.

NASDIM Abbreviation of ***National Association of Security Dealers and Investment Managers***.

National Advisory Council on International Monetary and Financial Policies (NAC) US government organization that coordinates the participation of the USA in international financial institutions and practices associated with them. Members of the council are drawn from the Treasury, the Federal Reserve, banks, commerce and trade.

National Association of Security Dealers (NASD) US national self-regulatory organization that regulates the ***National Association of Securities Dealers Automated Quotation (NASDAQ)*** and the over-the-counter (OTC) market.

National Association of Security Dealers and Investment Managers (NASDIM) Former UK organization established in 1979 (as the Association of Licensed Dealers) that represented licensed security dealers, who have since become members of various ***self-regulating organizations (SROs)***. NASDIM ceased to exist in 1987.

National Association of Securities Dealers Automated Quotation (NASDAQ) US computer-based system, established in 1971, that deals with orders and provides information for the US over-the-counter (OTC) market. More than 500 market-makers deal in actively traded securities of more than 4,000 US companies.

national debt Debts owed by the UK government, i.e. the sum of government borrowing, including such things as National Savings, Treasury bills, and government bonds. The US equivalent is called the Federal Debt.

National Development Bonds Former UK government bonds, introduced in 1964 and available through the Post Office or Trustee Savings Banks. The last issue has now matured, and no further interest is payable.

National Economic Development Council (NEDC or **Neddie)** UK government organization, established in 1962, that patrolled general industrial development and encouraged economic growth, whose responsibilities were split among various sub-committees (Little Neddies) in 1964. It became part of the British Technology Group in 1981.

National Economic Development Office (NEDO) UK government organization, established in 1961, that involved industrialists and trade unions in forward government planning. It proved to be ineffective and was later disbanded by a subsequent Conservative government.

National Freight Consortium plc Privately-owned organization established in 1982 to buy the National Freight Corporation from the

UK government. It now includes British Road Services, National Carriers and Pickfords. Now known as NFC plc, it also operates in Australia and the USA.

National Institute for Economic and Social Research (NIESR) UK non-profit making organization, established in 1938, that works with the Treasury in trying to predict future economic trends (today using computer models).

National Insurance (NI) Various benefits to employed and unemployed people that are the responsibility of the UK government's Department of Social Security (DSS). It is financed by the ***National Insurance Fund.***

National Insurance Contribution (NIC) Contributions to the UK ***National Insurance Fund*** paid by employers, employees and self-employed people.

National Insurance Fund UK government fund into which the self-employed, employees and their employers pay contributions. The fund is administered by the Department of Social Security (DSS) and provides state retirement pensions and various social security benefits, including invalidity benefit, unemployment benefit, maternity benefit, sickness benefit and widow's benefit.

nationalization Government policy whereby industries previously in private ownership are taken over by the state and subsequently controlled by the government. *See also* ***privatization***.

National Market System (NMS) Computerized real-time US system, established in 1975, that provides information about the prices of stocks.

National Research Development Corporation (NRDC) UK organization, established in 1949 by the then ***Board of Trade***, to develop and exploit new ideas from government and private research facilities. It has now become part of the British Technology Group.

National Saving Bank (NSB) UK government savings bank, established in 1861, as the Post Office Savings Bank. Its name changed in 1969 but it is still operated through the Post Office, where savers may withdraw money and invest in various National Savings products.

National Securities Clearing Corporation US clearing house, established in 1977, owned jointly by the ***American Stock Exchange***, the ***National Association of Security Dealers*** and the ***New York Stock Exchange***.

National Trade Data Bank (NTDB) Bank of data on international economic and export information, as supplied by 19 different US agencies.

natural monopoly Type of monopoly that arises where such is the scale of business operations that is sensible to have only one supplier of the service (such as ***nationalized*** or ***privatized*** energy and water utilities).

natural rate of interest Interest rate at which the demand for and supply of loans is equal.

natural wastage Method of reducing the work force of an organization without resorting to enforced redundancies. As far as possible, the employer does not replace employees who die, retire or resign.

NAV Abbreviation of ***net asset value***.

NBV Abbreviation of ***net book value***.

nearby delivery In the commodity market, indication that delivery will be made in the next calendar month.

nearby futures Futures contracts that are closest to maturity.

near money Liquid asset that can be transferred immediately (such as a bill of exchange or cheque), although not as liquid as cash. It is also known as quasi-money.

near-term Short-term; in the near future. US securities markets have been criticized for near-termism, the practice of examining price performance over a period of days rather than years.

NEDC Abbreviation of ***National Economic Development Council***.

Neddie Familiar abbreviation of ***National Economic Development Council***.

NEDO Abbreviation of ***National Economic Development Office***.

negative cash flow Cash flow in which the outgoings are greater than income.

negative equity Asset that is curently worth less than the money borrowed to pay for it. An all-too-common example is a house whose current market price is less than the remaining value of the mortgage taken out to buy it.

negative income tax (NIT) System of taxation by which those earning less than a specific income receive tax credits to bring their income in line with a guaranteed minimum income.

negative interest Charge made by a bank or other financial institution for holding funds for a certain time.

negative pledge Contractural undertaking by a borrower not to use the same assets to obtain another loan elsewhere (without the lender's permission).

negligence Breach of duty to take reasonable care. Professional people frequently guard against actions brought for negligence by taking out professional indemnity insurance.

negotiable In law, describing an asset whose owner has complete and undeniable right for its transfer, free from equities or defences that could be raised against the transferor. In a broader sense, the term describes a price that the seller is willing to modify in discussion with a potential buyer.

negotiable instrument Document that may be freely exchanged, usually by ***endorsement***, and which entitles the bearer to a sum of money. Negotiable instruments include ***bills of exchange***, ***certificates of deposit***, cheques and ***promissory notes***.

negotiable security Security that is easily passed from one owner to another by delivery. Very few instruments are negotiable in this way in the UK (*see* ***negotiable instrument***).

negotiation Method of arriving at a decision by bargaining, such as between a buyer and a seller of goods or services, or between management and workers (discussing wages or working conditions).

net assets Difference between a company's assets and its liabilities (sometimes termed owners' equity).

net asset value (NAV) Value of a company's shares determined by dividing its net assets by the number of issued shares. It is seldom the same as the market value.

net book value (NBV) Alternative term for ***depreciated cost***.

net cash flow In any accounting period, the difference between cash entering a company and cash leaving it. *See* ***cash flow***.

net current assets Difference between current assets and current liabilities, equal to a company's ***working capital***.

net loss For a given accounting period, the amount by which all expenses and losses exceed all revenues and gains; sometimes called negative net income.

net margin Difference between the selling price of an item and the total cost of making and selling it.

net monetary position Company's total monetary assets less total monetary liabilities.

net present value (NPV) In a discounted cash flow, the present value of cash outflows from a company less the present value of cash inflows. The worth of a future project can be assessed by discounting all future cash flows to the present to see if a desired rate of return would be achieved. A negative NPV would indicate that the project is not viable.

net profit Company's income that remains after deducting all expenses.

net realizable value (NRV) Amount that could be obtained for an asset (less direct selling costs). Or the sales value of a company's stock (less cost of sales). Both may be less that actual cost.

net weight Actual weight of goods, ignoring the weight of any packaging. Of a vehicle, it is generally taken to mean its total empty weight and without any fuel in its tank. Including the weight of fuel gives its kerb weight.

net worth Value of a company after liabilities have been deducted from the true market value of its assets.

new issue Issue of shares by a company that is seeking listing on a stock exchange for the first time. The term may also apply to the issue of equities or loan stock by an existing listed company in order to raise additional capital.

new issue market Part of the money market, principally the stock exchange, that supplies long-term capital to a company (*see* ***new issue***). It is also known as the primary market.

new product development (NPD) All the activities a company employs to identify, develop and market a new product (goods or services).

new time On the London Stock Exchange, the last two days of an ***account***. Transactions conducted in new time are settled at the end of the next account; for this reason, new time is effectively part of the next account period.

New York Futures Exchange (NYFE) US subsidiary of the New York Stock Exchange, established in 1979 in competition with the domination of futures trading by the Chicago Mercantile Exchange.

New York Mercantile Exchange (NYMEX) US commodity market established as the Butter and Cheese Market of New York in 1872. It changed its name to the New York Metals Exchange in 1887. It adopted its present name after merging with the Commodity Exchange (COMEX) in 1994. The NYMEX division deals mainly in futures in crude oil and oil products (including petrol), palladium and platinum; the COMEX division deals in other metals, such as aluminium, copper, gold and silver; it also trades in coal.

New York Metals Exchange *See* ***New York Mercantile Exchange (NYMEX)***.

New York Stock Exchange (NYSE) Biggest stock exchange in the world, established in 1792, which trades in stocks, shares, bonds, warrants, rights and options. More than 2,000 companies and 5,000 securities are listed. Situated in Wall Street, it is colloquially called Big Board (after the huge illuminated display of share prices on the floor of the exchange).

NI Abbreviation of ***National Insurance***.

NIC Abbreviation of ***National Insurance Contributions***. *See also* ***National Insurance***.

niche marketing Selling in a sector of the market that caters for a well-defined and usually small group of customers.

niche player Generally small financial institution that deals with a specialized sector of the market (*see* ***niche marketing***).

NIESR Abbreviation of ***National Institute for Economic and Social Research***.

NIF Abbreviation of ***note issuance facility***.

Nikkei Average Short form of ***Nikkei Stock Average***.

Nikkei-Dow Jones Average Former name of the ***Nikkei Stock Average***.

Nikkei Stock Average Share index of the Tokyo Stock Exchange, published since 1949, based on the 225 major equities quoted on the market. It is determined by Nihou Keizai Shimbun, commonly called Nikkei.

nil basis Way of calculating earnings per share (after tax) that assumes there is no distribution of profits as dividend.

nil paid New issue of shares for which the issuing company has yet to be paid. The term is most commonly applied to rights issues.

NIT Abbreviation of ***negative income tax***.

NL Abbreviation of ***no liability***.

NMS Abbreviation of ***National Market System*** and ***normal market size***.

no-brainer Fund that tracks the performance of a stock index. Its manager buys all the stocks listed on a major index, and hence no discretionary investment decisions are required.

no liability (NL) Australian equivalent of a ***public limited company (plc)***.

no-load share Share sold at ***net asset value*** with no commission charge.

no-loan fund Form of US unit trust that employs no salesman and therefore pays no commission or distribution costs. An investor thus avoids paying a commission on shares purchased, the only expense remaining being a relatively modest management fee.

nomad Colloquial name for a nominated adviser, a firm of stockbrokers that has London Stock Exchange approval to advise and sponsor companies on the ***Alternative Investment Market (AIM)***.

nominal capital Another term for ***authorized capital***.

nominal interest rate Rate of interest without an allowance for inflation.

nominal partner Partner who lends his or her name to a firm, but who has invested no capital and does not take an active part in the partnership. Her or she remains liable for the partnership's debts.

nominal price Minimal price assigned to an item so that a transaction may be accounted for.

nominal value Alternative term for ***face value***.

nominated adviser *See* ***nomad***.

nominee Person or institution in whose name assets are transferred but who has no beneficial interest in the asset concerned.

nominee shareholder Usually an institution that acquires shares in a company on behalf of somebody else (the ***beneficial owner***). This enables the true shareholder's identity to be concealed and is often used when a person wishes to build up his or her shareholding prior to a takeover bid.

non-business days Sundays and bank holidays when most financial institutions are closed for business. They are not included in days of grace, and bills of exchange that fall due on a non-business day are postponed until the following day.

non-cumulative preference share Type of preference share for which unpaid interest (dividend) is not carried over until the next year.

non-equity investment Any investment in securities except in company shares (equities).

non-executive director Member of a company's board of directors who plays no active part in the day-to-day running of the company. He or she may attend board meetings and offer advice. Non-executive (or outside) directors are often well-known public figures whose appointment lends cachet to a company, or whose presence on the board is valued for their expertise, impartiality or wide-ranging contacts.

non-participating preference share Type of preference share in which holders are paid a dividend before ordinary shareholders but do not receive additional dividends in a very profitable year.

non-performing asset Part of a company's capital that is currently yielding no return, and on which none is expected. Fixed assets are generally classified as non-performing.

non-performing loan Loan whose interest payments are very overdue (usually taken to be 90 or more days in the USA).

non-price competition Any type of competition in business except that involving pricing (such as advertising and packaging).

non-profit making organization (NPO) Company or organization that has a legal obligation not to make a profit. The term is most usually applied to registered charities.

non-recourse finance Loan in which the lender is entitled to repayment only from the profits of the venture the loan is funding (and not from any other assets the borrower may have).

non-tariff barrier Hidden trade barrier, often achieved through regulations that are difficult for importers to comply with.

non-taxable income Income that for one reason or another is not subject to normal income tax. In the UK it includes dividends, money received by charities and interest on bank deposit accounts.

non-voting shares Shares that carry no voting rights. They are issued to raise additional capital for a company, while permitting existing shareholders to retain control. Such shares are often known as A-shares and generally rank ***pari passu*** with voting shares in respect of other rights.

no par value (NPV) Describing shares that have no stated value, but are valued at the current stock exchange price.

normal goods Goods whose sales increase as people's spending power increases (as opposed to inferior goods, whose sales increase when spending power decreases).

normal market size (NMS) Method of classifying shares, introduced in 1991, equal to 2.5 times the average daily customer turnover last year divided by the price of the share. It has replaced the classification into alpha, beta, gamma and delta shares.

North American Development Bank (NADBank) Bank run by the governments of Mexico and the USA that finances deals resulting from the *North American Free Trade Agreement (NAFTA)*.

North American Free Trade Agreement (NAFTA) Agreement for the establishment of a free trade area established in 1989 between Canada and the USA, with Mexico joining in 1992 (coming into force in 1994).

nostro account Account kept by a bank with an overseas bank, usually in the foreign currency.

notary public Official (usually a solicitor) licensed to attest the validity of documents and of the signatures on them by signing and/or attaching a seal to them. Dishonoured or protested bills also require the seal of a public notary.

note issuance facility (NIF) Type of medium-term credit guarantee in which a bank provides funds to an issuer of promissory notes before the notes are actually issued; the guarantor usually buys any unsold notes.

note of hand Alternative tem for a *promissory note*.

note purchase facility Alternative tem for a *note issuance facility (NIF)*.

notice day In commodity markets, the day when notice must be given of the intention to supply a commodity (under contract to be delivered that month).

notice in lieu of distringas Notice issued by a shareholder and supported by a statutory declaration that formally advises the issuing company of his or her holding. Such notices prevent any attempt by the company to transfer the shares in question to a third party.

noting and protest First two stages in dishonouring a *bill of exchange*. The bill is first "noted", or witnessed, by a *notary public*, who thereby testifies to its existence but not necessarily to its validity. It is then presented again, and if refused for a second time it is protested by being returned to the notary, who then testifies to its refusal. Noting must be completed within one working day of the bill first being dishonoured.

not negotiable Description applied to a document to which a transferee has no better claim than any previous bearer. A bill of exchange may be crossed "not negotiable" as a safeguard against theft.

novation The making of a contract between the parties to an original contract and a third party in which it is agreed that the third party shall replace one of the original parties.

NPD Abbreviation of ***new product development***.

NPO Abbreviation of ***non-profit-making organization***.

NPV Abbreviation of ***net present value*** *and* ***no par value***.

NRDC Abbreviation of ***National Research Development Corporation***.

NRV Abbreviation of ***net realizable value***.

NSB Abbreviation of ***National Saving Bank***.

NTDB Abbreviation of ***National Trade Data Bank***.

null and void Describing an invalidated contract.

NV Abbreviation of ***naamloze vennootschap***.

NYFE Abbreviation of ***New York Futures Exchange***.

NYMEX Abbreviation of ***New York Mercantile Exchange***.

NYSE Abbreviation of ***New York Stock Exchange***.

O

OAT Abbreviation of ***obligation à trésorerie***.

OBL Abbreviation of ***ocean bill of lading***.

obligation Debt; or a debt instrument (such as a bond).

obligation French for bond.

Obligation German for bond.

obligation à trésorerie (OAT) French for treasury bill.

obligation d'état French for government bond.

OBSF Abbreviation of ***off balance sheet finance***.

obsolescence Loss of the value of something when it becomes out of date (or out of fashion). In accounting, obsolescence refers to an asset that has to be written off, not through deterioration but when its continued use would be economic. For example, a piece of machinery may be superseded by a new, faster version; it is therefore uneconomic for the company to continue to use it, and the asset becomes obsolete.

OBU Abbreviation of ***offshore banking unit***.

obvious damage Goods damaged in transit where the damage can be seen by external examination (as opposed to hidden damage).

ocean bill of lading (OBL) Document that acts as a receipt for a cargo and a contract between the shipper and the carrier for its carriage. It may also be used to establish ownership of the cargo (and can be made negotiable).

odd lot Collection of stocks and shares that is so small and varied that they inconvenience the broker who agrees to sell them, and which he or she will therefore buy at only a low price. In the USA, an odd lot of fewer than 100 shares is dealt at a higher commission rate than larger quantities.

OECD Abbreviation of ***Organization for Economic Cooperation and Development***.

OEEC Abbreviation of ***Organization for European Economic Cooperation***.

OEIC Abbreviation of ***open-ended investment company***.

off balance sheet finance (OBSF) Type of company finance such that some or all of it (and associated assets) do not appear on the company's balance sheet. Although legally allowable, the practice can give a very distorted view of a company's financial status.

offer Statement that one party is willing to sell something, at a certain price and under certain conditions. If a particular buyer is unwilling to buy at the offer price or under the conditions of the offer, he or she may make a bid against the seller's offer.

offer and acceptance by post Proof that an offer has been accepted (when there is proof of posting of an acceptance letter). It stands even if the acceptance letter does not reach the offerer.

offer by prospectus In contrast to an ***offer for sale***, an offer by a company to sell its shares or debentures directly to the public by issuing a prospectus, instead of selling shares to an issuing house.

offer by tender Offer by a company to sell its shares to people who tender for them, at a price above a stated minimum.

offer for sale Offer by a company to sell its shares to an issuing house, which then publishes a prospectus and sells shares to the public.

offer period During a take-over, the length of time an offer for shares must remain open (at least 21 days).

offer price Price at which a market-maker is prepared to sell a security. The equivalent US term is asked price.

offer to purchase Alternative term for ***take-over bid***.

offering circular Document in the USA that contains information regarding offers of shares exempt from ***Securities and Exchange Commission*** regulations and registration.

off exchange Small volume of share dealing that is not recorded by an official stock exchange (and thus does not attract commission payments to exchange dealers).

Office of Fair Trading (OFT) UK government organization, established after the ***Fair Trading Act 1973***, which encourages fair competition among UK businesses. It investigates anti-competitive and restrictive practices, and whether take-over bids should be referred to the ***Monopolies and Mergers Commission***.

Official List Formally the Stock Exchange Daily Official List (SEDOL), the official publication of the *London Stock Exchange* which appears daily at 5.30 p.m. detailing price movements and dividend information for almost all the securities quoted on the exchange.

official price Also known as the settlement price, on the *London Metal Exchange* it is the price attained in the day's first trading session, then used as a basis for most world trade for the following 24 hours.

official quotation Figure quoted daily for almost all securities on the *Official List* of the London Stock Exchange.

Official Receiver Person appointed by the courts to supervise the affairs of a company that has gone into liquidation, or the winding up of the estate of a bankrupt.

official reserves Gold and currency reserves kept by a country's government.

offshore Describing business carried out (in, e.g., London) between foreigners in foreign-denominated currency. The term is also used to describe a business that operates from a tax haven.

offshore banking unit (OBU) Foreign bank that deals in eurocurrency and foreign exchange settlements, located in a tax-favourable offshore banking centre.

offshore financing Raising capital in countries other than one's own.

offshore fund Investment scheme operated from a tax haven, by which investors may benefit from the haven's tax privileges without leaving their home country.

OFT Abbreviation of *Office of Fair Trading*.

ohne Dividende German for ex dividend.

ohne Kupon German for ex coupon.

old-to-market (OTM) Describing a large company whose manufacturing capability has significant foreign funding (and which has significant export sales).

oligopoly Industry in which there are many buyers but few sellers. Such conditions give the producer or seller a certain amount of control over price, but leave him or her especially vulnerable to the actions of competitors.

on-balance-sheet financing Obtaining company funding, using internal or external sources, that shows up on the company's balance sheet.

on-board bill of lading Document which certifies that a specified cargo has been loaded onto a named vessel, signed by the vessel's master.

on consignment Describing goods sent by their owner (consignor) to an agent (consignee) to be sold by the agent. The consignor is entitled to payment of a pre-agreed amount or return of the goods if they are not sold.

oncost Additional expense, such as that from employing staff (wages oncost) or storing goods (storage oncost). The term has also been used a synonym of ***overheads***.

on demand Describing a ***bill of exchange*** that is payable to the bearer immediately on presentation, such as a cheque.

one-man Describing a business, company or operation that involves only one person.

one-month money Money placed on the money market that cannot be withdrawn without penalty for one month.

one-off profit Monetary surplus that is unlikely to accrue again (because a recurrence of the event that gave rise to it is unlikely).

one-year money Money placed on the money market that cannot be withdrawn without penalty for one year.

on-floor Describing transactions that are conducted and concluded on the floor of an exchange in the usual manner.

on stream When something (such as an asset, investment or production process) begins to function, it is said to come on stream.

on the run Describing the most recently issued Treasury bills (with 3, 6 or 12 months to run).

OPEC Abbreviation of ***Organization of Petroleum Exporting Countries***.

open account Trade between an exporter and an importer without any built-in guarantee or payment. The exporter submits an invoice and expects to be paid in due course, as is the case with any normal domestic transaction.

open contract Contract that has been bought or sold on a financial futures market, but has not been closed by making an offsetting transaction or taking delivery of the financial instrument involved. *See* ***open position***.

open credit Credit extended by a financial institution that requires no security (because of the high creditworthiness of the borrower).

open-end fund Alternative term for a US ***unit trust***.

open-ended investment company (OEIC) Open-ended fund listed at a single unit share price on a stock exchange, common in the USA.

open general licence Import licence with no restriction on the type of goods or their country of origin.

open indent Order for goods that does not specify a particular supplier. The agent receiving the indent may purchase suitable goods from any manufacturer or supplier at his or her discretion.

opening bank Bank that opens a ***letter of credit***, instructed by an importer to pay a foreign exporter.

opening bid First bid at an auction.

opening price Price of a share at the beginning of a day's business on a stock exchange. This may differ from the previous evening's closing price, generally because the price has been adjusted to take into account events that have occurred overnight and the performance of other exchanges.

opening range On a financial futures market, the highest and lowest prices recorded at the opening.

opening sale Sale of an option contract where the seller becomes in effect the writer of the option by assuming responsibility for its performance.

open market Market in which goods are available to be bought and sold by anybody who cares to. Prices on an open market are determined by the laws of ***supply and demand***.

open market desk Familiar US term for the part of the New York Federal Reserve bank that carries out open market dealing for the ***Federal Reserve Board***.

open-market operations Intervention by a central bank to control the amount of money in circulation or to stablize interest rates (e.g. by the large-scale purchase of securities).

open order Alternative term for an order ***good-till-cancelled***.

open outcry Trading method for commodities or securities in which dealers shout out buy or sell offers on the main floor of the exchange. Potential buyers or sellers also shout, and eventually one of each type get together to make a trade.

open position Exposed position of a speculator who has bought or sold without making any hedging transactions, and who therefore gambled that the market will rise or fall as he or she predicted.

operating margin Company's ***operating profit*** expressed as a proportion of price or operating costs.

operating profit or loss Profit or loss made by a company through its main activity, calculated by taking operating costs away from trading profit (or adding operating expenses to its trading loss). It excludes interest on loans, returns on other investments, or any other extraordinary items.

operational research (OR) Application of mathematical techniques to determine, for example, how the various activities within an industry may be regulated to coexist with maximum efficiency.

operation of law Way in which a contract may be discharged, by obtaining a judgement in court.

operator's licence Licence that in the UK a carrier must have in order to transport goods by road (in a vehicle of more than 1½ tons unladen weight).

opportunity cost Revenue foregone by using an asset for one purpose rather than another. For example, a company owning a building which it uses as storage space could rent it to someone else. That rent is the opportunity cost of the building.

option An investor may pay a premium in return for the option to buy (a call option) or sell (a put option) a certain number of securities at an agreed price (known as the exercise price), on or before a particular date. The dealer may exercise his or her option at any time within the specified period and normally does so at an advantageous time depending on market prices. Otherwise the dealer may allow the option to lapse.

Options Clearing Corporation New York clearing house for over-the-counter derivatives.

Options Market London Exchange Options market, established in 1989, that trades in Norwegian and Swedish equities derivatives, to which wood pulp futures were added in 1997.

option to purchase shares Option to buy shares in a company, often to its employees, by a specified date and at a predetermined price (which generally has to be paid up front).

option writer Person who sells call options, thereby agreeing to supply shares, or a person who sells put options, agreeing to buy shares.

OR Abbreviation of *operational research*.

order and disposition In bankruptcy, a means whereby a bankrupt's creditors may seize property to which the bankrupt has no title. Order and disposition comes into effect only if title is not obviously someone else's and if the bankrupt has led a third party into believing the goods are his or hers in order to receive credit.

order book Total of outstanding orders from customers, usually in a given period of time.

order driven Describing an economy, industry or trading on a stock market that reacts in relation to the flow of incoming orders.

ordinary resolution Resolution passed by a company's shareholders at a meeting (usually the annual general meeting), generally by a majority of those present unless the articles of association say otherwise.

ordinary shares Company shares whose holders are the owners of the company. They are entitled to a dividend (at the discretion of the directors) after other preferential payments have been made. Ordinary shares are sometimes classed as either voting or non-voting shares, and are often also known as equities.

Organization for Economic Cooperation and Development (OECD) International organization established in 1961, mainly to coordinate aid to underdeveloped countries. Its members include the European countries, Australia, Canada, Japan, New Zealand and the USA.

Organization for European Economic Cooperation (OEEC) Post-World War II organization of European countries established to coordinate attempts to bring about a recovery of the European economy. Its main source of funds was the USA through the Marshall Plan. It was incorporated into the ***Organization for Economic Cooperation and Development (OECD)*** in 1961.

Organization of Petroleum Exporting Countries (OPEC) Organization of African, Middle Eastern and South American oil-producing countries which act as a cartel to control the international price of crude oil. Its influence, greatest in the 1970s, waned somewhat with discoveries of offshore fields of oil and gas in North America and western Europe.

originating bank In international transactions involving a foreign branch of a bank (with a head office in, say, London), the originating bank is the foreign branch at which the transaction originated.

OTC market See ***over-the-counter market***.

OTM Abbreviation of ***old-to-market***.

outcry market On commodity markets, trading is recorded from the outcries of the traders on the floor, although deals are sealed by private contract. Markets on which trading is carried out in this noisy manner are known as outcry markets and the style of trading is known as open outcry.

out of the money Describing an option to buy shares (call option) for which the current price is lower than when the price was fixed. Equally, it describes an option to buy (put option) for which the market price has risen above the agreed exercise price. In either case, the dealer makes a loss if he or she exercises the option.

output tax In a value-added tax system, the tax that is charged by a supplier to a customer.

outright purchase/sale In the USA, the purchase or sale of financial instruments in the money markets by the Federal Reserve, not for immediate resale and therefore affecting the reserves of the banking system.

outside broker Stock and share dealer who is not a member of any exchange.

outside director Alternative name for a ***non-executive director***.

outsourcing Passing the management and key functions of a company's development, such as information technology, to an outside organization.

outwork Work done by an outside worker, usually operating at home. It often pays a company to employ workers to work at home, normally producing goods or providing services at a low rate of pay.

overbought If there are many buyers on a market, prices (e.g. of shares) are pushed to artificially high levels and the market is said to be overbought.

overcapacity Situation in a market where the maximum capacity of the producers to produce is much higher than demand, current or future. It generally results in cuts in overheads, reductions in retail prices or the financial collapse of some producers.

over-capitalized Describing a company that has more capital than it can profitably employ.

over entry certificate Document issued by customs to acknowledge that too much duty was paid at prime entry.

overexposure Overabundance of risk. For example, if a stockbroker is paid a salary largely dependent on the performance of the company and maintains a substantial shareholding in that company, he or she is overexposed to the possibility of a downturn in the company's business.

overfunding Situation in which a government sells more debt (such as bonds) to the non-bank sector to meet its public sector borrowing requirement in a particular year.

overhead Also called overheads, the costs incurred in the everyday running of a business and not variable according to its output. Also known as indirect costs, fixed costs or supplementary costs, or "burden" in the USA, overhead costs include heating, lighting and energy costs, administration, insurance, rent and rates. Cost of sales and research and development costs are also usually included.

overnight money Money that is lent – placed in the money market – and which has to be repaid the following day. It is usually secured by a ***bill of exchange*** and given by a bank to a ***discount house***.

overriding commission Commission paid to a broker in return for finding underwriters to an issue of shares.

overseas company Company that is incorporated outside the UK but with a British place of business.

overshoot Describing price trends on a currency market that continue to rise above levels anticipated by analysts.

oversold Describing a market in which there are too many sellers, with the result that prices fall to an artificially low point, too rapidly.

oversubscribed Describing the situation in a sale of shares by application and allotment where the number of shares applied for exceeds the number of shares available. The distribution is then often made using a ballot.

over-the-counter (OTC) market Market on which securities not listed on any stock exchange may be bought and sold. In practice, the OTC market is operated by a limited number of market-makers, often on the basis of matched bargains.

overtime ban Type of industrial action in which workers refuse to do overtime, thus maintaining their basic wages while disrupting production (if overtime is regularly worked).

overtrading Potentially dangerous situation in which a company tries to take on more business than its working capital will allow.

overvalued currency Currency that trades on foreign exchange markets at a price that makes exports uncompetitive, usually leading to a balance of trade deficit.

own brand Also called own label, a large retailer's private brand name for goods that would normally be sold, at a higher price, under another well-known brand name (often obtained from the same manufacturer or supplier).

own label *See own brand.*

P

packaging Cost (including design, printing etc.) of the package that protects a product and presents it at point of sale.

packing Colloquial term for the practice of adding (e.g. to the repayments on a loan) charges for services such as insurance etc. without the borrower requesting them, or indeed being fully aware that the charge is being made. It is illegal.

packing list Document that lists the numbers and types of good in a consignment.

pac-man defence Method of defending against a hostile take-over bid, in which the target company makes a tender offer for the shares of the aggressor (named after an early US computer game in which pac-man gobbled up his attackers).

pagare Spanish for ***promissory note***.

paid-in capital In the USA, owners' equity in a company, i.e., the total amount invested during and since its incorporation.

paid-in surplus In the USA, excess received by a company over and above the par (standard) value of its issued shares.

paid-up share capital Capital obtained by a company for a share issue in which the shares are fully paid.

painting the tape Method of creating an impression of activity around a share, by reporting fictitious transactions. It is illegal.

pair French for ***par***.

palletization Using pallets to carry a number of individual packages for shipment.

P & L *See* ***profit and loss account***.

pan-European marketing Selling the same products in the same manner throughout Europe, i.e. treating the whole of Europe as a single market.

paper Any type of security or loan, particularly a short-term loan such as a ***Treasury bill***. Most paper is negotiable and can be bought and sold like any other commodity.

paper company Company established, often with little capital, merely for financial purposes.

paper currency Another name for ***paper money***.

paper gold Colloquial term for ***special drawing rights (SDRs)***.

paper money Any legal tender in the form of a document, with a stated value but with no intrinsic value (such as a banknote).

paper profit Apparent increase in the value of an asset or investment, not realizable until it is sold.

par Equal to the face value, or to current rate of exchange.

parallel financing Provision of funds for different parts of the same project by two sources of finance.

parallel imports Imports taken into a country and sold at a lower price than the one that normally prevails there (because they are cheaper in the country of origin).

parallel market Market outside the normal one for a particular financial instrument (such as American depositary receipts).

par bond Bond that trades at par (usually related to the new issue price).

parcel Block of shares that change hands in a single deal, or bargain.

parent company Company that owns or part-owns, but more importantly controls, one or more subsidiary companies.

parities Currency exchange rates.

pari passu Latin for with equal step, indicating simultaneous effect, often applied to new share issues. In this context, it means that the designated share will rank equally for dividends with comparable existing shares.

Paris Bourse France's principal and, since 1991, only stock exchange (incorporating those at Bordeaux, Lille, Lyons, Marselles, Nancy and Nantes). It has had an electronic trading system (*Cotation Assistée en Continue* (CAC), based on Totonto's Computer-Assisted Trading System (CATS)) since 1988, later upgraded to SUPERCAC.

Paris Inter-Bank Offered Rate (PIBOR) French equivalent of the UK's ***London Inter-Bank Offerred Rate (LIBOR)***.

parity Equality (in value).

partial shipment Incomplete order as requested by the purchaser (but which can be shipped if the purchaser agrees).

participating preference share Type of ***preference share*** that has additional rights to a further share of profits after dividends have been allotted to ordinary shareholders.

particular lien Right to take possession of specified assets in the event of a default. A particular lien relates only to the debt arising over which the lien is held.

part load In the carriage of goods, a consignment that does not completely fill the transport but which shares the space with another part load going to the same (or a nearby) destination.

partly paid Describing securities and shares for which the full nominal value has not been paid and on which the holder is liable to pay the balance either on demand or on specified dates. Formerly, it was common for a company to call up only a part of the nominal value of each share, retaining the right to demand the balance when it became necessary to increase its capital. This gave the company access to capital without the need for a new share issue. The term also applies to new issues in which the price is to be paid in instalments.

partner Person engaged in a business enterprise jointly with, and generally with the same status and responsibilities as, another or others. *See* ***partnership***.

partner's drawing Payment to a partner, which is charged against his or her share of revenue.

partnership Formal business association, in the UK normally formed between two to twenty partners. The partners are jointly liable for the debts of the partnership, so that if one partner dies or decamps, the remaining partners are responsible for any debts.

partnership at will Partners are normally bound by a formal agreement; if not, the partnership is termed a partnership at will, and may be broken at any time by any partner.

part payment Interim payment or instalment; payment of part of the sum due under a debt or contract, in itself of no legal significance (unlike ***payment on account***).

par value Alternative term for ***face value*** or nominal value.

passed dividend Dividend that is not paid in a particular year (because the company has insufficient funds).

passing a name Providing a seller with the name of a potential buyer. A broker often "passes a name" in this way, but rarely guarantees the buyer's solvency when doing so.

passive income Income a company receives from its operations in a *tax haven*.

passive management Form of mutual fund management, increasingly popular in the USA, in which a fund's investments are selected automatically to match the exact performance of a stock index.

pass-through US term to describe a type of security that represents an interest in an underlying pool of mortgages. Payments received on the underlying pool are passed through to the security investor.

pathfinder Brief *prospectus* that gives a short account of a company's prospects and history, sent before a full prospectus in an attempt to raise investors' interest.

pawnbroker Person who lends money secured against goods, called a pledge, and issues a formal receipt for them. Loans are normally made for a period of six months and seven days and, if not repaid in that time (with interest), the pawnbroker is entitles to sell the pawned goods.

payables Informal term for a company's short-term debts (debtors).

payable to bearer *Bill of exchange* on which the payee or, if the bill has been endorsed, the endorsee is not named. The bill is payable to the bearer.

payable to order *Bill of exchange* payable to an existing payee or order and not endorsed in blank. Only a bill payable to a payee or "bearer", a fictitious payee or endorsed in blank will be payable to bearer and therefore transferable by delivery without endorsements.

pay-as-you-earn (PAYE) System of income tax collection in the UK in which tax is deducted from current earnings at source. The employer is responsible for collecting the tax, and the employee receives only net wages. A similar system is called pay-as-you-go in the USA.

payback period Time that elapses before a new project's cash inflows equal its cash outflows. In the USA it is also called payoff or payout.

pay day Account day; a colloquial term for the day on the *London Stock Exchange* when settlements are due.

PAYE Abbreviation of *pay-as-you-earn*.

payee Person or people to whom money is paid (in the case of a cheque also called the drawee).

payer Person who authorizes payment (in the case of a cheque also known as the drawer, the person who signs it).

paying agent Bank or other institution that pays capital or interest to holders of bonds, for which the agent may charge a fee.

payment for honour supra protest Payment of a ***bill of exchange*** (that is not paid and is protested) by somebody who is not named on the bill.

payment in advance Payment for goods or services made before they are received. Under the accruals concept, it is accounted for as a deferred debit.

payment in kind Payment, generally of wages, made in goods or services rather than in money. Payment of total wages in kind was made illegal in the UK in the 19th century, but part-payment in kind still occurs (for example, luncheon vouchers and the use of a company car are payments in kind).

payment on account Part payment of an outstanding debt, usually coupled with an agreement to repay the balance by a specific date. For long-term contract work, payment on account (also called progress payment) denotes a stage payment for work completed by a certain specified time.

pay-out ratio US term for a dividend expressed as a percentage of the available company profit, known in the UK as dividend cover.

payroll List of people employed (usually full-time) by a company and of the amount that each is due to be paid.

payroll tax Tax on a business undertaking levied in relation to the number of people employed, or as a percentage of the total wages bill. It is sometimes used to control the relative elasticities of the supply and demand for labour. Its imposition deters companies from employing more workers than they currently require.

pay slip Small form included in an employee's pay packet, giving details of how the net pay has been calculated. Employee's paid directly into a bank account receive a similar document.

peculation Embezzlement, particularly the appropriation of public money or goods by an official.

peg To fix a currency's exchange rate.

P

PEG Abbreviation of ***price-earnings growth factor***.

pegging the exchanges Maintenance of a fixed currency exchange rate, by government intervention in the markets. Pegging the exchanges is generally resorted to in order to prevent an unfavourable rise or fall in the value of a currency.

penalty clause Clause in a contract stating that if one party breaks the contract (e.g. by late delivery of goods) it will be liable to pay a penalty, usually in money.

penny shares/stock Shares/stock in a company that are traded in low denominations (usually under 50p). Penny shares are often highly volatile.

PEP Abbreviation of ***personal equity plan***.

peppercorn rent Very low ground rent imposed merely to establish that property is leasehold, not freehold.

P/E ratio *See* ***prices-earnings ratio***.

PER Abbreviation of ***prices-earnings ratio***.

per capita Latin for "by the head". It usually indicates that a sum will be divided equally among a group of people. Thus per capita income is calculated by dividing the total income received by a group by the number of people in the group; it is thus the average income.

per contra Latin for "by the opposite side". In accounting, it is an entry on the opposite side of an account or balance sheet, and therefore a self-balancing item.

per diem Latin for "by the day". It usually applies to allowances, rental or charges made on a daily basis.

perfect competition Idealized situation in a market in which all rival products are the same (so the buyers have no preference), there are many small buyers and sellers (so that none can on its own control price) who all try to maximize profit and can leave or join the market whenever they like, and buyers pay only the lowest price.

perfecting the sight Supplying the full details demanded on a ***bill of sight***.

performance Earnings or losses made on a security or by a company.

performance bond Also known as a contract bond, a bond delivered by a contractor to a public authority for a sum in excess of the value of a contract, and which is to be paid in the event of a breach of contract. It is therefore a form of guarantee.

performance ratios Financial ratios that are used to measure the performance of an entity, division, department or personnel. They can, for example, provide insights into a financial institution's profitability, return on investment, capital adequacy and liquidity.

performance-related pay (PRP) Salary increase or bonus awarded to an employee in recognition of good performance at work.

period bill Fixed-period ***bill of exchange*** payable on a specified date, and not on demand.

perishable goods Goods that are likely to deteriorate over a relatively short period of time. The term is most frequently applied to foodstuffs.

period costs Alternative term for ***fixed costs***.

perks Abbreviation of perquisites, i.e., casual benefits. In general terms perks are ***payments in kind***, but are more specifically applicable to informal rather than formal agreed benefits. *See also* ***fringe benefits***.

permanent interest-bearing shares (Pibs) In the UK, a type of building society investment involving shares that can be redeemed only when the society is wound up (i.e. they are perpetual).

permission to deal Authorization issued by a stock exchange that permits dealings in the shares of a company. It must be sought three days after the issue of a prospectus.

perpetual debenture Debenture that may not be repaid on demand.

perpetual floating rate note Type of ***floating-rate note (FRN)*** that is not to be repaid, i.e. it has no maturity and is mainly used as an investment instrument.

perpetual succession Continuation of a company after the departure or death of its members. A company is an individual legal entity which exists irrespective of its personnel, and which ceases to exist in law only after its liquidation.

personal allowance Amount that a person may earn before he or she is liable to pay income tax.

personal equity plan (PEP) Former method of tax-free saving introduced by the UK government in 1987 in which money was invested in stocks and shares (equity). They ceased to be available after April 1999 with the introduction of ***individual savings accounts (ISAs)***.

Personal Investment Authority (PIA) A UK self-regulatory organization (SRO) established in 1993 that oversees businesses that deal with private investors. It is a self-regulating organization (SRO) and took over responsibilities from the Financial Intermediaries, Managers and Brokers Regulatory Association (FIMBRA) and the Life Assurance and Unit Trust Regulatory Organization (LAUTRO). In 1997 it was itself incorporated into the Financial Services Authority (FSA).

personal loan Generally unsecured loan made (usually by a bank but now increasingly by registered brokers) to a private individual. This form of loan is generally fairly modest and intended for some specific purpose, such as the purchase of a car.

personnel department/management Company department or management area that deals with employees and their relationship to the company (particularly with regard to pay and working conditions). It may also be responsible for recruitment and training.

PERT Abbreviation of ***programme evaluation and review technique***.

petrocurrency Money (usually US dollars) paid to the exporters of petroleum in exchange for their product. After the OPEC countries markedly increased prices, the amount of petrocurrency in circulation exceeded the oil-exporting countries' economies to absorb it. As a result, much of it was invested in the world's financial markets, where it helped to offset the trade deficits caused by the OPEC price rises.

petrodollars Petrocurrency denominated in dollars.

petroleum revenue tax (PRT) UK tax on the profits of oil companies (which can be deducted from corporation tax).

petties Abbreviation of ***petty cash***, used most commonly on an invoice to denote charges for various small items not separately enumerated.

petty cash Money in notes and coins kept for payment of small bills and day-to-day expenses. *See also* ***float***.

PFI Abbreviation of ***private finance initiative***.

physical Type of commodity, available on a commodity market for very early or immediate delivery (as opposed to a future).

physical price Also known as actual price or cash price, the price an immediately available commodity.

PIA Abbreviation of ***Personal Investment Authority***.

PIBOR Abbreviation of ***Paris Inter-Bank Offered Rate***.

PIBS Abbreviation of ***permanent interest-bearing shares***.

picketing Action of strikers (usually members of a trade union) who stand outside a place where there is an industrial dispute such as a strike, trying to persuade non-strikers and other workers, such as those delivering to the place, not to cross the picket line. Mass picketing, defined as more than six pickets, is illegal in the UK. *See also* ***secondary picketing***.

picket line *See* ***picketing***.

piece-rate Method of paying a worker in accordance with the number of items (pieces of work) that he or she produces; the sum paid per piece is the piece-rate. Sometimes a bonus is also paid for production in excess of a pre-set target.

piecework Work that is paid per unit of output (instead of per hour of time worked). *See* ***piece-rate***.

piggyback exporting Type of exporting in which two producers sell their (non-competing but complementary) products together.

pilferage Loss or damage to stock in a warehouse or to cargo in transit. In the case of loss it is usually because of theft.

pilot study Early stage in market research employed to test the effectiveness of a questionnaire, before it is widely used.

PINC Abbreviation of ***property income certificate***.

pink sheet Daily US publication, by the National Quotation Bureau, that lists bid and offer prices of brokers who deal in American Depositary Receipts (ADRs) and over-the-counter stocks (OCTs).

pit On a commodity exchange, the equivalent of a stock exchange trading floor. It derives its name from the nickname for the floor of the Chicago Commodities Exchange; the term now applies to the floor of any open outcry exchange.

pitch Area in which a trader operates.

pit trader Dealer on the floor of a commodity market or stock exchange that trades by open outcry.

placement Another term for ***placing***. The French *placement* means investment.

placing Process of issuing shares through an intermediary, usually a stockbroker or syndicate. The intermediary "places" the shares with clients, frequently institutional investors, or with members of the public. A certain proportion of any share quoted on the London Stock Exchange must be made available to the public through the Exchange.

plain vanilla Colloquial term for the most basic form of a financial instrument (with no added ***bells and whistles***).

planned obsolescence Alternative term for ***built-in obsolescence***.

plant Fixtures (services) or machinery used in an industrial process, or a general term for a factory or industrial complex.

plant register List of a company's plant and machinery, usually including information about date and cost of purchase, depreciation and any sale or scrap value received.

PLC (also **plc, Plc)** Abbreviation of ***public limited company***.

pledge Transfer of personal property from a debtor to a creditor as security for a debt. Legal ownership of the property remains with the pledger. *See also* ***pawnbroker***.

ploughed-back profit Alternative term for ***retained earnings***.

poaching Persuading skilled workers to leave their current employer (often a competitor) and join your company.

point Unit of price in which stocks are traded. One point usually equals £1 or $1.

point-of-sale (POS) Point at which ownership of goods passes from the seller to the buyer. It is also where value added tax (VAT) becomes payable.

poison pill Technique used by companies facing a hostile take-over bid to make their stock as unattractive as possible to the aggressor. Stock may be diluted by new issues and company articles changed to require the approval of a greater proportion of the shareholders for the take-over. Expensive subsidiaries may be purchased to reduce the attractiveness of the company's balance sheet, and provision is often made for ***greenmail*** payments and for ***golden parachutes***.

polarization Under the terms of the UK Financial Services Act, a regulation that does not allow financial intermediaries to act as advisers about financial products and at the same time sell their own products. They must act either as independent advisers, recommending the best product for their client from all those available, or as tied agents, selling only their own products – i.e. they must polarize.

political and charitable contributions Under the UK Companies Act 1967, companies must reveal such contributions (over a certain amount) and their recipients in their accounts.

political risk In trading in securities, the risk that an investment may be harmed by changes in government policy towards such things as currency controls, interest rates, quotas, state ownership, tariffs, taxation and so on. Devaluation of a country's currency is not normally regarded as a political risk.

political union Agreement among nations to create a trading bloc with no trade, monetary or taxation barriers between the members.

poll Vote at a shareholders' meeting, usually by ballot, with each shareholder having a number of votes in proportion to his or her holding.

poll tax Tax charged to every adult in a community, generally as a means of raising revenue for local government. The term was also applied to the defunct community charge in the UK (now replaced by ***council tax***).

Ponzi scheme Scheme in which depositors are paid interest by using capital from the later depositors. It is fraudulent (and therefore illegal).

porcupine provision Provision written into a company's articles of association, or into a corporate charter or bylaw, designed to act as a deterrent to hostile take-overs. A ***poison pill*** defence is one example.

portfolio Selection of securities held by a person or institution. Portfolios generally include a wide variety of stocks and bonds to spread the risk of investment, and the contents of the portfolio are generally managed – that is, continually adjusted in order to maximize income or growth.

port of entry Port at which goods from overseas pass into the receiving country.

POS Abbreviation of ***point of sale***.

position In general terms, the place of a dealer or investor (in terms of financial commitment) in a fluctuating market. *See also* ***long position; open position; short position***.

post-date To affix some future date to a financial instrument, most commonly a cheque, thereby preventing the occurrence of actions or transactions concerning that document before the specified date.

post-entry Describing events or developments that occur after a company's entry to a stock market.

post-tax profit Company's profit after corporation tax has been deducted, also called its earnings.

post-war credit Promised refund of a tax levied in the UK between 1941 and 1946, partly paid and since 1959 accruing interest. Men over 60 and women over 55 can get full repayment from the Inland Revenue on application.

pot is clean Term indicating that all the shares allocated during an issue for offer to institutional investors have been taken up.

pound cost averaging Lower average cost per share that results from investing a fixed sum of money regularly in a share, compared with buying a fixed number of shares at the same frequency (because more shares are purchased at low prices than at high prices). In the USA it is termed dollar cost averaging (equal to a constant dollar plan).

power of attorney Written legal agreement giving one person the authority to act in legal matters on behalf of another.

PPP *See* ***purchasing power parity exchange rates***.

PR Abbreviation of ***public relations***.

predator Company attempting a hostile take-over bid for another company, also called an aggressor.

predatory dumping Selling an exported product on a foreign market at less than market value, to beat local competition. Once competition is eliminated, the price generally rises.

predatory pricing Policy of setting a price for a product at less than market value to drive out competition (and deter new entrants to the market).

pre-emption Right to purchase shares before they become generally available, usually offered in the case of new issues to existing shareholders. Rights of pre-emption are often proportional to the value of an existing holding.

preference shares Also known as preferred stock, preference shares offer the shareholder preferential claims to dividends, usually at a fixed rate, and a prior claim to ordinary shareholders on the company's assets in the event of liquidation. The market price for the preference shares tends to be more stable than that of ordinary shares. Preference shareholders may not vote at meetings of ordinary shareholders. Preference shares fall into five categories: cumulative, non-cumulative, redeemable, participating and convertible. They are known as preferred stock in the USA.

preferential creditor Creditor who gets paid in preference to others in the event of a company's liquidation (such as, in the UK, the Inland Revenue, for taxes outstanding, and Customs and Excise, for VAT).

preferential debt In bankruptcy or liquidation, a debt owed to a *preferential creditor*.

preferential trade area (PTA) Region in which member countries have preferential tariff arrangements for goods imported from certain other countries.

preferred stock US term for *preference shares*.

preliminary announcement Also called preliminary statement, an announcement of a company's full year results a month or two before publication of its annual report.

preliminary expenses Expenses incurred in setting up a new company (such as the cost of printing share certificates and issuing them).

preliminary statement Alternative term for *preliminary announcement*.

pre-market Describing trading in commodities before the main market opens.

premium In general, any price, payment or bonus valued higher than the norm. More specifically, it is the difference in price between the offer price of a new share issue and the price at which it begins trading, if the latter exceeds the former. The term is also used to describe the positive difference between the face value and redemption value of any stock or bond. The premium is also the price paid for insurance. *See also premium on a lease*.

premium brand Brand of a product that sells at a higher price than most others of the same type, usually because of some perceived quality.

premium on a lease Lump sum paid, in addition to rent, on taking up a lease (sometimes called key money).

prepayment *See payment in advance*.

pre-placement Activity that occurs before a share has been placed (*see placing*).

pre-preferential debt In bankruptcy or liquidation, a debt that ranks before even preferential debts (such as money held on trust by a bankrupt).

pre-refunding Practice of issuing shares to re-fund (i.e. pay for debts that are about to mature), not immediately before maturity of the old issue, but in advance of it, in order to take advantage of favourable interest rates.

present value Assessment of the current net cost or value of future expenditure or benefit. Most frequently it is used to measure return on capital investment.

president Chief executive of a US company, equivalent to a managing director in the UK.

prêt French for loan.

pre-tax profit Profit calculated before allowance is made for tax (such as corporation tax and capital gains tax).

preventative maintenance Programme for the ongoing maintenance of equipment and machinery that is built into a production schedule, to prevent any delays caused by sudden breakdowns and so on.

Prevention of Fraud (Investments) Act 1939 UK legislation that requires dealers in shares to be licensed (unless a member of a stock exchange) and banning the making of misleading statements about or unsubstantiated claims for shares (as was once done by share pushers).

price Cost of purchasing a unit of goods or services. Very broadly, prices are generally set by the producer and retailer, taking into account all fixed costs and variable costs and allowing for a profit margin.

price control Method of controlling inflation or allocation of resources in a centrally-planned economy by pegging prices within specified limits. Market forces make it difficult to control prices in this way in the long term, and the method is normally used only for short-term crisis management.

price discrimination Practice of charging different prices for the same product to different buyers (i.e. charging more to people whom the seller thinks can afford it, and charging less to people with less purchasing power, for example children's fares and admission charges).

price-earnings growth factor (PEG) Ratio of the predicted ***price-earnings ratio (P/E ratio)*** of a share to its anticipated growth rate in ***earnings per share***, devised to help in choosing investments (the higher, the better).

price-earnings ratio (P/E ratio) Current market price of a company's ordinary shares divided by the ***earnings per share*** (the higher, the better).

price elastic Describing a good or service that sells in proportionately smaller quantities compared to the proportionate increase in its price; i.e. a price increase has a more serious effect on sales than expected. *See* ***price elasticity***.

price elasticity Measure of the way in which a change in the price of a good or service affects the numbers sold. It is defined as the percentage change in numbers sold divided by the percentage change in price. The value of this ratio is greater than one for things that are ***price elastic***, and less than one for those that are ***price inelastic***.

price index Series of numbers that represent average prices over a period of time, relative to a base (usually 100 or 1000) assigned to the first period. *See also* ***share index***.

price inelastic Describing a good or service that sells in proportionately larger quantities compared to the proportionate rise in its price; i.e. a price increase has less serious effect on sales than expected. *See* ***price elasticity***.

pricing Method used to set a ***price***, specifically by equating supply with demand.

price leader Also called price maker, a product that can dictate the price within its market (because of its perceived value), which rival products have to undersell.

price maker Alternative term for ***price leader***.

price mechanism Operation of the laws of ***supply and demand***, which determine prices.

prices and incomes policy Government policy for controlling prices and wages as a means of checking inflation.

price sensitive Describing goods or services whose sales are greatly affected by a change in price; similar to ***price elastic***.

prices policy Generally part of a ***prices and incomes policy***.

price taker Company whose products are not readily distinguished from the competition, whose prices it must therefore undercut in order to obtain a market share.

price variance In standard costing, the difference between actual and standard cost per unit multiplied by the quantity purchased. It measures the change in revenue caused by a change in price. It is also termed value variance.

primage Cost of loading or unloading a vessel, normally part of freight charges.

primary capital Capital that is used in the start-up of a business.

primary commodity Commodity that is essential to a nation, such as food, fuel and raw materials for industry.

primary dealer Regulated dealer in US government securities, or a market-maker in UK gilt-edged securities (gilts).

primary efficiency ratio Alternative term for ***return on capital (ROC)***.

primary market Market in new security issues, also known as the ***new issue market***.

prime cost Combined cost of ***direct expenses***, ***direct labour*** and ***direct materials***, as assigned to a product.

prime entry In international trade, describing imported goods on which customs duty is levied as soon as they enter the country, and which are impounded until the duty is paid.

prime lending rate Preferential interest rate charged in the USA for short-term loans made to people or organizations with a high credit rating. It is approximately equivalent to the banker's base rate in the UK.

prime rate Alternative term for ***prime lending rate***.

principal In finance, the original sum invested or lent, as distinct from any profits or interest involved. A principal is also a person who gives instructions to an agent.

principal-only bond Bond, issued at a discount, on which no interest is paid. The full face value is paid on maturity.

prise de contrôle French for take-over.

private Describing a person or organization that is independent of the public or government sector.

private carrier Carrier who transports goods only on specific contracts, i.e. does not make a general offer to carry to the public.

private company Privately-owned company whose shareholders' liability may be limited or unlimited. *See* ***private limited company***.

private enterprise Undertaking by an individual or private group working without significant support from the state.

private equity Investment in an unlisted company by an institutional investor.

private finance initiative (PFI) Programme of construction projects in the private sector to which the UK government contributes some of the finance.

private label Alternative name for ***own brand***.

private limited company Company with share capital of at least £50,000 whose shares are not available to the general public through the medium of a stock exchange (i.e. it is unlisted), and whose members do not exceed 50 in number. The shareholders' liability is limited the value of their shareholding. *See* ***public company***.

privately held Describing a company, capital or other possessions that are in the hands of a person or a group of people.

private placement Alternative term for ***private placing***.

private placing Sale of the whole of a new issue of shares to a financial institution.

private sector That part of the business activity of a country that is financed and controlled by individuals or private companies (i.e. mainly shareholders and institutional investors).

private trading system US computerized trading system used by dealers and institutional investors who, for various reasons, do not wish to deal through a stock exchange.

privatization Practice of offering shares in previously state-owned industries or enterprises for sale to the general public. British Aerospace, British Rail and British Telecom are privatized companies in the UK. It may also be called denationalization.

prix d'offre French for ***reserve price*** (of a new issue of securities).

proactive Describing an action or decision that produces a response in others (rather than responding to others' actions or suggestions).

probate price Share price calculated for tax purposes by taking the lower of the bid and offer prices and adding to it one-quarter of the difference between the two. The process is known as quartering up.

pro bono Short form of *pro bono publico*, Latin for in the public good, used to describe unpaid-for (professional) work.

procuration Power given to somebody to sign documents on behalf of another. The signatory usually gives the name of the authorizer, prefixed by the letters *pp* (meaning *per procurationem*).

produce Agricultural produce, i.e. goods that are grown or derived from farm animals.

product Something that is produced, either in terms of goods or services or in terms of income.

product awareness Percentage of a target market that is aware of a specific product (although not necessarily purchasers of it).

product differentiation Extent to which a product is perceived as being different from its rivals by potential purchasers. A product with little differentiation has to be sold at a lower price than its rivals in order to obtain market share.

product diversification Decision to begin manufacturing new products, usually by ***horizontal*** or ***vertical diversification***. The main purpose is to lessen the risk of commercial failure caused by a sudden fall in demand for a particular product. Diversification is also attractive to companies that are dependent on seasonal or cyclical business.

production Broadly, the practice of manufacturing goods or providing services for sale. It may be measured in units of production, labour costs, or the time (machine or labour hours) taken to produce it.

production chain In manufacturing, the whole sequence of activities that covert raw materials into finished goods and then distribute and sell them.

production line In manufacturing, organization of production activities in such a way that part-finished products move sequentially from one stage to the next, usually with each worker repeating the same operation at his or her own stage in the process.

productivity Measure equal to the output of any of the factors of production (land, labour and capital) per unit of output. It may be enhanced by the improvement of any one of these three factors, most usually by the introduction of new technology or an incentive scheme. Productivity of land is generally measured in output per hectare or acre, that of labour in output per working hour, and that of capital as a percentage per annum.

productivity bonus Also called an incentive bonus, extra money paid to an employee to encourage him or her to work harder (and therefore more productively).

product life cycle Sequence in the production and sales of a product over its lifetime, generally taken to occur in five stages: development, introduction, growth, maturity and decline. Cash flow does not usually become positive until towards the end of the growth phase, with sales maximized at the middle of maturity.

product portfolio Mix of a company's brands or products, providing diversified sources of income (and a hedge against a sudden fall in demand for one of them).

product range All the products produced by a company or offered for sale by a retailer.

professional valuation For the purposes of a company balance sheet or a prospectus, a valuation of assets made by somebody who is experienced or qualified to do so.

profit Surplus money, after all expenses have been met, generated by a company or enterprise in the course of one accounting period. *See also* ***disposable income***.

profitability Measure of a company's record of producing revenue that exceeds its expenditure.

profitability ratio Measure of a company's profit in terms of net assets or sales income.

profit and loss account (P & L) Annual summary of a company's financial operations, required by law to be submitted to the UK Registrar of Companies by every trading company over a certain size (*see* ***small company***). The profit and loss account has three sections: the trading account, the profit and loss account, and the appropriation account. The profit and loss section takes the (gross) profit or loss figure from the trading account, and after accounting for income not concerned with trading and expenses such as those incurred in administration, deducts tax from the final net profit or loss figure.

profit and loss account reserve Reserve containing the balance of retained earnings that are to be carried forward to the next accounting period (or distributed in whole or in part to shareholders).

profit and loss appropriation account Account that details how a company's net profits have been allocated. *See* ***profit and loss account***.

profit and loss sharing ratio The part of net income (or loss) that is allocated to a partner in a partnership.

profit centre Part of an organization that creates revenue and to which costs can be assigned. *See also* **cost centre**.

profit margin Sales less all expenses (outgoings), usually expressed as a percentage of net sales or as simple net profit. Company policy generally specifies some profit margin below which it would be hardly worthwhile producing goods. *See also* **gross margin; net margin**.

profit-related pay Method of paying employees a basic salary/wage plus a percentage of the company's profits.

profit sharing Distribution of some or all of a company's profits to its employees as a bonus. The distribution may be in the form of cash or shares.

profit-sharing ratio (PSR) Ratio in which an organization's profits (or losses) are shared, often specified in a partnership agreement.

profits tax Tax levied on a company's profits.

profit-taking Selling stock and taking a profit on the transaction, instead of waiting for a better price. It occurs when dealers believe that the market will not improve much more, at least in the short term.

pro-forma invoice Type of invoice submitted before goods are despatched, used to confirm an order and advise of despatch.

programmed trading Using computers to decide when to trade in shares or foreign currency.

programme evaluation and review technique (PERT) Continual review of a company's procedures and performance (based on critical path analysis) in order to make early decisions and improve efficiency.

progressive tax Tax that is levied at various levels for different "bands" of income (the higher bands attracting the higher levels of tax), as with UK income tax.

project finance Method of raising money for large capital projects (usually in the construction industry), using the expected future cash flow as collateral.

projection Estimate of future developments made on the basis of, or projected from, a knowledge of past events.

promissory note Document that states that a person promises to pay a certain sum of money on a certain date. It is also known as a note of hand.

promoter Entrepreneur, especially a person involved in the organization or launch of a business.

promotion Forming a new company (*see* ***promoter***), or using advertising and other means to increase the sales of a product (often called a *sales promotion*).

prompt date In a commodity futures contract, the delivery date.

property Legally, property is divided into real and personal property. Real property may defined as land and buildings held freehold. Personal property consists of other personal possessions. More specifically, property is sometimes defined as something that appreciates in value or yields income.

property company Company that develops, invests in or trades property (buildings).

property income certificate (PINC) Tradable share in the ownership of a building (capable of providing capital growth and income).

proposed dividend Dividend that is proposed by a company's directors, which has to be approved at the ***annual general meeting (AGM)***.

proprietary company (Pty) Name of a private limited company in Australia and South Africa (Pty is used in a similar way to Ltd in the UK).

proprietor Owner of a business or property.

pro rata Latin for in proportion. For example, the total amount of dividend received by a shareholder is pro rata to his or her shareholding.

pro rata freight Part of the freight payable on a shipment when it is delivered (with the owner's consent) at a port not as close as the agreed destination.

prospectus Document that describes a proposal, such as that issued to prospective shareholders by a company that intends to make a public issue of shares, giving details of past and present performance and of prospects.

protected bear Alternative name for ***covered bear***.

protectionism Policy based on self-interest, for example one that shields an industry against foreign competition, usually by the imposition of selective or general quotas and tariffs.

protest Certificate (drawn by a notary) confirming that a ***bill of exchange*** has been dishonoured (i.e. not paid on the due date).

prototype Sample of a product made to test its design, manufacturing method and sales potential.

provision Allowance for some eventuality, such as a sum written off to provide for depreciation or replacement of assets.

proviso clause Clause in a directive given to the US open market desk after each meeting of the ***Federal Open Market Committee***, specifying the level of free reserves that must be maintained (as long as bank credit proxy does not increase excessively).

proxy Authorization given by a voter to another person to allow that person to vote on his or her behalf. For example, a shareholder may give somebody proxy to vote at a company meeting that the shareholder is unable to attend.

PRP Abbreviation of ***performance-related pay***.

PRT Abbreviation of ***petroleum revenue tax***.

prudence concept Concept that calls for a cautious view in accounting, such as the exclusion on the balance sheet of money owed but not received, and the inclusion of all liabilities, whether or not they must be met immediately. It therefore postulates a worst-moment scenario.

PSR Abbreviation of ***profit-sharing ratio***.

PSBR Abbreviation of ***public sector borrowing requirement***.

PTA Abbreviation of ***preferential trade area***.

Pty Abbreviation of ***proprietary company***.

public Describing something that is in the hands of the people and, as such, managed or controlled by the government; or that which is open to anybody.

public company Company that is limited by guarantee or shares, which has more than £50,000 share capital and is referred to as a public company in its ***memorandum of association***. It must be registered at Companies House and carry the words "public limited company" or the abbreviation "PLC" or "Plc" after its name. Its shares are available to the general public through a stock exchange.

public corporation Formal term for a nationalized industry.

public dividend capital Long-term UK government finance for nationalized industries which pays dividends (rather than interest).

public expenditure Spending on goods and services by public corporations and by central and local government.

public finance Money for ***public expenditure*** raised by government borrowing and taxation.

public limited company (PLC or **plc)** *See* ***public company***.

public offer New issue of shares or securities on offer to members of the general public. *See* ***offer for sale.***

public relations (PR) Various methods of using the media to obtain favourable publicity for a company. Direct advertising is generally excluded from the definition.

public sector That part of the business activity of a country that is financed and controlled by the central and local government. State public sector industries are often known as nationalized industries.

public sector borrowing requirement (PSBR) Difference between the government's expenditure and revenue, generally financed mainly by issuing ***gilt-edged securities*** (gilts) and other long-term loans.

public trustee Person appointed by the state who undertakes to act as a trustee, executor or investment adviser to any member of the general public.

puisne mortgage Mortgage that has not been protected by depositing the title deeds of the property concerned. The lender may instead register the property with the Land Register or the Land Charges Register; this ensures that any transaction concerning the property must have the approval of the lender.

pullback After a period when market prices have been fluctuating erratically, the movement or return to more recognizable and predictable trends.

pull to maturity Tendency of gilt-edged stocks (gilts) to approach par value as their redemption date draws near.

pumping Method by which the US Federal Reserve causes a fall in interest rates by adding greatly to bank reserves before then cutting the discount rate. It is disliked by the money markets.

purchase allowance Reduction in selling price, usually because the goods or service supplied were not exactly as ordered.

purchase documents Documents that confirm or place an order for goods or services.

purchaser Legally, somebody who takes a title to goods from somebody else, whether or not money changes hands. The term is much more commonly used to mean anybody who buys something (*see next entry*).

purchaser for value Somebody who has paid in cash or in kind in return for goods.

purchase tax Former tax levied in the UK on most goods made and sold in the UK. Manufacturers making taxable goods were licensed with the *Customs and Excise*. It was replaced by ***value added tax (VAT)***.

purchasing agent Agent who buys goods or services for large overseas buyers.

purchasing manager Person in an organization whose job is to buy supplies and ensure that they arrive on time (and at the best price).

purchasing power parity (PPP) exchange rate Exchange rate that is based on the relative prices of the same group of goods in two countries, thus taking account of relative local purchasing power.

put band Period for which a ***put option*** is valid.

put option *Option* to sell shares, commodities or financial futures at an agreed price on or before an agreed future date.

put-through Stock exchange dealing procedure used in cases of very large orders, where a stockbroker finds both a seller and a buyer and is therefore able to "put the shares through the market" in a single quick transaction.

pyramid selling Practice of selling distributorships, or the right to sell distributorships. The pyramid seller makes his or her profit from the sale of franchises and leaves the franchisee to dispose of the goods. In a typical system, each franchisee must guarantee to purchase a certain quantity of goods, which he or she then disposes of by recruiting distributors. Those at the bottom of the pyramid usually sell (or fail to sell) to family and friends.

Q

qualified report Also termed a qualified audit report or qualified opinion, an auditor's report in which he or she qualifies the financial statements (because he or she does not sanction the way in which some matters are treated or because the scope of the audit has been limited for some reason).

qualifying loss Trading loss that arises because of corporation tax calculations.

qualifying shares Fixed number (or percentage) of shares a person must hold before he or she is entitled to a position on the ***board of directors*** or to a ***bonus issue***.

quality control On a production line, the process of checking the quality of a product (or samples of it).

quality of bills of exchange One of the three grades of ***bills of exchange***: trade bills, agency bills or bank bills.

quango Abbreviation of quasi-autonomous non-governmental organization, which in the UK covers many semi-permanent public bodies set up to investigate certain cases or to deal with special problems. Examples are the ***Advisory, Conciliation and Arbitration Service (ACAS)*** and the ***National Economic Development Council (NEDC)***.

quantitative fund management Method of making investment decisions based on a mathematical analysis of the market.

quantity discount Also termed quantity rebate, a reduction in purchase price granted because of the large amount of goods or services being purchased.

quantity rebate *See* ***quantity discount***.

quantity restriction (QRs) Limit to the amount of goods that can be imported or exported; a quota.

quanto option Option on a foreign security that is guaranteed to be free from exchange rate risk.

quantum meruit (Latin for as much as he has earned.) If a supplier only half-completes the work he or she has been contracted to do, the supplier may in some cases claim payment in proportion to the amount of work completed, known as payment *quantum meruit*.

quartering up *See* ***probate price***.

quasi-autonomous non-governmental organization *See* ***quango***.

quasi-contract Contract judged by the Courts to be applicable (at least in part), even though no legal written contract exists.

quasi-equity Loan stock or debit instrument that offers its holder rights and befits similar to those offered to holders of shares. *See also* ***mezzanine finance***.

quasi-loan Benefit received by a director from a company instrument (such as personal purchases made using a company credit card), which he or she must repay the company.

quasi-money *See* ***near money***.

quick assets Alternative term for ***liquid assets***.

quick ratio Alternative term for ***acid-test ratio***.

quid pro quo Latin for this for that. The principle of *quid pro quo* underlies all contracts in that a contract is an agreement to exchange something such as services for something else, such as cash.

quiet time Time between the registration of a new share issue and its being offered for sale.

quorum Minimum number of people who have to be present at a meeting for it to go ahead and the decisions made to be valid. In the UK, the quorum for a members' meeting is noted in a company's ***articles of association***.

quota Amount of something (e.g. goods) allowed to one person or company, normally fixed by a body in authority. Some countries impose import quotas on the quantity of certain goods that may be imported.

quotation Appearance of a company's shares on the ***Official List*** of the stock exchange.

quotation spread Difference between the offer price and the bid price on a security. It is also known as the bid-offer spread.

quoted company Company that has received a listing on a stock exchange; or a quoted price; or the price at which a given market-maker will trade.

quoted currency Rate of exchange determine by relating two currencies. The base currency is assigned the numerical value one; the other is the quoted currency. Thus if the exchange rate between sterling and the Deutschmark is quoted at 3.5, sterling is the base currency and the Deutschmark is the quoted currency.

quoted investment Investment in shares or debentures that are quoted on an official exchange.

quoted price Price of a security as it is quoted on an exchange. The quoted price may fluctuate from day to day, or even minute to minute.

quote driven Describing a stock market that reacts (in terms of prices) to the quotations of market-makers rather than to the number and flow of incoming orders.

quote machine Colloquial term for a computer that allows a broker access to up-to-the-minute information on quoted prices.

quote sheet In the USA, an analysis of costs that a company employs when deciding on a selling price for goods or services.

quotient cours bénéfice French for ***price-earnings ratio***.

R

raid To buy significant numbers of a company's shares, usually as a prelude to a ***take-over bid***.

raider Person or group initiating a hostile ***take-over bid*** by buying quantities of the target company's shares.

rallonge Extension of the term for which ***short-term monetary support (STMS)*** is available.

rally Rise in market price of a share (or of market prices in general) when prices have stagnated or consistently fallen, usually followed by a further fall.

ramp To artificially push up the price of a share (usually by buying them and thus making them look sought after). It is illegal for a company to buy its own shares for this purpose.

R and D Abbreviation of ***research and development***.

random walk theory Theory of stock movements developed in the 1950s and 1960s, which states that share prices move in a random way, and so their movements up or down cannot be predicted.

ratchet Device used by a venture capitalist to encourage management by giving it a large share in the equity if the company performs well.

rateable value Value of a property for the purpose of calculating ***rates***, based on an estimate fo the rent the property would command (the annual value) on the open market with vacant possession.

rate capping Method used in the UK by the Secretary of State for the Environment to discourage high-spending local authorities, by reducing the amount they can raise in ***rates***.

rate of exchange Also called exchange rate, the rate at which various currencies are exchanged for each other.

rate of interest *See* ***interest***.

rate of return Amount of money made on an investment (in the form of interest or dividend), normally expresses as a percentage of the amount invested. The revenue a company receives for investing resources in some commercial activity is also known as its rate of return.

rate of return pricing Using a required ***rate of return*** as a method of setting the selling price of a product.

rate of turnover Usually annual frequency at which a company asset or investment is turned over. For example, the ratio of sales revenue to the average value of stock gives the stock turnover figure.

rates In the UK, a local government tax levied on householders and occupiers of commercial premises to pay for local works and services, expressed as a certain amount in the pounds of ***rateable value***. For private property, rates have been replaced by ***council tax***, which is payable by the occupant.

rate support grant Payment made by the UK government to local authorities to support council services that are neither self-financing nor receive any other form of grant.

ratification Official approval, giving something (e.g. a document or an agreement) validity.

rating Method of classifying various financial instruments, based on an assessment of whether payments of capital and interest will be made when they are due. For example, Standard & Poor's ratings in the USA range from triple A (AAA), the best, to DDD (the worst: a debt that is in default).

rating agency Organization that rates the quality of issuers of securities or commercial paper (*see* ***credit rating; rating***).

rationalized production Policy of an organization to produce different products, or parts of them, in different locations, even globally. In this way it can take advantage of lower local costs of materials and labour.

raw material Any material purchased for and employed directly in a production process. Raw materials, such as chemicals, metal sheet and timber, are generally at a low level of finish compared to the manufactured product that results from consumption.

reaction Fall in market prices after a period of continuous price rises. The opposite of a ***rally***.

reaction function Adjustment made to its monetary control by the US Federal Reserve in reaction to general changes in the economy.

real Describing a monetary quantity that is quoted after taking into account the effects of inflation (such as real income or real interest rate).

real-estate investment trust (REIT) Publicly-quoted US trust that issues bonds with a package of commercial property as security.

realignment Effectively a devaluation of a currency occurring under as fixed exchange rate system when one country's currency gets out of line (thus favouring its exports).

real income Income after taking into account inflation. For example, a 10% pay rise when inflation is running at 6% is worth only 4% in real terms.

real interest rate Interest rate after taking into account the effects of inflation. For example, if an investment pays 5% interest and inflation is running at 4%, the real interest rate is only 1%.

realizable account Also termed realization account, an account opened when a company is being wound up and its assets are being realized in order to pay creditors, or a partnership is being dissolved. Proceeds from the sale of assets are placed in the realizable account.

realizable assets Alternative term for ***liquid assets***.

realizable value Amount that can be obtained by selling an asset; market value.

realization Selling of assets for cash.

realization account Alternative term for ***realizable account***.

real property Property that consists of freehold land (as opposed to personal property).

real value Value of something after taking into account the effects of inflation.

rebate Sum of money returned to a payer because he or she has paid too much (such as a tax rebate), or a ***discount*** on the price of something.

rebate of duty Also known as drawback, a government rebate of duty that was paid on imports that were later re-exported.

rebate rate Rate of interest that is deducted when a ***bill of exchange*** is paid in advance of its maturity date.

recapitalization Euphemism for an injection of cash into a company that has insufficient of its own to continue trading safely.

receipt Document stating that money has been paid or goods have been received. The acquisition of money is also termed the receipt of money;

such acquisitions are called receipts or revenue (as opposed to expenditure).

receipts *See* ***receipt***.

receipts and payments basis Accounting basis in which accounts are drawn in terms of cash actually received or paid (as opposed to the ***accruals concept***).

receivables Any collectibles, whether or not they are currently due, such as claims for goods, services or money.

received for shipment Wording on a ***bill of lading*** that indicates that goods have been received alongside but not loaded or shipped.

receiver Official into whose hands a company with financial difficulties is placed to ensure that, as far as possible, creditors are paid.

receivership Company's state when a ***receiver*** is called in.

receiving order Court order placing a company into the hands of a ***receiver***.

recession Stage in a trade cycle in which the decline in economic activity accelerates, causing investment values to fall, companies to have to deal with adverse trading conditions, and unemployment to rise and so income and expenditure to fall. A recession may end in a depression unless there is a recovery.

reciprocal quote One divided by the direct quote of a rate of exchange (i.e. divided by the number of local currency units exchanged for one unit of the foreign currency).

reciprocity Reduction in import duties, quotas or tariffs in exchange for similar concessions from another country. Other similar mutual arrangements (such as the setting up of financial institutions in two countries) are also termed reciprocity.

recognizance Contract between a court and a person by which the person is bound to perform a certain act, such as to appear in court on a certain date, to be of good behaviour so as not to cause a breach of the peace, or to stand bail for somebody else.

recognized investment exchange (RIE) Market that has been authorized by the UK ***Securities and Investment Board*** to carry out investment business. Its individual members must also be authorized, in accord with the ***Financial Services Act***.

recognized professional body (RPB) Organization of which membership is sufficient to comply with the terms of the UK ***Financial Services Act*** with regard to investment activities and giving financial advice, without having to belong to a ***self-regulating organization (SRO)***.

recommended retail price (RRP) Retail price of a product as suggested by its manufacturer (which is seldom legally enforceable, although some manufacturers have other ways of getting retailers to comply with their wishes). The RRP is often specified on the packaging to indicate to customers that the retailer is not overcharging and to allow a comparison to be made between the prices of competing brands.

reconciliation Calculation that demonstrates how one figure (such as a balance) is derived from another or others.

recourse agreement In ***hire purchase*** transactions, an agreement that enables the seller to repossess the goods in the event of the purchaser being unable to make the payments required.

recoverable advance corporation tax ***Advance corporation tax*** that has already been paid but which can be set off against the current year's liability for gross corporation tax.

recoverable amount For an asset, its value in use or its net realizable value, whichever is the greater.

recovery Upturn in the financial position of a company, a market or the economy in general.

recovery shares When a company's performance is improving after a period of difficulty, its share price is likely to go up. Shares in such a company are known as recovery shares.

rectification of the register If a court believes that an official list (for example, a company's list of its shareholders) is incorrect, it can make an order, known as a rectification of the register, to have the list amended.

recycling Sorting of waste products so that they can be reused. The term was also used in the mid-1970s for the practice of banks of taking surplus funds from OPEC countries and investing them elsewhere (so that the recipients could spend it with OPEC).

Red Book Colloquial tern for the UK government's *Financial Statement and Budget Report* (issued on Budget Day).

red chip Describing a company listed on the Hong Kong stock exchange that is controlled by an organization in mainland China.

red-circle rate Rate of pay in the USA that is higher than usual for the job undertaken.

red clause Clause on a ***letter of credit*** that allows an exporter to receive the total amount due before the goods are shipped. It is traditionally typed or printed in red.

redeemable preference shares Preference shares for which the issuing company reserves the right to redeem (but only out of distributable profits).

redeemable security Security (stocks or bonds) that are repayable at par value at a specified date or dates (or in the event of something specified happening).

redemption Repayment of an outstanding loan or debenture stock by the borrower.

redemption date Date on which a loan or debenture is to be repaid. Redemption dates (plural) are those on a stock which is redeemable at par. In the case of UK Treasury stocks, the precise date of repayment is decided by the government.

redemption fee Premium paid to shareholders who surrender redeemable shares when asked to do so by the issuing company.

redemption price Price at which forms of indebtedness (e.g. bills of exchange or bonds) are redeemed by the institution or government that issued them.

redemption yield Also called yield to maturity, for bonds with a fixed ***redemption date***, the yield taking into account capital gain upon redemption plus the dividend, related to the market price of the bond.

red goods Goods, such as food, that are produced and consumed quickly.

red herring On Wall Street, an initial prospectus for a share issue, circulated before the price has been fixed and the issue has been ratified by the appropriate regulating authority.

redundancy Dismissal from employment through no fault of the employee, which in the UK entitles a full-time ex-employee to compensation ranging from half a week's pay to one-and-a-half week's pay per year of employment, depending on the age of the ex-employee (after two years service). *See also* ***dismissal***.

re-export To import goods from one country and then export them to another.

refinance credit Credit for a foreign buyer who does not wish to pay cash and who cannot obtain credit from the UK exporter, which is made available at a foreign bank in London. The deal is concluded using a sight draft (to pay the exporter) and a bill of exchange on the buyer (paid into the foreign bank).

refinancing Taking out a loan to pay back other borrowing, known as refunding in the USA. Early repayment of a debt, however, may incur a penalty.

reflation Government action that attempts to boost a country's economy. It is done by increasing the money supply, usually by reducing interest rates and taxation.

refunding Another term for ***refinancing***.

regiocentrism Exporting policy that recognizes the needs of regional markets.

regional stock exchange Smaller stock exchange that deals in shares of local companies as well as those listed on the main exchange. Only Germany and Switzerland still maintain significant regional exchanges.

regional test Test marketing of a product in a limited area, to judge its potential market share and help in deciding whether to launch it nationally.

regional trading arrangement Agreement about trade between countries in a given region, usually regarding common tariffs and free movement of labour and currency.

registered bond Bond that is registered in the name of the holder. It may be transferred to another holder only with the consent of the registered holder.

registered office Company's official "residence" as registered with Companies House in Cardiff, and the address to which legal documents have to be delivered. It need not be on the company's premises (it may, for example, be at the offices of its accountants or auditors). It is the keeping place of the company's register of members (share register, listing the names of shareholders and so on) and company seal.

registered representative US equivalent of a financial adviser who is registered with the ***Securities and Exchange Commission***. He or she passes on the client's instructions to a stockbroker, in return for a percentage of the broker's commission.

registered security Security whose holder is registered with its issuer. *See inscribed stock; registered bond*.

registered stock Alternative term for *inscribed stock*.

register of charges List of charges payable by a company on its property, such as mortgages and debentures. A copy of this list must be filed by all UK companies with Companies House in Cardiff.

register of companies List of UK companies kept at Companies House in Cardiff, detailing registered addresses and names of directors.

register of debentures List drawn up by a UK company of those people who hold *debentures*.

register of directors List drawn up by a UK company detailing the names (and former names), addresses, nationalities, dates of birth and business occupations of its directors. Any other existing or previous directorships held must also be listed. A copy has to filed with the *Registrar of Companies*.

register of members Also called share register, a list of a UK company's shareholders (names and addresses) and their holdings, kept at the company's registered office.

registrar Person who keeps a register. In business finance the registrar is the company or person who keeps the register of members (share register).

Registrar of Companies Person who keeps a record at Companies House in Cardiff of all UK joint-stock companies. The registrar also holds their *memorandums of association* and copies of the annual report and accounts.

regressive tax Tax that is levied as a smaller proportion of income the greater the income is. Even a fixed tax (such as the duty of petrol) can effectively be regressive because it represents a smaller proportion of a high-income earner's spending than that of a low-income earner.

regulated loan Loan of £15,000 or less, regulated by the UK *Consumer Credit Act 1974*, that is not exempt under the 1974 *Finance Act* (which exempted loans for the alteration, improvement, purchase or repair of a private dwelling).

Regulation Q US Federal Reserve rule that sets a ceiling on banks' rates of interest paid to depositors.

reinvoicing Way of reducing a tax bill used by a domestic company that also has an offshore subsidiary. Goods are imported by the subsidiary, which then reinvoices them to the parent company at a higher price (increasing the offshore company's profits and reducing the domestic company's tax liability). The profit can then be returned to the domestic company as a tax-free loan.

REIT Abbreviation of ***real-estate investment trust***.

relative strength Measure of an individual share's performance compared with the market as a whole.

remitting bank Also called collecting bank, a bank that accepts a ***bill of exchange*** (such as a cheque) for credit of an account.

remuneration Pay, such as a salary or a fee for professional services.

remuneration committee Committee of non-executive directors that decides a company's policy on the payment of executive directors, as recommended by the Greenbury Report.

rendement French for ***profit*** or ***yield***.

Rendite German for ***profit*** or ***yield***.

rendu Form of contract by which an exporter pays to have goods delivered to a buyer's warehouse. It is also known as a franco or free contract.

rent Money paid for the occupation or use of something for a period of time (such as a building, factory, office, car or television set). *See also* ***lease***.

rent back To sell property (offices, factory space, etc.) on the understanding that the new owner will lease back the property to its original owner. It is a way of raising capital by realizing property assets without having to vacate the premises.

Rentenanleihe German for a ***government bond***.

renunciation Act of giving up rights to a rights issue of new shares (and assigning them to somebody else).

repackaging Dividing a security into different parts and selling them as separate financial instruments (such as repayment of principal and payment of interest).

repatriation Act of transferring capital from overseas to the home market.

repayment supplement Payment of interest on overpaid tax (by the *Inland Revenue*).

RPI Abbreviation of ***retail price index***.

replacement cost For a given asset, the current market price of another similar asset.

replevin In a case of distraint, the return of goods to their owner while the court is deciding whether the restraint was lawful.

REPO Abbreviation of repossession, or of ***repurchase agreement***.

reporting dealer Official US term for a ***primary dealer***.

repudiation Act of informing the other party in a contract that one does not intent to honour the contract. The term may also refer to the repayment of a debt, or to the termination of any form of agreement.

repurchase Situation that occurs when an issuer buys its own securities. It is most frequent in unit trust holdings.

repurchase agreement (REPO) Transaction between a bond dealer and a bank. The dealer sells government securities while at the same time agreeing to buy them back at a specified time at a price high enough to allow the bank a profit margin. In this way, the repro may be looked upon as a form of loan.

reputed owner Person who acts as the owner of a property, even if he or she is not. If the reputed owner becomes bankrupt, the property is divided among the creditors.

resale price maintenance Practice whereby a supplier refuses to sell goods to a retailer unless the retailer agrees to sell them at a certain price, or above a minimum price. Resale price maintenance may be applied to prevent retailers from using the product as a loss leader. In the UK, resale price maintenance is allowable under the Resale Prices Act 1976 if the supplier can prove that it is in the interests of the consumer, as in the case of books and some pharmaceuticals.

resale price method Method officially allowed in the USA in determining an arm's length transaction, which takes the price received by the reseller less a suitable mark-up.

rescheduling debts Method used by a company or even a country with financial problems, in which existing loans are converted into others with a more remote repayment date (or instalment dates), sometimes insisted on by the lender and backed by a third-party guarantee.

rescission Cancellation of a contract and restoration of both parties to their original positions, usually because of misrepresentation on the part of one of them.

research and development (R and D) Activity that aims to discover or invent new products or services. It covers pure scientific and technical research, applied research, product improvement and technological innovation.

reserve Part of a company's undistributed capital (excluding share capital) resulting from retained profits or the issue of shares at above nominal value.

reserve accounting Allowable transfer of items into reserves without their having passed through the profit and loss account (perhaps because of prior-period adjustments).

reserve capital Also termed reserve liability, a part of a company's capital deemed not capable of being called up unless the company is wound up.

reserve currency Foreign currency held by a central bank in order to fund foreign trade.

reserve for bad debts Money put aside by a company against the possibility of unpaid debts (i.e., bad or doubtful debts).

reserve for obsolescence Money put aside to cushion a company against the possibility of its ***fixed assets*** becoming obsolescent or uneconomic.

reserve liability Alternative term for ***reserve capital***.

reserve price Minimum price for shares sold by tender. It is also a general term for the lowest price at which somebody is prepared to sell something or accept a bid at auction.

reserves *See* ***reserve***.

reserves market Method by means of which the US Federal Reserve implements its monetary policy, through the transactions of its open markets desk with dealers and brokers in instruments that comprise the reserves of the banking system.

residual cash Cash remaining at the end of a company's trading period or an order's trading cycle.

residual income (RI) Also called residual return, the net income generated by a subsidiary company or division after having paid a percentage return for the book value of the assets it controls.

residual interest Owners' equity in a company's assets after deduction of liabilities and any other higher priority claims.

residual return Alternative term for ***residual income***.

resolution of members When a motion put before a meeting of a company's shareholders is agreed upon, it becomes a resolution.

rest day Method of paying employees in which pay is for a seven-day period, including one or two designated rest days.

resting order Alternative term for an order ***good-till-cancelled (GTC)***.

restitution Either the giving back of something to somebody, or a compensatory payment.

restrictive business practice *See* ***restrictive practice***.

restrictive covenant Term in a contract that restricts one party from doing something during or after the term of the contract (such as a non-competition clause in a contract of employment).

restrictive endorsement Endorsement on a ***bill of exchange*** that limits the power of the endorsee to negotiate the bill.

restrictive practice Agreement made between two companies that aims to make restrictions regarding the supply of their goods or services, on such things as price, quantities, processes, geographical area, and so on. On the whole, restrictive practices are assumed by the law to be against the general public interest.

Restrictive Practices Court UK court established in 1956 to apply the Restrictive Trade Practices Act 1956 to trade agreements. From 1964 it was also responsible for applying the restrictive trade practice provisions of the Resale Prices Act 1964.

restructuring Usually voluntary rearrangement of a company's capital and financial structure. It may also involve changes to the management and workforce (sometimes resulting in redundancies). *See also* ***rescheduling debts***.

retail Sale of goods or services to the general public, or describing the sector of the service industries that is concerned with selling (also called the retail trade).

retailer Shop or store that sells goods to the general public.

retail margin Profit that a retailer makes on each item sold, generally expressed as a percentage. It takes no account of overhead costs (i.e. it is the gross margin).

retail price Price at which goods or services are actually sold through a retailer (higher than the wholesale price because of the retailer's mark-up).

retail price index (RPI) Analysis of trends in retail prices, expressed as an index number and used to evaluate changes in retail prices with reference to inflation (and thus a measure of the cost of living). It is usually related to a basket of particular goods and services. In the USA it is called the consumer price index (CPI).

retail selling price (RSP) Same as ***retail price***.

retail trade *See* ***retail***.

retained earnings That part of a company's post-tax earnings not distributed to shareholders, and thus retained by the company to finance its day-to-day activities and any future expansion. Retained earnings are added to ***reserves*** and thus appear on the company's balance sheet. They are also called retentions, retained income, retained profits or ploughed-back profits.

retained income Alternative term for ***retained earnings***.

retained profits Alternative term for ***retained earnings***.

retention money Part of a contracted price for a job kept back on completion of the work in case there is any faulty workmanship to be remedied.

retentions Alternative term for ***retained earnings***.

retiring a bill Withdrawing a bill from circulation by having the acceptor pay it, either on or before the due date.

return Profit and income from transactions or investments. The term is also used for a document (usually describing a financial situation) sent to an authority, such as a tax return.

returned without action (RWA) Description applied to an export licence application that is incomplete or in respect of a product that cannot be granted a general licence.

return load Load sought by a carrier who has to carry goods to a particular place (rather than return with an empty vehicle).

return on assets (ROA) Revenue that results from employing (fixed) assets, a measure of how well a company is using them.

return on capital (ROC) Also called return on capital employed (ROCE), a measure of how well a company's capital is used, equal to 100 times the trading profit (before tax and interest) divided by the average capital employed.

return on equity (ROE) Measure of a company's performance equal to 100 times its pre-tax profit divided by the shareholders' funds (share capital and reserves).

return on investment (ROI) Mainly USA term for ***return on capital employed (ROC)*** or ***return on equity (ROE)***.

return on sales (ROS) Measure of a company's performance equal to 100 times its pre-tax profit divided by the number of units sold.

revaluation Practice by means of which a company puts a new value on its ***fixed assets***, because nominal values and real values of such assets as property and machines have changed significantly.

revaluation account Account in which historical values and current values (revaluations) of assets and liabilities are recorded after a partner enters or leaves a partnership. The resulting profit or loss is shared among the partners (in the profit-sharing ratio).

revaluation method Method of calculating depreciation on a fixed asset. The asset is revalued annually, and any loss written off as depreciation (charged against the profit and loss account).

revaluation of assets *See* ***revaluation***.

revaluation reserve Reserve fund raised by a company by revaluing assets (at market price or replacement cost). Funds can also be raised by issuing shares at a premium above their par value.

revenue Money received from any transaction or sale (including interest on investments); income. *The* Revenue is short for ***Inland Revenue***.

revenue account Accounts of a business that state the amount of money received from sales, commissions, and so on.

revenue expenditure Expense written off to the profit and loss account in the period in which it occurs, as opposed to ***capital expenditure*** (to acquire an asset or pay a liability).

revenue spending All company spending except for that on fixed assets.

reversal Change in the fortunes of a company and/or its shares (from being profitable to being unprofitable, or vice versa).

reverse arbitrage Paying off a bank loan by borrowing from the money market.

reverse auction Method used to reduce the number of bonds at issue by the issuer inviting holders to offer prices at which they may be bought back.

reverse imports Products of an overseas subsidiary that are exported to the parent company in the home country.

reverse monetization Theory that the US Federal Reserve will restrict bank reserves in times of large federal deficits.

reverse repo Similar transaction to a ***repurchase agreement (REPO)*** in which the dealer buys the bonds instead of selling them, so that in essence they are a security on bank loan.

reverse take-over Purchase of control of a public company by a smaller, private company. This is often done in order that the private company may obtain a listing on a stock exchange.

reverse yield gap Situation in which low-risk assets provide greater returns than high-risk assets.

reversion Return of property, goods or rights to their original owner; or the difference between the amount owing on a mortgage and the market value of the property (i.e. the equity in the property).

revocable credit Credit facility extended by a banker who is willing to take ***bills of exchange***, but ones that are revocable (i.e. repayable) at any time.

revolver US term for ***revolving credit***.

revolving credit Lending made by a bank that is automatically renewed at the start of each period (or as soon as the sum is repaid). For example, a bank may arrange to lend a company a certain amount each month. It will stop any borrowing above that limit once it is reached, but allow borrowing to go on at the start of the next month. The US term for this arrangement is revolver.

reward packaging Method of presenting goods and other products to a potential purchaser so that the most desirable elements are evident immediately, from the best fruit at the top of a box in retailing to the best-selling (and most profitable) product in a financial proposal.

rework Extra cost incurred (materials and labour) in correcting defects in a product, especially on a production line.

RIE Abbreviation of ***recognized investment exchange***.

rigging the market Action that influences a market, by overriding market forces. For example, it may be done by one dealer buying a substantial number of shares or a significant quantity of a commodity, thus pushing up the market.

right of resale Right of a seller, in certain circumstances, to reclaim goods from a buyer and resell them, for example if a stoppage in transaction or a lien occurs and the goods are likely to perish as a consequence. In this case, the seller may sell to another buyer and give a lawful title to the goods.

rights issue Practice of offering existing shareholders the opportunity to buy more shares (i.e. subscribe more capital), in order that a company may raise additional capital. Rights issues act as a protection for the shareholder, in that the total number of shares issued increases without decreasing the percentage holding of each shareholder.

ring In general, a group of people who get together in order to illegally rig the market, for example by acting in concert to push prices up or down. A ring is also a method of trading on the London futures market or metals exchange (*see* ***ring trading***).

ring trading Trading in commodities when dealers assemble around a ring, calling out their bids and offers. It is thus a type of outcry market.

risk Amount a buyer or seller potentially stands to lose by a transaction. There are various identifiable risks in financial trading, including ***credit risk***, ***exchange rate*** risk, ***interest rate*** risk and ***political risk***. People who do not (want to) take risks are described as risk-averse.

risk arbitrage Practice of buying in to a ***take-over bid*** in the expectation that share prices will rise.

risk-averse *See* ***risk***.

risk capital Capital invested long-term in a company, or security, that presents a risk (i.e. the possibility of a loss or, indeed, a gain). The term is also used as an alternative to ***venture capital***.

risk management Measures adopted to minimize financial risk (for example through insurance, hedging or spreading the risk).

risk premium In the currency markets, the difference between the forward exchange rate and the expected future spot rate.

risk reversal Combination of selling a call option and simultaneously buying a put option, to minimize potential loss.

ROA Abbreviation of ***return on assets***.

ROC Abbreviation of ***return on capital***.

rocket scientist Colloquial name for a mathematician who uses statistical methods (and computers) to analyse financial markets.

ROE Abbreviation of ***return on equity***.

ROI *See* ***return on investment***.

rolled-up coupon Coupon (representing the interest payment on a security or other financial instrument) that is reinvested in the instrument rather than being passed to the holder.

rolling over Practice of carrying over debts into the future rather than paying them at the due date, by arrangement with the lender (usually for an additional fee).

rolling settlement system Method of paying for shares (purchased on a stock exchange) a pre-set number of days after the deal. It has been suggested as an alternative to the ***account*** system on the ***London Stock Exchange***.

roll-over Movement of an investment from one institution to the owner of another institution; or the transfer of a derivative from one delivery month to another.

roll-over certificate of deposit (CD) Method of splitting a certificate of deposit's maturity period into shorter-term periods, for which other CDs are issued.

roll-over relief Reduction in ***capital gains tax*** on the sale of a company's fixed assets if it is buying other assets in order to replace the first ones, a form of deferred taxation.

roll-up fund Offshore investment that reinvests interest so that it becomes part of the capital, thus providing potential tax advantages.

Roosa bonds Bonds that were issued by the US Treasury in the early 1960s. They were denominated in currencies other than US dollars and held as non-marketable securities by central banks (to help to finance the federal deficit).

ro-ro ship Short for roll-on/roll-off ship, on which cargo loaded in lorries can be driven on and off a ramp or ramps at the bows and/or stern.

ROS Abbreviation of ***return on sales***.

rotation of directors Process whereby at each ***annual general meeting (AGM)*** of a public company, a certain number of the directors retire (normally one-third), although they may then be immediately re-elected to the board. This enables shareholders to change a director without having to dismiss him or her.

round lot Number of (possibly mixed) shares or bonds traded at the same time, as a lot. The commission charged on a round lot is generally slightly less than on an ***odd lot***.

round tripping On a futures market, the practice of buying and then selling the same investment, or vice versa. The term is also used to describe the practice of a creditworthy company that borrows money using a bank overdraft and then lends it on the money market at a profit.

round turn Entire futures transaction from start to finish.

round-up stage Time at the US Federal Open Market Committee's monthly meeting at which each of the 19 members is asked for comments.

Royal Commission Formally, a body set up in the UK by royal warrant to investigate and report on a matter of public importance. In practice, it is usually set up by the government to look at an area that might be affected by proposed legislation.

Royal Mint UK government department, located in Llantrisant in Wales, with the sole responsibility for the minting of coins and printing of banknotes, under the control of the Chancellor of the Exchequer. It also makes medals, and money for other countries. The US equivalent is the Bureau of the Mint.

RPB Abbreviation of ***recognized professional body***.

RRP Abbreviation of ***recommended retail price***.

RSP Abbreviation of retail selling price. *See* ***selling price***.

Rule 415 issue *See* ***shelf registration***.

Rule 535 London Stock Exchange rule concerned with permitted dealings. Clause (i) lists the items that can be dealt. Clause (ii) permits

R

dealings in shares not listed, but with certain restrictions. Clauses (iii) and (iv) apply to overseas companies and exploration companies, respectively.

run Panic rush to withdraw money from a bank or sell currency or shares, because investors fear that there is to be a sudden significant fall in their value.

running ahead Personal trading in a share by a broker immediately before following a client's instructions to do the same. It is illegal in the USA.

running broker Somebody who acts as an intermediary between those who issue bills and the discount houses.

running days Number of consecutive ***lay days*** including weekends and public holidays.

running margin Difference in rates of interest on money borrowed and on the same money invested.

running yield Alternative term for ***flat yield***.

run to settlement Describing the sale contract for a commodity that has run to the date when physical delivery is due.

Russell 2000 New York Stock Exchange share price index of smaller companies.

RWA Abbreviation of ***returned without action***.

S

SA Abbreviation of *Sociedad Anónima* and *Société Anonyme*.

safe haven currency National currency that is secure politically.

safety margin Difference between demand for a product and its maker's break-even level of output.

saitori Intermediary on the Japanese Stock Exchange who deals only with members.

safe investment Investment certain to yield the expected return.

salary Money paid to an employee, normally expressed as so much per year (per annum, p.a.), but usually paid monthly by cheque or directly into the employee's bank account.

sale Formally, the act of transferring goods or services from one person to another, accompanied by the exchange of money (the price).

sale and leaseback Sale of property where the buyer agrees to lease the property back to its former owner. In this way, the seller is able to turn the property into liquid capital while at the same time remaining *in situ*.

Sale of Goods Act 1979 UK legislation that defines the contractual arrangements involved in buying goods. Among other things it requires that the goods should be of merchantable quality and fit for their stated purpose. Further regulations were incorporated in the Supply of Goods (Implied Terms) Act 1973.

sale or return Arrangement whereby a distributor or retailer takes goods from a manufacturer or wholesaler on the understanding that he or she may return them if they are not sold within a specified period of time.

sales Colloquial name for the department within a company that deals with the sale of its goods or services. Alternatively, the term can be short for sales revenue, synonymous with turnover, as represented on a company's profit and loss account (especially in the USA).

sales account Document presented to a consignor when goods are sent to a foreign country for sale through an agent. The agent submits to the consignor an account of the sales made, along with details of the agent's commission, expenses and final net profit on the sale.

sales audit Method of calculating the state of a retail trade, by comparing the throughput of money against stock.

sales commission Money paid to sales staff (in addition to any basic salary), usually based on a percentage of the value of sales.

sales conference Meeting at which a company's sales staff are told about new products and their promotion (and thereby motivated to sell them).

sales documents Documents relating to the fulfilment of customers' orders, including an order, delivery note and invoice.

sales drive Effort to improve sales and create demand for a product. Techniques include reducing prices, increasing the sales force or its commission, providing free samples and distributing point-of-sale advertising material.

sales force Alternative name for a company's sales staff.

sales promotion Use of incentives to get people to buy a product. *See sales drive.*

sales representative Alternative name for a salesman or woman or, more formally, an agent responsible for the distribution, servicing and selling of goods on behalf of an overseas seller.

salinating Usually illegal method of hiding a company's assets overseas, to evade taxation.

sample Product, or part of a product, that is sent or given to a prospective purchaser so that he or she can judge whether or not to buy.

samurai bond Bond denominated in yen and issued by a non-Japanese company in Japan.

sanction Type of embargo in which a country or group of countries refuse to trade with another country that is violating international law or endangering peace and security.

sandbag Defensive tactics for a take-over bid in which the target company agrees to negotiate a take-over, but lengthens the talks in the hope that a ***white knight*** might ride by in the meantime.

S and L Abbreviation of ***savings and loan association***.

S & P 500 *See* ***Standard and Poor's 500***.

sans recours *See* ***without recourse***.

SAP Abbreviation of ***Structrural Adjustment Programme***.

SàRL Abbreviation of ***Société à Responsibilité Limitée***.

savings and loan association (S & L) US equivalent of a UK building society in which people invest personal savings and often earn interest. Often notice of withdrawal must be given.

savings bonds US government bonds issued at a discount to their par value, which is their maturity value. They provide a capital gain and interest on maturity.

SBIC Abbreviation of ***small business investment company***.

scale of production Measure of the level of a company's output, generally compared with the usual trend or with its competitors.

Schatzbrief German for ***savings bond***.

Schatzschein German for ***Treasury bill***.

Scheduled Territories Also known as the Sterling Area, pre-1979 term for areas where sterling was the official currency (and so there were no exchange control restrictions). In the end it consisted only of Great Britain, the Channel Islands and the Isle of Man.

Schlusskurs German for ***closing price***.

SCM Abbreviation of ***smaller companies market***.

scorched earth Defensive tactics for a hostile take-over bid in which the target company sells its most attractive assets, or initiates adverse publicity about itself in an effort to make it seem a less desirable acquisition.

SCOUT Abbreviation of ***shared currency option under tender***.

scrip issue Also called bonus issue or capitalization issue, extra shares issued to existing shareholders free of charge. It is done by transferring reserves into the company's share account. In this way, the company increases its capitalization while at the same time reducing its share price and increasing the number of shares on the market.

SD Abbreviation of ***standard deviation***.

SDRs Abbreviation of ***special drawing rights***.

SEAF Abbreviation of ***Stock Exchange Automatic Execution Facility.***

seal Metal design impressed on melted wax on or over the join of a flap on a document. Every company has to have a common seal, used on certain documents, with its use recorded in a seal book.

SEAQ Abbreviation of ***Stock Exchange Automated Quotations System***.

seasonal adjustment Method of removing (often misleading) seasonal variations from data in order to expose the underlying trend.

seasonal unemployment Unemployment caused by seasonal fall-off in demand for workers because of the nature of the occupation (for example, the agricultural industry needs crop pickers only at harvest time).

seat Membership of an exchange (for commodities or securities), which may be bought or sold.

SEATO Abbreviation of ***Southeast Asia Treaty Organization***.

SEATS Abbreviation of ***Stock Exchange Alternative Trading Service***. *See also* ***Australian Stock Exchange***.

SEC Abbreviation of ***Securities and Exchange Commission***.

secondary boycott Boycotting of a company because it has had dealings with another company that is already boycotted.

secondary market Market in securities that have been listed for some time, rather than in new issues. Secondary market trading occurs on a stock exchange.

secondary picketing Illegal setting up of a picket line at a place other than that at which the industrial action originated. *See* ***picketing***.

secondary production Production of goods that have been manufactured, as opposed to the production of raw materials or foodstuffs.

second marché The second-tier Belgian or French unlisted securities market.

second mortgage Remortgage on a property that is already mortgaged. The inevitable high risk (because the first mortgagee holds the security) results in high interest rates, and a second mortgage may not be granted unless the property has sufficient value to act as security for both loans.

second-tier market Market for shares in companies that do not have a listing in the main market (i.e. an ***unlisted securities market***).

S

second via Second (duplicate) document in a ***bill of exchange*** in a set, which is sent by a different route to insure against loss.

secret profit Undisclosed profit made because of a working relationship with somebody else (such as an agent or partner acting on his or her own account, or a director who places business with another company in which he or she has an interest). The activity is usually in breach of a contract and may result in a legal claim for damages.

secret reserve Alternative term for ***hidden reserve***.

sectorial privatization Transfer of a business in a particular industry from state ownership to private ownership. *See* ***privatization***.

sectorial reciprocity Lessening of import restrictions in a particular industrial sector in exchange for similar concessions from another country.

secured creditor Creditor (such as a bank) that has a legal charge on one of the debtor's assets.

secured liability Debt in which the lender is safeguarded because the borrower has put up sufficient assets as security in the event of non-payment.

secured loan Loan secured by specified assets that revert to the lender if the loan is not repaid. It generally attracts lower interest than an unsecured loan.

securities *See* ***security***.

Securities and Exchange Commission (SEC) Government organization founded in 1934 that regulates the securities market (brokers and stock exchanges) in the USA. It also controls auditing practices and the financial reporting of companies.

Securities and Futures Authority (SFA) Self-regulatory organization (SRO) established in the UK in 1991 to regulate the conduct of people who deal in debentures, futures, options and shares. It was formed by combining the functions of The Securities Association (TSA) and the ***Association of Futures Brokers and Dealers (AFBD)***.

Securities and Investments Board (SIB) UK financial watchdog, set up in 1986 by the Department of Trade and Industry to oversee the UK's deregulated financial markets. The US equivalent is the ***Securities and Exchange Commission (SEC)***.

Securities Association, The (TSA) Former UK self-regulatory organization, established in 1986, for dealing in securities. It was formed from the London Stock Exchange and the International Securitues Regulatory Organization (ISRO), and in 1991 merged with the Association of Futures Brokers and Dealers (AFBD) to form the ***Securities and Futures Authority (SFA)***.

Securities Exchange Act 1934 UK legislation that seeks to outlaw misrepresentation, manipulation and other abusive practices in securities markets and to establish and maintain "just and equitable principles of trade which would be conducive to open, fair and orderly markets".

Securities Investor Protection Corporation (SIPC) US compensation scheme for investors should there be a failure of dealers or market-makers.

securitization Tendency of companies to use security markets to raise finance rather than the more traditional financial intermediaries such as banks.

securitized paper Financial instrument created by converting a bank loan into a negotiable security.

security Anything (usually property) pledged as collateral against a loan, or the document that sets out the terms of such collateral. A security is also any financial instrument that is traded on a stock exchange and that yields an income. It represents a loan that will be repaid at some time in the future. Such securities include bills of exchange, bonds, debentures, gilt-edged securities, options, shares, stocks and unit trusts (but not insurance policies).

seedcorn capital Minimum capital needed to start a new business. *See* ***front money; venture capital***.

seed money Alternative term for ***front money***.

segundo mercado Also called *bolsa secundaria*, the Spanish ***unlisted securities market***.

seignorage Difference between the face value of a coin and the value of the metal it contains.

self-assessment Scheme introduced in 1996 (for the year to 5 April 1997) by the UK ***Inland Revenue*** that makes a taxpayer responsible for calculating his or her own liability for income tax. The calculation can, however, be delegated to the Revenue. After 1 July 1999 a similar scheme was introduced for companies.

self-employment Being in business on one's own account. The self-employed include those who run their businesses, either alone or in partnership, and professional people such as doctors and lawyers.

self-liquidating asset Asset that has a predetermined lifetime and liquidates itself at the end of that period. For example, in the investment trust sector, a closed-end fund with a stock exchange listing is self-liquidating.

self-liquidator Sales promotion that produces enough revenue to pay for itself (such as an item in exchange for cash plus two packet tops; the customer makes two purchases, and the item's cost is covered by the cash payment).

self-regulatory organization (SRO) Sometimes called a self-regulating organization, a non-governmental organization in the UK, set up under the ***Financial Services Act 1986***, that governs a particular area of business activity, laying down codes of practice and protecting consumers and investors. There have been various mergers among the original SROs until there are currently four: the ***Financial Intermediaries, Managers and Brokers Regulatory Organization (FIMBRA)***, the ***Investment Management Regulatory Organization (IMRO)***, the ***Life Assurance and Unit Trust Regulatory Organization (LAUTRO)*** and the ***Securities and Futures Authority (SFA)***.

sell at best Instruction to a broker to sell shares or commodities at the best price possible. I.e., if the broker is selling , he or she must find the highest selling price; or if buying, the lowest price.

sellers' market Market that is more favourable to sellers than to buyers. Such a market often arises when demand is greater than supply.

seller's option On the New York Stock Exchange, an option that enables the seller to deliver the relevant security at any time within a period of 6-60 days.

sellers over Market condition on a stock exchange where there are more sellers than buyers.

selling cost Extra expenditure required to increase sales of a product.

selling, general, and administrative (SGA) expenses Total cost of these activities: direct selling costs (e.g. advertising, warranties), indirect selling costs (e.g. postal charges, telephone charges) and general and administrative costs (e.g. costs of heat, light, rent and non-sales personnel).

selling out If a person who agrees to buy shares cannot close the deal, the seller is entitled to sell the shares for the best price possible and then charge the person who made the original tender the difference between the selling price and the original tender price, plus any costs.

selling price Broadly, the cash price a buyer must pay for securities, goods or services.

selling short Practice of making a bargain to sell securities or commodities the seller does not own. The seller does this in the hope that before settlement is due, the price of the item will fall and he or she will be able to buy enough to cover the bargain at the lower price, thereby making a profit. It is also known as shorting or short selling.

sell-side People who are on the market to sell, rather than to buy.

semi-fixed costs Also termed stepped costs, costs that increase step-wise with increasing activity. For example, an extra member of staff may be required each time production exceeds a certain level, and the labour cost on that job becomes a semi-fixed cost.

semiprivatization State-owned parts of a specific industry transferred to private ownership.

semi-variable costs Costs that increase in a linear manner, over and above an initial fixed cost, with increasing activity. Thus the fixed cost remains even when activity is zero.

senior debt Oldest existing debt owed by a person or company, hence the debt that should be paid first in normal circumstances.

separate legal entity Once a business becomes incorporated as a limited company, it is legally separated from its owners (shareholders). Thereafter the company is liable (e.g. for its debts), not the owners.

separate trading of registered interest and principal of securities (STRIPS) Separating a bond into its capital and its coupons. The capital can then be traded as a zero-coupon bond and the coupons as interest-only securities.

sequestration Act of seizure of property or other assets by the courts until a dispute has been settled.

series Call or put options on the same underlying financial instrument with the same striking price and maturity.

service Something provided, usually for a fee, that may not be classed as manufacturing or production in any form (such as legal advice, brokerage, agency services and financial advice).

service charge Extra charge added to a bill to pay for the service element (as in a restaurant), supposedly instead of expecting the customer to pay a (voluntary) ***gratuity***.

service contract Contract of employment for senior managers and directors of a company.

service industry Businesses engaged in the service, or tertiary sector, of an economy, such as a bank, shop or restaurant.

servicing a debt/loan Paying interest on a debt/loan.

SES Abbreviation of ***Singapore Stock Exchange***.

set of bills Alternative term for bills in a set, foreign bills of exchange made out in triplicate and sent to the drawee separately to insure against loss. The copies are known as a set of bills.

set-off Two parties that have an indebtedness to each other may set off both debts against each other by assuming that one debt has paid off the other and *vice versa*. Such an arrangement is termed a set-off.

SETS Abbreviation of ***Stock Exchange Electronic Trading Service***.

settlement Act of paying in full for goods or services received, or of repaying a debt or loan.

settlement date Alternative term for ***account day***.

settlement day Alternative term for ***account day***.

settlement discount Discount offered for early or prompt settlement of an account.

settlement price Alternative term for ***official price*** on the London Metal Exchange.

settlement risk Risk in securities trading that after one party to a deal delivers securities or pays cash the other side delays payment or delivery.

seven-day money Funds that have been invested in the money market for seven days.

sever To terminate a contract, especially a contract of employment. *See* **severance pay**.

severance pay Sum of money paid to an employee when he or she is made redundant.

Sex Discrimination Act 1975 UK legislation that banning discrimination (against either sex) in relation to employment, including recruitment, appointment, terms and conditions, training and promotion.

Sex Discrimination Act 1986 UK legislation that established a common age of retirement for women and men (in 1993 fixed as age 65).

SFA Abbreviation of ***Securities and Futures Authority***.

SFS Abbreviation of ***Summary Financial Statements (SFS)***.

SGA Abbreviation of ***selling, general and administrative expenses***.

shadow director Person who, although not named as a company's director, nevertheless gives directions and instructions that are acted upon.

shakeout When a market cannot support the number of suppliers it has attracted, many of the less profitable suppliers leave the market, with only the more healthy operators remaining. In the USA, this process of "natural selection" is known as a shakeout.

share broker Broker who charges commission on each share, rather than on a total transaction.

share *See* ***shares***.

share capital Capital raised by a company through an issue of shares. *See also* ***authorized capital; issued share capital; uncalled capital.***

share certificate Document that proves a person's ownership of a company's shares.

shared currency option under tender (SCOUT) In situations where a foreign currency contract is under tender from several companies, SCOUT allows them to share a single hedge in the form of a currency option.

share exchange Alternative term for ***stock exchange***.

share exchange scheme Arrangement by which investors can use an existing portfolio of shares (instead of cash) as an investment in an investment trust or unit trust.

shareholder Person who holds shares in a company (and is thereby one of its owners).

shareholder derivative suit Legal action taken in the USA by a shareholder or group of shareholders against the directors of a company for mismanagement or breaches of responsibility.

shareholder relations Department within a US company, rather like customer relations, that concentrates on keeping shareholders up-to-date with company performance, and so on.

shareholders' equity Equity in a company held by shareholders rather than by the company itself.

shareholders' funds Share capital and accumulated profits (reserves) that are owed by a company to its shareholders.

shareholders' rights Legal rights of ordinary shareholders in a company (such as the right to attend the annual general meeting, to take part in a vote of confidence in the chairman and to vote on the appointment of new directors, and the right to receive a copy of the company's annual report).

shareholder value Principle that all management decisions should be aimed at maximizing shareholders' equity in a company (such as disposing of unwanted subsidiaries).

share index Index that shows the average change in value of a number of individual shares. Share indexes therefore give an overall guide to movements in the financial markets. Examples include the ***Financial Times Stock Exchange 100 Index (Footsie)***, the Nikkei-Dow Average and the Dow Jones Industrial Average.

share issue Method of raising capital used by a limited company, which may issues shares value at a fraction of the company's total value. The shares are generally placed on the market by a stockbroker acting on behalf of the company in question and may, in most cases, be purchased by financial institutions, other companies and members of the public.

share option UK scheme that gives employees the option to buy shares in their company at attractive prices (normally well below market price) at a specific future date. It therefore constitutes a type of profit-sharing scheme.

share perk Benefit granted by a company to its shareholders (such as discounts off the price of its products).

share premium On a new issue of shares, a premium charged on the nominal value of the shares if it seems that the real value is likely to be much higher.

share pushing *See* ***Prevention of Fraud (Investments) Act 1939***.

share register Also known as register of members, a register of shareholders that is held by a company (and viewable at its registered office), giving names, addresses, details of shareholding, and so on.

shares Forms of security that represent a shareholder's stake in a company. Income on shares is in the form of a dividend rather than interest, and is declared depending on the company's financial performance over a year. In the USA shares are known as common stock.

share shop In the UK, a government-appointed bank, building society or stockbroker that deals with shares in a newly privatized industry. For the duration of the public share offer, share shops sell shares directly to the public without a commission charge (which the government pays to the shop).

shares in trust Shares held in trust for somebody else are generally registered in the name of the trustees.

shares issued at a discount In the UK, shares cannot be issued at a discount under the terms of the Companies Act 1980 (which in this respect superseded the provisions of the Companies Act 1948).

share split If the market price of a share is thought to be too high, a company may decide to issue extra shares to its shareholders (known as a ***bonus issue***), increasing the number of shares on the market and thus decreasing the price of each share. The process is known as a share split.

share transfer Formal transfer of the right of ownership of a share when it is sold or otherwise disposed of. It is done by sending a completed transfer form and the share certificate to the registered office of the company concerned, which then amends its share register.

share warrant Certificate of ownership of shares, presented after shares are fully paid. It does not include the shareholder's name and so ownership can be transferred to somebody else by giving him or her the warrant.

shark Informal term for a person or company that may be preparing to make a take-over bid.

shark repellent Informal term for defensive tactics resorted to in the event of a take-over bid.

shark watcher Informal term for a consultant who studies the buyers of a company's shares in an effort to identify potential ***sharks***.

shelf registration System whereby a large US company can file details of all planned security issues (undated) with the ***Securities and Exchange Commission (SEC)***, and when they want to make an issue to raise capital they can do it "off the shelf" without waiting for clearance from the SEC. The relevant SEC rule is Rule 415, and for this reason such issues are also sometimes known as Rule 415 issues.

shell company Company that does not produce anything in the usual sense, but exists only in name. Shell companies may be set up and sold to people who are unfamiliar with the procedure for doing this (for their convenience), or may be remnants of a defunct company that has been sold on to somebody else. They may also be set up for use at some future time, or to operate as the holder of shares.

shelter Investment instrument that gives little in the way of return but allows the investor to reduce income tax liabilities.

Sherman Antitrust Act One of the fundamental US ***Antitrust Laws***, the pioneer federal statute in this field (passed 2 July 1890), and a cornerstone in the legal expression of public policy against restraint of trade and monopoly or attempts to monopolize.

shift work Work at non-standard hours (such as the night shift, often 8 p.m. to 2 a.m.). Unsociable hours may be compensated for with higher rates of pay.

ship-broker Also termed shipper's agent, shipowner's agent who sells cargo space and obtains cargo for shipment.

shipment Formally, all cargo carried under one ***bill of lading***. More generally, any cargo or freight carried by land, sea or air.

shipped bill ***Bill of lading*** that proves goods have been loaded onto a ship.

shipper Person responsible for shipping goods, as named on the shipping document.

shipper's agent Alternative term for ***ship-broker***.

shipping agent General agent who deals with, among other things, the documentation concerning the import or export of goods.

shipping weight Gross weight of a cargo, including all wrappings and containers.

ship's husband Old term for a shipowner's agent who looks after a ship while it is docked.

ship's manifest List of individual shipments that make up a ship's cargo, as signed by the master of the vessel.

ship's master Captain of a merchant vessel.

ship's papers Various documents pertaining to a ship and carried on it, such as the ship's articles, its certificate of registry, ship's log and manifest.

shogun bond Bond issued on the Japanese market by a non-resident and denominated in a foreign currency (i.e. not yen).

shop assistant Person who sells goods in a shop (acting as the shop owner's agent).

shop-floor Place where shop assistants and factory workers work.

shop steward Person who is elected to represent a trade union's members in discussions with the management.

short *See* ***selling short*** and the following entries.

short bill ***Bill of exchange*** that is payable on demand or on sight, or in less than 10 days.

short bond ***Bond*** with less than five years to maturity.

short covering When a person is ***selling short***, the purchase of the security concerned in order to cover the bargain.

short credit Loan that must be repaid over a short timescale.

short-dated gilt ***Gilt-edged security*** with a redemption term of less than five years.

short-dated security Fixed-interest security that has a redemption date of less than five years.

short end That part of the market that deals with securities with relatively little time to go before payment is due. The amount of time varies from a few days up to five years, depending on which security is being traded.

short hedge Hedge against a rise in interest rates on the futures market.

shorting Alternative term for ***selling short***.

short interest Interest rate charged on loans over a period of three months or less.

short position In the position of having sold more commodities or securities than one owns. *See* ***selling short***.

shorts Alternative term for ***short-dated securities***.

short sale Sale of a security that the seller does not own, or any sale that is consummated by the delivery of a security borrowed by or for the account of the seller.

short-term Broadly, something (in the financial world, a security) with only a short time left before maturity. In the USA, short-term generally means something with less than a year to run. A US alternative is near-term.

short-term capital Capital raised for a short period (such as an overdraft), usually to cover temporary cash-flow problems.

short-term deposit Funds deposited (e.g. with a bank, building society or finance house) that can be withdrawn at short notice, usually reflected in the comparatively low interest rate paid.

short-term investment Investment for a short period. In the City, it refers to an investment for a period of days; elsewhere, the period may be up to three months. Short-term investments are usually made in return for interest rates slightly lower than those available on long-term investments.

short-termism Policy of favouring short-term investments that yield immediate profit, rather than (possibly more secure) long-term investments.

short-term monetary support (STMS) *European Monetary System (EMS)* intervention mechanism by means of which a country with balance of payments difficulties gets its central bank to borrow (for three months) from other members' central banks. An extension to the agreed term is called a rallonge.

show stopper Informal term for a court injunction initiated by the target company of a hostile take-over bid and taken against the raider, stopping it from taking action any further.

shrinkage Mainly in retailing, a euphemism for theft (of goods or stock) by employees.

shunter Broker who deals on two different exchanges (usually a provincial exchange and a main exchange) in securities that are quoted on both.

SIB Abbreviation of ***Securities and Investment Board***.

SIC Abbreviation of ***standard industrial classification***.

SICAV Abbreviation of ***Société d'invessement à capital variable***.

sight deposit Known in the USA as a demand deposit, money ***at call***; or money deposited overnight.

sight draft ***Bill of exchange*** payable on presentation (i.e. on sight).

silent partner Person who invests in an enterprise but takes no active part in its management; a ***sleeping partner***.

silver wheelchair Terms sometimes written into the service contract of a company's top management or directors, whereby the employee receives a large sum in compensation if he or she loses his or her position as a result of a take-over. If the terms are generous enough, the silver wheelchair may act as a disincentive to raiders.

simple debenture Debenture that gives the holder no guarantee that repayment will be received by a specified date. In such a case, the holder of an unsecured debenture must wait until the company has been wound up before claiming payment. For this reason, most debentures are secured against company property or financial assets. It is also known as a naked or unsecured debenture.

simple interest Rate of interest calculated by keeping interest that has already accrued separate from the capital sum. Thus, when calculating the next interest payment, the capital sum only (excluding the interest already accrued) enters the calculation. In mathematical terms, simple interest equals $Atr/100$, where A is the amount invested or borrowed, t is the time in years and r is the interest rate as a percentage per annum. *See also* ***compound interest***.

sine die Latin for indefinitely, usually relating to fixing a date for a future event.

Singapore Stock Exchange (SES) Stock exchange established in 1973 with the separation of the exchanges of Malaysia and Singapore (although the two still maintain close links). Dealing is through a computerized system.

single capacity System that formerly operated on the UK stock market, with separate functions for jobbers and stockbrokers, but ended with deregulation in October 1986. A jobber was not allowed to deal with the general public and a stockbroker could not trade in shares except through a jobber. The two functions may now be amalgamated (duel capacity) in the person of a single ***market-maker***.

single currency Objective of the ***European Monetary System (EMS)***, as defined by the 1991 Maastricht Treaty, under which a single central bank would issue currency that could be used anywhere in the EU. The target date for its implementation, 1999, has already passed.

single-currency peg Exchange rate regime in which a country pegs its currency to the US dollar or some other stable currency and makes very few adjustments to the parity.

Single European Act European legislation of 1987 that planned for the establishment of the ***single European market*** by 1 January 1993.

single European market Agreement between EU member states to eliminate trading differences between them from 1 January 1993 (i.e. with no tariffs or customs controls and common taxation). It has yet to happen in its entirety.

single market *See* ***single European market***.

single sourcing Company policy to buy from only one supplier, which may offer advantages of bulk purchase and a long-term working relationship, although there is no competitive pressure on the supplier and no back-up should supplies fail.

sinking fund Sum of money set aside for a specific purpose and invested so that it provides the required amount at the right time. The fund's earnings are liable for tax.

SIPC Abbreviation of ***Securities Investor Protection Corporation***.

SITC Abbreviation of ***standard international trade classification***.

six-month money Funds invested on the money market for six months.

skimming the market Policy of setting the price of a new product so high that only enthusiasts or trend-setters will buy it.

skinny bid Alternative term for ***thin bid***.

skip day US term for settlement of a security purchase two days after the deal.

skittish Colloquial term describing a market that is extremely volatile.

skunk costs US term for costs already ascribed to a project, which will not be clawed back if the company decides to abort the project.

slate bull Non-profit making stock that is kept for a long time.

sleeping partner Partner who invests capital in a firm but takes no active part in its management. He or she does, however, remain liable for the partnership's debts.

sliding scale Scale of charges that is based on the value of the thing upon which the charges are to be made, for example rates of income tax. *See also **ad valorem**.*

slippage Underperformance of a start-up company, which may lead to the need for additional capital.

slump Period of time during which the economy is poor, with high levels of unemployment and reduced economic activity.

small business investment company (SBIC) US company established in 1958 using low-cost funds with tax advantages from the federal government which invests in small businesses.

small cap stocks Shares in smaller companies quoted on the US stock markets (usually with a capitaliazation of less than $250 million).

small company UK company that meets various criteria and is thereby permitted to issue less detailed annual reports to shareholders and file abbreviated accounts with Companies House. Its turnover has to be less than £2.8 million, its balance-sheet total less than £1.4 million and its number of employees less than 50. If its turnover is less than £90,000 and balance-sheet total less than £1.4 million, it is exempt from a statutory audit of its accounts.

smaller companies market (SCM) Republic of Ireland's equivalent of the UK ***alternative investment market***.

small company fund Fund that puts unit trusts or other collective investments in the shares of various small companies.

small loan company US term for a ***finance house*** that provides funds for consumer credit.

smurfing Colloquial term for the practice of transferring into a single (often offshore) account many small sums of money from many different bank accounts. It may be a device for money ***laundering***.

snake Popular term for the European monetary system that links the following currencies: Belgian and French francs, Danish krone, Irish punt, Dutch guilder, German deutschmark and Italian lira. Its purpose is to control (within 2¼ %) day-to-day fluctuations in exchange rates against the US dollar.

SNC Abbreviation of ***Societa in Nome Colletivo*** and ***Société en nom Collectif***.

sobashi Japanese for speculator (the type that ***ramps***).

social chapter Part of the social charter agreed by EU member states under the terms of the Maastricht Treat (except for the UK).

social charter Raft of measures agreed by members of the EU under the terms of the Maastricht Treaty intended to harmonize social legislation throughout the Union.

social grade Method of classifying people (and by inference their families) in one of six bands according to occupation, much used in marketing. The grades are:

A top professionals and company directors

B senior managers

C1 clerical workers

C2 skilled workers

D semi-skilled or unskilled workers

E people dependent on the state

social ownership Ownership of some or all of a countries industries by the state (on behalf of society in general).

Sociedad Anónima (SA) Mexican for ***public limited company***.

Sociedad de Capitales Spanish for ***public limited company***.

Sociedad en Comandita Simple (S. en C.) Spanish for ***limited partnership***.

Sociedade de Capitais Portuguese for ***public limited company***.

Societa in Nome Collettivo (SNC) Italian for ***general partnership***.

Società per Azioni (SPA) Italian for ***public limited company***.

Société Anonyme (SA) French for ***public limited company***.

Société Anonyme de la Bourse Name of the Luxembourg Stock Exchange.

Société à Responsabilité Limitée (SRL, or SàRL) French for ***private company***.

Société d'invessement à capital variable (SICAV) French for ***unit trust***.

Société du Nouveau Marché Name of an unlisted stock market established in Paris in 1966 (dealing mainly in high-growth hi-tech stocks).

Société en Commandité Simple French for ***limited partnership***.

Société en Nom Collectif (SNC) French for ***general partnership***.

socks and stocks Because US Federal Reserve regulations do not permit branch banking, some US banks (popularly known as socks and stocks) have been set up to deal with either current account facilities or commercial lending, but not both.

SOFFEX Abbreviation of ***Swiss Options and Financial Futures Exchange***.

soft arbitrage Movement of funds between the money market and bank deposits to benefit from the difference in interest rates.

soft commodity Also called softs, any commodity other than metals (though usually applied to agricultural products).

soft currency Currency of which there is a surplus on the market and which is therefore relatively cheap.

soft dollars Dollars traded on the foreign exchange markets for which demand is persistently low because of a US trade deficit. The value of soft dollars tends to fall.

soft goods Goods made from textiles, or the textiles themselves.

soft loan Loan that carries an unusually low rate of interest, often advanced as a form of foreign aid.

softs Popular name for traded commodities other than metals (e.g. foodstuffs).

sola ***Bill of exchange*** that does not have a duplicate as in bills of a set.

sold contract note Alternative term for a ***sold note***.

sold note Document sent by a broker to his or her client, confirming that a sale has been made. It is also known as a sold contract note.

sold short *See **short position***.

sole agency Agreement by which one party (the agent) represents a principle either in a certain capacity or in a particular geographical area.

sole proprietorship Non-company business owned by one person (i.e. not limited for liability).

sole trader Person who trades on his or her own behalf and has not registered as a business. In the financial world, a sole trader is somebody who is involved in buying and selling securities short-term, for his or her own account; or it is somebody who specializes in buying and selling securities on behalf of a broker or dealer, usually working as an employee; or it is a person who buys and sells contracts in financial futures without a hedge in the appropriate cash market.

solvency State of a person or company that is cash positive, and able to pay all bills as they fall due; i.e. its assets are more than its liabilities. Its converse is ***insolvency***.

solvency ratio For any financial institution, its own funds divided by its liabilities. *See also* ***gearing; liquidity***.

solvent Describing a person or company in a state of ***solvency***.

source and disposition of funds Company statement outlining how it has raised funds and used them in a particular period.

Southeast Asia Treaty Organization (SEATO) Mutual defence pact signed in 1955 by Australia, France, New Zealand, Pakistan, the Philippines, Thailand, the UK and the USA. It was intended to resist Communist activity in the area, but was abandoned in 1977 through lack of support.

sovereign risk Alternative term for ***political risk***.

SPA Abbreviation of ***Società per Azioni***.

special agent Agent with authority to perform one particular action on behalf of another.

special buyer Bank of England official who runs the open market trading in Treasury bills (working though a discount house).

special drawing rights (SDRs) Form of credit extended by the ***International Monetary Fund (IMF)*** to its member countries as an addition to the credit they already hold. SDRs do not represent actual money, they are simply a form of credit, but they do not have to be repaid to the IMF and thus form a permanent addition to the reserves of each member country. Originally they were allocated in proportion to a country's subscription to the IMF, but since then additional allocations have been made. At first SDRs were valued in relation to the value of gold, but have since been valued in relation to the member country's own currency. SDRs may be exchanged between member countries or between those countries and the IMF.

special endorsement Endorsement in the name of a particular person on a ***bill of exchange***.

specialist Member of the New York Stock Exchange who buys all available stock of a number of companies and sells all that he is asked to sell.

special Lombard rate Interest rate charged by the German Bundesbank when lending against the ***Lombard rate*** is suspended.

special manager Person with the requisite experience appointed by the court to run a business that is in liquidation.

special resolution Resolution (to the shareholders of a company) that is defined by the majority it needs and the notice that must be given. For example, a special resolution to change the ***articles of association*** of a company must usually be passed by a three-quarters majority.

speciality debt Debt that is not barred until after 12 years.

special situation fund Fund that places unit trusts or other collective investments in a range of shares that are expected to rise sharply in value (perhaps because of a merger or take-over) or are believed to have bottomed out and are expected to recover.

specie Coins, rather than banknotes or bullion.

specific performance order Order made by a court to one party of a contract to fulfil the obligations to which that party is contracted. It may be made, for example, instead of awarding damages.

speculation Broadly, in finance, the practice of making investments or going into a business that involves risk. The term is sometimes used with pejorative undertones to apply to investment for short-term gain. In certain markets, such as commodities and financial futures, speculation is clearly distinguished from transactions undertaken in the normal course of trading (physical buying or selling) or hedging (where the specific purpose is to minimize overall gains and losses arising from price movements).

spillover effect Awareness of a product in a country where it is not marketed resulting from advertising in a neighbouring country (whose media may cross the national boundary).

spin off Company that is formed from part of or separated from the ownership of a larger company; or merchandise that is produced to take advantage of one high-profile product (such as a book or T-shirts from a television programme); or a technology or product that arises as a by-product of another.

split Marketing exercise in which a company issues more shares to existing shareholders in order to reduce the price per share. *See also* ***bonus issue***.

split-level trust Type of investment company or trust in which the capital is split into capital shares (which benefit from increases in the capital value of the investments) and income shares (which benefit from the income on the investments).

spoilage Alternative term for ***wastage***.

sponsor Alternative description of an ***issuing house*** for a new issue of securities.

sponsorship Provision of funds for an event (cultural or sporting) in return for prominent display of the name of the sponsor or one of its products.

spot Something that is carried out at once, on the spot. The term is most often used on futures markets, where its opposite is forward or highest (as in highest prices).

spot deal Deal for currency exchange that must be completed within two business days of signature (at the rate prevailing at that time).

spot exchange rate Exchange rate quoted for immediate delivery (within two business days).

spot goods As opposed to futures, commodities that are available for immediate delivery, rather than forward delivery.

spot market Market in which the goods sold are available for immediate delivery. It is also known as the non-contract market.

spot month First month for which contracts are available for futures.

spot price Price quoted for goods available for immediate delivery, usually higher than the forward price because it takes into account all costs except delivery.

spot rate Alternative term for ***spot exchange rate***.

spot transaction Dealing for cash (rather than credit) or in futures.

spread Broadly, the difference between two (or sometimes more) prices, rates or values.

SRL Abbreviation of ***Société à Responsabilité Limitée***.

SRO Abbreviation of ***Self-Regulatory Organization***.

SSE Abbreviation of ***Stockholm Stock Exchange***.

SSP Abbreviation of ***statutory sick pay***.

stabilizer Something that acts to keep, e.g., the economy or prices stable. Also known as a built-in stabilizer, it is also the part of a system that stabilizes it to keep fluctuations to a minimum without direct intervention.

stable-valued money Stable currency from a country with low inflation.

staff association Organization that represents employees in discussions with management.

stag Person who buys new issues of shares in the hope that he or she will be able to make a fast profit by selling them soon after trading opens on a stock exchange. With the UK privatization programme of the late 1980s, the number of stags increased. It is not to be confused with STAGS (short for ***sterling accruing government securities***).

stagflation US term for a combination of high inflation and economic stagnation.

stagging Practice of buying shares in a company flotation to make a fast profit by selling them on a stock exchange. *See* ***stag***.

STAGS Abbreviation of ***sterling accruing government securities***.

stakeholder Person who holds the stake (or stakes) for a wager, pending its outcome, and then pays the winner(s). Because wagering contracts have no validity in law, the stakeholder cannot normally be sued for recovery of the money. In company finance, a stakeholder is a person or group that, because of its investment, has a direct interest in a company's performance.

stale bull Dealer who has bought in the expectation that prices will rise but cannot then sell at a profit, either because prices have remained static or fallen, or because nobody wants to buy.

stamp duty Duty levied on the completion of certain transfer documents. For example, stamp duty is paid (on property over a certain value) when a person signs property transfer documents.

Standard and Poor's 500 (S & P 500) US share index based on the weighted prices of 500 securities quoted on the New York Stock Exchange.

Standard and Poor's Ratings Classification of US securities in terms of risk, varying from AAA (Triple A), the highest, to DDD (in default).

standard cost Predetermined cost (usually per unit) that is assigned to a product and should be attained. It is also termed target cost.

standard costing Method of determining and controlling product costs by means of **standard costs**, which are regularly compared with actual costs.

standard cost system Alternative US term for ***standard costing***.

standard deviation (SD) In statistics, a measure of the spread of the elements in a sample given by the square root of the variance.

standard industrial classification (SIC) Method of classifying US business, manufacturing and all commercial activity for statistical purposes.

standard international trade classification (SITC) International trade classification system adopted by the United Nations in 1950.

standardization Use or production of components that are identical and therefore fully interchangeable, a necessity for successful mass production (and the subsequent repair of such goods).

standard of living Measure of people's ability to purchase the goods and services they want.

standard time In standard costing, the time allowed for a given production task, expressed as either the output achieved in standard hours or the standard time allowance.

standby arrangements Conditional arrangement, extending up to 3 years, that guarantees an ***International Monetary Fund (IMF)*** member a specified amount of credit.

standby credit Form of back-up credit guaranteed by a Euronote facility or other note issuance facility.

standby letter of credit (LC) Contractual arrangement guaranteeing economic or financial performance involving three parties: the "issuer" (bank), "account party" (bank customer) and "beneficiary". The bank guarantees that the account party will perform on a contract between the account party and the beneficiary. *See also* ***letter of credit***.

stand on velvet Colloquial term for making a profit from speculation in stocks.

standstill agreement When bidding for shares in a target company, an agreement that no more bids will be made for the time being.

staple commodity Alternative name for primary commodity.

start-up Normally used to describe a company that is beginning from scratch. A start-up often needs ***venture capital*** financing to help it on its way.

state enterprise Undertaking initiated and controlled by the government, generally for the benefit – direct or indirect – of all its citizens, for example a nationalized industry.

statement in lieu of prospectus If a UK company proposes to make a new issue of shares or debentures and does not issue a prospectus, its must pass a statement in lieu of prospectus to the registrar of companies at least three days before the issue is to take place.

statement of account Document issued by a creditor (to a debtor) detailing transactions to date and any balance still due.

statement of affairs Type of ***statement of account*** that details a person's or company's financial position at a given time, particularly the assets and liabilities of a company in liquidation (or a person in bankruptcy).

statement of changes in financial position Term used in the USA for a statement concerning changes in a company's working capital during an accounting period. It is also known informally as a funds statement.

state trading enterprises (STEs) Government-established organizations that produce, export and/or import certain products (with various exclusive or special trading privileges).

Stationery Office Full name Her Majesty's Stationery Office (HMSO), organization that publishes, distributes and sells official UK government publications, as well as some more general material.

statute-barred debt Debt whose time limit (normally 6 years) has elapsed and cannot therefore be recovered at law. If the debtor makes a part payment or acknowledges the debt in writing, the time limit can begin to run again.

statutory books Books that a company has to keep by law, which include books of account and registers of charges, directors and members.

statutory company Company set up by Act of Parliament to produce essential services such as the provision of power and water.

statutory instrument UK legislation initiated by a government minister (under the terms of an existing Act of Parliament).

statutory requirements Legal requirements that every UK company has to meet.

statutory sick pay (SSP) Sickness benefit provided in the UK through *National Insurance* to employed people who are too ill to work and are off work for more than 3 days (as long as they normally pay National Insurance contributions).

stay of proceedings Suspension of winding-up proceedings against a company after receipt of a petition by the court.

step-function costs Alternative term for stepped costs; *see semi-fixed costs*.

step-lock option Alternative term for *ladder option*.

stepped costs Alternative term for *semi-fixed costs*.

stepped preference shares Shares in a *split-level trust* that benefit from both capital growth and income.

sterling accruing government securities (STAGS) Form of zero-coupon bonds, denominated in sterling and backed by Treasury stock.

sterling area *See scheduled territory*.

sterling bloc Countries of the British Commonwealth that fix the exchange rate of sterling to favour trade within the bloc. *See scheduled territory*.

sterling warrant into gilt-edged stock (SWING) Option to buy or sell a specific gilt-edged security (gilt), obtainable from an apppointed dealer and first authorized by the Bank of England in 1987.

STEs Abbreviation of *state trading enterprises*.

STI Abbreviation of *Straits Times Index*.

stick to the knitting Colloquial piece of advice reminding companies to concentrate on doing what they do best (rather than diversifying into the unknown).

stipend Another term for *salary*.

STMS Abbreviation of *short-term monetary support*.

stock Fixed-term security denominated in units of £100; or the raw materials or manufactured goods held by a manufacturer, wholesaler, retailer or end-user (also known as stock-in-trade or inventory). Generally in the USA, and sometimes in the UK, stock is also an alternative term for ordinary share.

stock appreciation Increase in the worth of a company's stock (inventory), generally because of inflation.

stockbroker Formal name agency broker, somebody who gives advice and buys and sells stocks and shares on a stock exchange on behalf of clients.

stock control Processes used to make sure that the ordering, delivery and handling of a company's or retailer's stock (inventory) is done efficiently.

stock dividend Issuing of a company's stock instead of a dividend. *See* ***scrip issue***.

stock exchange Essentially a place where securities, stocks and shares are bought and sold.

Stock Exchange Alternative Trading Service (SEATS) Service that displays quotations and orders for illiquid stock in which only one (or no) market-maker is willing to trade.

Stock Exchange Automated Quotations System (SEAQ) Electronic system of the ***London Stock Exchange*** that displays in the offices of brokers and others up-to-date prices and information for all quoted securities. Only market-makers are permitted to quote prices on SEAQ, accepting certain obligations in return for the increased business that SEAQ offers.

Stock Exchange Automatic Execution Facility (SAEF) Computerized system on the ***London Stock Exchange*** that allows buying and selling of securities to be done at terminals in the broker's office.

Stock Exchange Council Governing body of the ***London Stock Exchange***, a function it shares to some extent with the ***Securities and Futures Authority (SFA)***.

Stock Exchange Daily Official List *See* ***Official List***.

Stock Exchange Electronic Trading Service (SETS) Service introduced in 1997 that computerized the work of market-makers in matching buying and selling orders for shares on the London Stock Exchange.

Stock Exchange of Hong Kong (SEHK) Exchange established in 1986 by merging the four previous stock exchanges in Hong Kong. It produces the Hang Seng index of 33 leading stocks.

Stock Exchange Pool Nominees (SEPON) Company that acted as a central pool for shares while they were being transferred from buyer to seller on the ***London Stock Exchange***. Sold stock was deposited into SEPON and buy orders were fulfilled from it, through the ***TALISMAN*** system. It was replaced by the Bank of England ***CREST*** system in 1997.

Stockholm Stock Exchange (SSE) Stock of exchange of Sweden, known locally as the Stockholm Fondbors. It became a limited liability company in 1993, with its shares available to the general public since 1994.

stock index future Future contract that is determined by share indexes.

stock-in-trade Alternative term for ***stock*** (inventory).

stockist Person or company that, in return for special purchasing terms (usually discount), keeps a minimum stock of a specified product, perhaps exclusively in a particular area.

stockjobber Alternative term for ***jobber***.

stock market Organized market in securities, stocks and shares; a stock exchange.

stock option UK term for an option to apply for or take a company's shares.

stockpiling Building up levels of stock, perhaps before launching a new product or in anticipation of a retail sale.

stock rotation Policy of using or selling older stock (inventory) first, to prevent deterioration, obsolescence or wastage – generally by using the ***first in first out (FIFO)*** system.

stocks *See* ***stock***.

stock split US term for a free bonus issue of shares to shareholders in some proportion to their existing holding, which has the effect of increasing the number of shares held but not the stake in the company.

stocktaking Task of counting (and often valuing) the stock-in-trade of an organization, such as a manufacturing company, wholesaler, retailer or end-user. The stock valuation appears in a company's financial records at the end of an accounting period. Some organizations carry out ***continuous stocktaking***, often with the aid of a computer program.

stock turnover Alternative term for ***inventory turnover***.

stock valuation *See* ***stocktaking***.

stop for freight Shipowner's or broker's instruction to a dock authority not to permit delivery of goods until freight is paid.

stop-loss Describing an automatic selling price assigned to a security that prevents any further losses to an investor.

stop-loss order Instruction given by a client to a stockbroker to sell securities should they fall below a certain price.

stop-loss selling Sale of shares or futures contracts in a declining market, usually at a predetermined price, in order to prevent further loss.

stop order Alternative term for ***stop-loss order***.

stopover Pre-agreed break in a carrier's journey.

stoppage in transitu Repossession of goods from a carrier by a seller because their buyer has become insolvent.

stop rate In a ***repurchase agreement (REPO)***, the US term for the lowest rate of interest that is accepted.

straddle Practice of simultaneously buying forward and selling forward a futures contract or an option in the same security in order to make a profit if the price of the security moves in either direction.

straight bill of lading ***Bill of lading***, with a directly named consignee, that is non-negotiable.

straight bonds/notes Securities that have a fixed rate of interest.

straight-line depreciation Method of calculating the rate of ***depreciation*** of an asset. A fixed proportion of the total original value of the asset is written off in each accounting period, making allowance for its current resale value either as a useful asset or as scrap (salvage value). Thus the depreciation at any one time is the asset's original cost less net residual value, divided by its predicted lifetime (in years).

Straits Times Index (STI) Share index on the ***Singapore Stock Exchange (SES)***.

strangle Practice of buying out-of-the-money call and put options that are close to expiry at a relatively low premium. If the price of the underlying future rises or falls suddenly, the buyer makes a profit.

strategic alliance Close cooperation between two companies, even to the extent of having a jointly-operated business division (*see* ***joint venture***).

street name Name of a broker in which shares are registered and who retains them (the real owner not taking actual possession), making it easier to sell the securities later if required.

Street, The Popular name for the ***New York Stock Exchange***, referring to its location, Wall Street.

street trader Person who sells goods in the street (usually out of a suitcase); he or she may or may not hold a requisite licence.

strict liability Legal principle, commonly applied in Germany and the USA, that somebody who causes loss or harm is liable, whether or not there was negligence or harmful intent. *See also* ***absolute liability***.

strike pay Money paid to workers on official strike by their ***trade union***.

strike price Also called striking price and exercise price, the price at which an option for the purchase or sale of a security is exercised.

stripping Practice of taking US Treasury bonds, stripping the interest-bearing coupon and selling that and the principal separately. Such securities are said to have been stripped.

STRIPS Abbreviation of ***separate trading of registered interest and principle of securities***. *See also* ***stripping***.

strong bear hug During a take-over, a situation in which there is a high level of publicity surrounding the bid, putting pressure on the target company.

Structural Adjustment Programme (SAP) World Bank programme that makes loans available to developing countries.

structural unemployment Unusually high level of unemployment caused by the change from a labour-intensive to a capital-intensive (often hi-tech) economy.

sub-assembly Assembly of components into a unit that will later be used in the assembly of the finished product.

subcontractor Person or company that makes part of all of a final product on behalf of another company. Some manufacturing contracts specifically do not permit the use of subcontractors.

subject bid/offer Bid/offer that is subject to stated conditions (as opposed to a firm bid).

subordinated Describing a loan or security that has an inferior claim for repayment, sometimes called a junior debt (as opposed to a senior debt, which has priority).

sub-prime lending Lending to somebody who has difficulty getting a loan elsewhere (because he or she is thought to be a bad risk), usually at higher than usual rates of interest.

subscriber Signatory to a company's ***memorandum of association*** (who also signs the ***articles of association*** and purchases shares).

subscriber capital Alternative term for ***issued share capital***.

subscription Sum paid to a company for shares in a new issue.

subsidiary Company that has more than 50% of its voting shares owned by another company (which is known as the parent or holding company).

subsidy Sum paid (by government) to companies in certain industries to enable them to sell their goods or services at a price close to the prevailing market price. A subsidy is also used to provide financial support to a commercial or quasi-commercial activity that would otherwise not be viable in narrow profit-and-loss terms, usually in order to sustain broader economic and social benefits.

subvention payment In the UK, payment from one company to another (related) company in order to give a better picture of the group's performance. In the USA, it is a grant made by the government, a company or other institution to a non-profit making organization.

suicide pill Defensive tactics in the event of a take-over bid. If the raider manages to acquire a certain percentage of the target company's shares, the remaining shareholders are automatically entitled to exchange their shares for debt securities, thus changing the company's equity to debt and making it seem less attractive to the raider.

summary dismissal Also called instant dismissal, on-the-spot dismissal of an employee because of behaviour that invalidates his or her contract of employment.

Summary Financial Statements (SFS) Shortened form of a company's report and accounts that, in the UK since 1 April 1990, may be sent to shareholders instead of the full report (as long as certain conditions are complied with).

sunlighting Practice of having two full-time jobs at once. *See also* ***moonlighting***.

sunrise industry Industry that supplies a rapidly growing market (such as biotechnology and information technology).

sunset industry Declining industry that supplies less-needed products using obsolete technology.

supermajority Among a company's shareholders, between 70% and 80%

S

of the voters. It is usual to demand a supermajority when deciding on such points as mergers or take-overs.

supermarket Large self-service retail outlet, but not as large as a hypermarket.

superstock Share issue in the USA that gives existing shareholders a large number of votes per share. Normally used as a defensive tactic during a hostile take-over bid, superstock must be held for a certain period of time before the extra votes are credited to the holder.

superstore Type of ***supermarket*** with a large car park.

supervisor Manager on the shop floor of an organization, in direct contact with workers.

supplementary benefit Payment made by the UK government to somebody who is either out of work but does not qualify for unemployment benefit, or is on a very low wage.

supplementary costs Alternative term for ***overheads***.

supplier credit Finance made available to an importer by the export-credit agency of the exporter's country.

supply Provision of goods or services, or the amount of these available on the market.

supply and demand Two market forces that in microeconomic theory determine the prices of goods, services or investment instruments. If supply is low and demand high, prices increase. Conversely, if demand is low and supply high, prices fall (unless price controls are in operation).

supply risk In limited recourse financing of a construction project, the risk that the materials required may not be available some time after the project has been started.

supporting a currency Practice of actively buying securities or foreign exchange by an "official" in order to stop their market value from falling. This most often happens when a central bank buys its own securities to stop the price falling and thus forestall a rise in interest rates.

surcharge Extra charge imposed on certain goods, such as an added tax on imported goods (when it may be referred to as surtax).

surety Alternative term for ***guarantee***.

surtax Higher rate of income tax formerly levied in the UK on high incomes, abolished in 1973. *See also* ***surcharge***.

sushi bond Bond denominated in a foreign currency and issued by a Japanese institution, when it then counts as a domestic bond.

suspense account Temporary account that records part of a transaction before complete analysis of that transaction or that records sums to correct errors.

sustainable income Part of distributable income that a company can expect to earn in the next accounting period if it continues at its present level of activity.

swap Financial transaction in which assets are exchanged by two people. *See also* ***bed-and-breakfast deal***.

swap arrangement Practice whereby two countries exchange currencies (thereby increasing reserves).

swap line Similar to a ***swap arrangement***, except that in return for currency the second central bank provides a forward contract.

swap rate Difference between a currency's forward rate of interest and its spot rate (expressed as a premium or discount on the spot rate).

swaption Colloquial term for an arrangement that gives the right to enter into a swap contract at predetermined rates at a specified future date.

sweating ones assets Colloquial term that emphasizes the need to attain a high asset turnover (by maximizing sales).

sweat shop Colloquial term for a workplace that is ill-equipped and crowded, with low-paid workers expected to achieve high productivity.

swing In a two-nation trade agreement, the provision of room for mutual extension of credit.

SWING Abbreviation of ***sterling warrant into gilt-edged stock***.

swing line In markets for domestic and Euro-commercial paper, an arrangement whereby different settlement dates can be reconciled, less important now that same-day settlement is becoming more common.

Swiss Options and Financial Futures Exchange (SOFFEX) Futures and options market established in 1988 by five Swiss banks in conjunction with the stock exchanges in Basle, Geneva and Zurich.

Swiss stock exchanges Main exchanges are Zurish, Geneva and Basle (in order of size), which are grouped under the *Schweizer Borse*. In 1988 the *deuxième marché* (second tier) was established, with the *avant-borse* for pre-market trading.

switching Practice of transferring investment from one security to another (in a comparable class) in order to take advantage of price fluctuations or to improve a tax position.

switching discount Reduction in offer price or discount on a unit trust that is offered to people who have invested in other unit trusts of the same financial group.

switch selling Salesperson's technique whereby, if a potential buyer resists a particular product, another (equally attractive) one is suddenly made available.

SWOT analysis Acronym of strengths, weaknesses, opportunities and threats, aspects that an organization should consider in analysing its present position and in planning for the future.

syndicate Group of people who come together to work for a common aim, for example managing the issue of a security or underwriting risks for ***Lloyd's of London***.

syndicated credit Credit, such as a large bank loan, made by a group of banks to a single borrower.

syndicated loan *See* ***syndicated credit***.

syndication Practice of dividing investment risk between several people or organizations in order to minimize individual risk.

synergy Additional benefits to be gained by the combination of hitherto separate activities. It is sometimes colloquially expressed as "2 + 2 = 5", and cited to justify the take-over or merger of companies with complementary or mutually reinforcing activities or resources.

systemic risk Risk that difficulties in any one financial market or institution may spread and cause problems for the whole system.

T

tacit agreement In marketing, collusion between companies regarding market share or pricing.

tail-gating Act of a broker who recommends purchase of a stock to one client on the basis of another customer having expressed faith in it by making a purchase. The term also includes the personal trading in a share by a broker immediately after taking an instruction from a client to do the same.

tail swallowing Selling enough of a deep-discounted rights issue (of company shares) to raise the money to buy the remainder at no cost.

tailspin Sudden plunge in market prices.

take back When a US company is sold, the take back is a situation in which the owner must accept payment in something other than cash.

take in Accept stocks as loan security in order to postpone a sale until the next settlement date.

take-over Buying of a proportion of another company's shares so that the purchaser gains control of the company or its assets. *See also* ***merger***.

take-over bid Offer by one company to buy the shares of another, thereby gaining control of the target company. It is often shortened to "bid".

take-over panel London Stock Exchange body responsible for seeing that the City Code on Takeovers and Mergers is observed by parties wishing to make a take-over bid.

take-over stock Shares that are bought by a raider during a take-over battle.

taker Person who purchases an ***option***.

taker-in Person who is willing to take up a commitment made by a bull dealer, in the event of the dealer being unable or unwilling to pay for it at that time.

TALISMAN Abbreviation of ***Transfer Accounting, Lodgement for Investors, Stock Management for Jobbers***.

tally Originally a notch made on a piece of wood as a record of a debt or payment, now most often referring to a distinguishing mark on an item of merchandise.

tallyman Person who gives credit to be paid in instalments (traditionally by going round housing estates door-to-door); or a person responsible for checking merchandise as it is loaded or unloaded from a vessel; or an accountant who works for a bookmaker on a race course.

talon Slip that accompanies a sheet of coupons of bearer bonds, which may be sent to the issuing company when more coupons are required.

tangible assets Literally, assets that may be touched, such as buildings or stock; also called tangibles. They may be contrasted with intangible (or invisible) assets, such as a company's goodwill or the expertise of its staff. *See also* ***fixed asset***.

tangibles Another term for ***tangible assets***.

tanstaffl US acronym for there ain't no such thing as a free lunch.

tap When the UK government makes a new issue on the gilt-edged security (gilt) market, it is very rarely fully subscribed. The remaining gilts in the issue are gradually released by the government broker and this action is known as a tap.

tap buying In certain circumstances, the government will buy back gilt-edged securities (gilts) before they have matured. This is known as tap buying.

tap issue Issue of government securities direct to government departments rather than onto the open market.

tap stock Gilt-edged stock released onto the market in a ***tap***.

tap dancing Unethical method of manipulating share prices in the USA in which a dealer reports a deal inclusive of his or her commission. This seems to make the share price higher.

TAPs Abbreviation of ***training access points***.

tare When the weight of goods is being established, the tare is the weight allowed for the packaging. It is also the weight of a (goods) vehicle without fuel; its unladen weight.

target Objective towards which somebody or an organization is working. In corporate finance, it is a company that is the object of a take-over bid.

TARGET Abbreviation of ***Trans-European Automated Real-time Gross Settlement Express Transfer***.

target audience Also called target market, the precisely defined customers a company wishes to sell to.

target market Alternative term for ***target audience***.

target price Theoretical selling price set annually or farm produce under the ***Common Agricultural Policy (CAP)*** of the European Commission. It may be achieved by purchasing goods at the ***intervention price***.

tarif French and Dutch for ***tariff***.

tarifa Portuguese and Spanish for ***tariff***.

tariff Generally, a list of charges made in return for goods or services. More specifically, it is the list of dutiable goods and duty payable, issued by (in the UK) Her Majesty's Customs. It is also a system of charges in which a certain rate is payable up to a certain point (e.g. a certain quantity of goods) and then the rate changes beyond that point.

tariffa Italian for ***tariff***.

tariff anomaly Situation in which the tariff on raw materials or semi-manufactured goods is larger than that on the finished product.

tariff barrier Tariff imposed by an importing country that restricts or prevents the free flow of such goods. It is also called a customs barrier.

tariff quota Imposition of a higher tariff on imported goods once a specified quantity has been imported (at a lower tariff).

tariff suspension Cancellation of a tariff to protect domestic industry from foreign competition.

TAURUS Abbreviation of ***Transfer and Automated Registration of Uncertified Stock***.

taux d'intérêt French for ***interest rate***.

tax Money paid to central or local government to finance its expenditure and implement its financial policy. Various kinds of taxes are collected by the ***Inland Revenue*** in the UK (the ***Internal Revenue Service*** in the USA), HM ***Customs and Excise*** (in which case the tax is known as ***duty***) and local government authorities. *See also* ***rates; value added tax (VAT)***.

tax abatement Reduction in the rate of tax. It should not be confused with a tax rebate.

taxable income Income on which taxes are levied. It is calculated by deducting personal allowances (and any other tax-deductible expenses) from gross income.

tax allowance Deduction from gross income to give taxable income.

tax and price index (TPI) Index introduced in 1979 to compare levels of taxation with retail prices and relate them to average wage levels. The TPI is used to calculate the real spending power of the nation.

tax assessment Calculation of a person's income tax liability made in the UK by the ***Inland Revenue***. If actual income figures are not available it may be estimated. *See also* ***self-assessment***.

taxation Imposition and subsequent collection of tax.

tax avoidance Legal avoidance of or reduction in income tax, achieved by arranging one's financial affairs so as to take advantage all possible concessions. Such a device is also termed a tax shelter in the USA. Tax avoidance should not be confused with ***tax evasion*** (which is illegal).

tax base Form of income upon which tax is calculated. For example, the tax base for income tax is a person's taxable income, for corporation tax a company's profits.

tax bracket The percentage of a person's income that he or she pays in tax depends on the level of income. Incomes are divided into brackets (ranges) for the purpose of calculating tax. The term is also applied to people in that bracket.

tax concession Allowance made by the ***Inland Revenue*** to UK taxpayers in certain categories, which means that these people or companies pay less tax than they would otherwise be liable for. For example, tax concessions are often used by government to induce companies to relocate in areas of high unemployment.

tax credit That part of a dividend payment on which a company has already paid tax, thus relieving the shareholder from the necessity of doing so.

tax-deductible Describing an amount that may be deducted from personal income or company profits to establish the tax liability.

tax deduction Money removed from a person's salary or wages to pay income tax. In the USA, however, the term means expenses that are deductible against tax.

tax deduction card In *pay-as-you-earn (PAYE)* income tax, a record of all deductions made by an employer at source, submitted for each employee to the ***Inland Revenue*** annually.

tax-effective Describing a reduction in tax by a method that is in accordance with tax law.

Taxes Management Act 1970 UK legislation concerning administration and collection of ***capital gains tax***, ***corporation tax*** and ***income tax***.

tax evasion Evasion of tax liabilities by providing false information to the Inland Revenue. It is a criminal offence in the UK. *See also* ***tax avoidance***.

tax exemption Not having to pay tax. In the USA, however, the term describes the proportion of income upon which tax is not payable.

Tax Exempt Special Savings Account (TESSA) Former type of tax-free investment, introduced in the UK in 1990 to encourage people to save. Up to £9,000 could be invested, and interest was tax free as long as no withdrawal was made for a period of five years. TESSAs lost their tax-free status in 1999, being replaced by ***individual savings accounts (ISAs)***.

tax exile Person who lives abroad in order to minimize liability for tax.

tax-free Describing any allowance, benefit or other income that is not subject to tax.

tax gap Difference between the amount somebody owes the Inland Revenue (Internal Revenue Service in the USA) and the amount he or she actually pays.

tax haven Country (such as the Bahamas, the Cayman Islands, Liechtenstein and Monaco) that has liberal tax and banking regulations. In some instances it benefits companies to set up their registered offices in such a country, to avoid paying taxes in their own country.

tax holiday Period during which a start-up company need not pay taxes.

tax invoice With ***value added tax (VAT)***, a detailed invoice that one taxable person sends to another when the taxable supply is worth £100 or more.

tax loss Loss sustained by a person or business which may, once incurred, be offset against a demand for capital gains tax, corporation tax or income tax. Tax losses are frequently incurred deliberately in an attempt to reduce the real cost of paying taxes.

taxman Informal name for an Inspector of Taxes.

taxpayer identification number (TIN) In the USA, a nine-digit number with no alphabetic characters, usually the same as a person's Social Security number or employee identification number.

tax period Period of time for which a return for ***value added tax (VAT)*** applies (usually three months). The return should be sent Customs and Excise within a month of the end of the period.

tax point Date on which goods or services are sent to a customer. It identifies the tax period in which ***value added tax (VAT)*** is accounted for.

tax rebate Repayment of tax that has already been paid (usually because it was assessed too high).

Tax Reform Act 1986 US legislation that increased personal income tax thresholds and abolished or reduced some deductions for business or personal tax.

tax relief Concessions made to taxpayers in respect of certain liabilities (such as, at one time, mortgages).

tax return Document submitted to the Inland Revenue annually, stating a person's earnings and expenses for the year and used to calculate a person's tax liabilities. *See also* ***self-assessment***.

tax shelter Investment instrument that does not attract tax. In the USA, the term is also used for ***tax avoidance***. *See also* ***tax haven***.

tax shield US term for non-cash items charged against income, thereby "shielding" that amount from tax. Depreciation is an example of a tax shield.

tax tables Tables used by employers to calculate the income tax payable by employees under the pay-as-you-earn (PAYE) method. The calculations are often computerized.

tax treaty Treaty between governments about what income is or is not taxable by the country in which the money is earned.

tax week Any whole week following 6 April, the start of the UK tax year (fiscal year).

tax year Another term for ***fiscal year***.

T-bill Abbreviation of US ***Treasury bill***.

TCV Abbreviation of ***total contract value***.

teaser Initial low rate of interest offered on an adjustable rate mortgage (ARM), which may seem very attractive at the time of the arrangement, but which inevitably rises.

technical analysis Detailed analysis of the changes in price of a company's stock, based on past movements in the value of its shares, as a basis for predicting future trends. It is a form of chartism.

technical insolvency Situation in which a company's losses outweigh its share capital (i.e. it has negative assets), perhaps because of the cost of fighting a take-over battle.

technical office protocol (TOP) Scheme aimed at standardizing computer systems that link design and engineering functions within manufacturing industries.

technical rally Sudden rise in the prices of commodities or shares for technical only reasons (perhaps a milestone level of a market index).

teddy bear hug Situation in which the target company approves of a take-over bid in principle but requires a higher price.

Ted spread Difference between the price of a US Treasury bill and the price of the Eurodollar.

TECs Abbreviation of ***Training and Enterprise Councils***.

telemarketing Advertising, selling or conducting market research over the telephone, person to person.

telesales Selling a product over the telephone, a branch of telemarketing.

teleshopping Service whereby a store's customers may order goods for delivery, either over the telephone or, increasingly, using a person computer (via the ***Internet***).

teletext output price information computer (TOPIC) Computerized system that provides stock dealers with up-to-the-minute information on market prices, sometimes called a quote machine.

teleworking Working at home but linked to one's employer through fax, telephone or computer modem.

temporary admission (ATA) carnet International customs document that permits a person (usually a commercial traveller) to take certain goods (usually samples) into a country without paying duty on them.

temporary exports Goods exported duty-free for use at exhibitions or as samples and then reimported. The term is also used of cash that is "exported" to an offshore locaction, often for the purposes of tax avoidance.

tenancy Either an agreement whereby a person is entitled to occupy a property, usually in return for rent, or the length of time agreed for such occupancy.

tenancy in common In principle, a situation in which two or more people are entitled to tenancy of the same property and may do as each wishes with their part of it. If one tenant dies, his or her share of the property is passed to the heir, rather than to the other tenant(s). Now, however, tenancy in common applies only to groups of four or more people. *See also* ***joint tenants***.

tender Generally, an offer to supply goods or services at a certain price and under certain conditions. A tender is usually submitted in response to an invitation to do so, normally in competition with other potential suppliers.

tender bill Treasury bill, issued by the UK government each week to cover short-term finance. Tenders for these bills are made by discount houses and financial institutions. *See also* ***tap***.

tender offer Offer for sale by tender. In the USA, it is an offer made to the shareholders of a public company to buy their holding at a certain price, normally above the current market price. This may be done by a company in order to effect a take-over.

tender panel Group of banks that are invited to subscribe credit for the euronote issuance facility.

tender pool One of a series of groups into which an acquisitive company may divide its target company's shareholders, in order more successfully to persuade them to take up a tender offer. It is a form of divide and conquer.

tenor Period of time before a ***bill of exchange*** has to be paid. In effect it is the "life" of the bill.

term Period of time during which something is valid.

terminal date Also called terminate date, the date of expiry of a futures contract.

terminal loss Business loss that cannot be carried forward (for taxation purposes) because the business is closing or being wound up. The Inland Revenue may therefore allow the loss to be carried back to offset up to three previous year's profits.

terminal market Financial market in futures.

terminate date Alternative term for ***terminal date***.

term loan Fixed loan made for a specified number of years, unlike a demand loan which a borrower may be asked to repay at any time.

terms Conditions attached to an agreement or contract.

term shares Funds deposited with a building society for a stated number of years, to earn higher than usual interest.

terms of payment Ways in which a company can be paid for goods or services sold abroad (such as a bill of exchange, letter of credit, and so on).

terms of purchase Also called terms of sale, the conditions that relate to the payment for goods or services. They may include a latest date for payment and discounts for prompt or cash payment.

terms of sale Alternative term for ***terms of purchase***.

terms of trade Indication of a county's trading prospects, based on a comparison of its imports and exports.

territorial waters Area of sea around a country over which it claims jurisdiction. The distance from shore varies widely among countries. For example, the UK claims up to 12 nautical miles (Territorial Sea Act 1987) for general purposes, but up to 200 miles for fishing rights.

territory Geographical area covered by a sales representative or by a company's operations.

tertiary market Market in listed securities traded by non-exchange brokers on the over-the-counter market.

tertiary sector Major part of a developed country's economy, concerned with service businesses. It is thus synonymous with the service industry.

TESSA Abbreviation of ***Tax Exempt Special Savings Account***.

test market Small defined geographical area in which a new product is launched to test its sales potential.

Texas hedge Transaction in derivatives that increases risk; i.e. the opposite of a proper hedge.

TGRs Abbreviation of ***Treasury investment growth receipts***.

The Opening Call-over at the start of each trading session on some exchanges. The term is also used to mean ***opening price***.

thin bid Take-over bid backed by an aggressor who holds only a small number of shares. It is also known as a skinny bid.

thin market Describing shares that are only rarely traded.

third-class paper Corporate debt issued by companies with a low credit rating. It can be a hazardous investment.

Third Market London Stock Exchange market introduced in January 1987, with less stringent entry requirements than the ***Unlisted Securities Market (USM)***. It is also known as the third tier.

thirteenth month Type of bonus in which an employee is paid an extra month's salary once a year.

three-six-three Late-lamented lifestyle of the US banker: "Pay interest at 3%; lend at 6%; be on the golf course by 3 p.m."

threshold Limit or point at which something changes.

threshold agreement Agreement between an employer and employees (or the representative trade union) that wages will increase only if the rate of inflation reaches or exceeds a certain level, the threshold.

threshold company Company that has moved out of the start-up stage and is moving towards becoming more profitable.

threshold price Price fixed under the ***Common Agricultural Policy (CAP)*** of the European Commission, below which the price of agricultural imports from non-member states is not allowed to fall.

thrift US shorthand for thrift and loans.

thrift and loans Financial institutions in the USA that are backed by an insurance fund and oriented towards the customer. They are also known as industrial banks. *See also* ***savings and loan association (S&L)***.

through bill of lading Single ***bill of lading*** that covers a cargo when two modes of transport are used for its shipment.

tick Minimum allowable price movement on a financial futures contract.

ticket day Also called name day, the day on the Stock Exchange when brokers give sellers the names of buyers so that deals can be settled (the names are written on slips of paper called tickets).

tied loan Loan made by one country to another on condition that the money concerned is spent in the lending nation. Tied loans are a common form of foreign aid because they create employment and have no effect on the lending country's ***balance of payments***.

tied outlet Retail outlet that is financially backed by a manufacturer on the condition that the outlet sells the manufacturer's goods (for example, in the UK most public houses are tied outlets).

tie-up Arrangement whereby a large company helps to finance a smaller company, thus gaining rights in some or all of its developments. Tie-ups most often occur when the receiving company is developing in high-technology areas.

tigers Colloquial name for ***Treasury investment growth receipts***.

tighten Describing what happens to the market price of a bond whose interest yield is lower than that at which it was issued.

tight money Money available only at a high rate of interest. It is created when the authorities reduce the money supply in an attempt to curtail the level of activity within the economy; funds therefore become scarce and thus attract higher interest rates.

time and a half One-and-a-half times the normal hourly rate of pay, sometimes paid to employees who work unsociable hours or for working on public holidays and at weekends.

time and motion Study of the way in which a particular job is carried out, in an effort to streamline the physical actions involved and so save time.

time bargain Deal struck on the understanding that settlement will be postponed until the next settlement date.

time charter Hiring of all or part of a ship for a specified period of time (during which any number of voyages may be made).

time deposit Cash deposited in a bank and earning interest (as opposed to a non-interest earning demand deposit).

time draft Draft that matures a particular number of days after the date on it or a particular number of days after it is accepted.

time office Office at company that keeps records of time worked by hourly-paid employees.

time preference Theory of interest that suggests that interest is the price paid by the borrower for immediate consumption, and compensation to the lender, who loses the opportunity to use the articles or money lent for his or her own purposes. Therefore, time preference is a person's preference for current rather than future consumption, or *vice versa*.

time rate Payment for work done based on the amount of time the job takes. *See also* ***piece-rate***.

times covered Number of times a company's profits exceed payments of interest, and therefore a measure of its ability to service a debt. It is also called income gearing.

time server Employee who has lost sight of any promotional ambitions and has no motivation to work with any interest or initiative. A time server usually freewheels until he or she retires.

time sharing In employment, the sharing of a full-time job by two or more people, each performing the same function but working at different times; it is also called job sharing. In property, time sharing is an arrangement whereby people buy time during which they are entitled to use a property (such as a two-week time share in a holiday villa abroad).

time sheet Document that records the time a worker or machine spends on each activity in a particular period, used mainly for costing purposes.

time value of money Theory which postulates that one's money is more valuable now than at any time in the future, whether it be in a hour's time, next week or next year. For example, the earlier money is received the sooner it can be invested to earn interest, and the later it is paid out the longer it will earn interest.

tip Cash given to somebody who has rendered a service, over and above the payment agreed. Tipping customs vary from country to country, but those who are normally tipped include taxi-drivers, waiting staff, beauticians and hairdressers. It is also known as a gratuity.

tip sheet Publication that gives details of stocks that are expected to do well, which can in itself affect the price.

title Person's right to (possess) something.

title deed Also known as deed of title, a degal document giving the holder title to land or (more loosely) to property. Title deeds are often accepted as collateral for a loan.

TNC Abbreviation of ***transnational corporation***.

toehold purchase First acquisition of up to 5% of a target company's shares in an attempted take-over bid.

Tokyo Stock Exchange (TSE) Second largest stock exchange in the world (after New York), which handles with 80% of share dealings in Japan (there are 1200 listed companies). There is still a trading floor, although most deals are computerized.

tolerance In manufacturing, the degree to which a product differs from the ideal specification, without giving grounds for it to be rejected.

toll Payment made for the use of a facility such as a bridge or tunnel. In some countries there are also tolls payable for the use of motorways. The toll is normally charged to cover the cost of providing and maintaining the service.

tombstone Informal term for an advertisement, placed in the press, giving details of those involved in a securities issue. A tombstone is not normally an offer of sale.

tonnage Size of a ship based on its cubic capacity, where 1 ton equals 100 cubic feet. It is not the vessel's carrying capacity.

tontine Type of annuity where a group of people contribute a lump sum to a fund, a sort of cooperative insurance (popular in the 17th century). When somebody dies, his or her money is shared among the surviving members. It ends when the last member dies.

TOP Abbreviation of ***technical office protocol***.

TOPIC Abbreviation of ***teletex output price information computer***.

Topix Index of the 1200 shares quoted on the Japanese stock markets, forming the basis for the Tokyo Stock Exchange futures contracts.

top up To improve the benefits gained from an existing arrangement, for example by increasing contributions to a pension or assurance scheme.

Toronto Stock Exchange (TSE) Exchange established in 1878 that today handles three-quarters of the deals done in Canada. It is regulated by the Ontario Securities Commission and since 1996 has produced the TSE 100 share index.

total assets Total of all of a company's assets (as opposed to net assets).

total assets turnover Turnover calculated as sales divided by total assets.

total contract value (TCV) Figure applied to futures markets calculated by multiplying the size of the contract (e.g. 10 tons of cocoa) by the market price (e.g. £1,000 per ton) to give the value of the contract (£10,000).

touch For any security, the difference between the best bid price of one market maker and the best offer price of another. *See also* ***spread***.

towage Charge for towing a ship.

toxic waste Informal US term rating a security as a very bad investment.

tracker Description of an investment fund that tracks a share index, such as the FT-SE 100 Index (Footsie).

tracker bond Lump-sum account invested in equities that guarantees the capital and often guarantees also a minimum return.

trade Business of buying and selling in general. In the USA, a trade may be another term for a bargain or deal.

trade acceptance Alternative term for ***accepted bill of exchange***.

trade agreement Agreement between two or more countries or two groups of countries regarding general terms of trade.

trade association Organization that represents the interest of companies within a particular industry, especially in discussions with government.

trade balance Alternative term for ***balance of trade***.

trade barrier Something that restricts or discourages trade, such as high levels of import duty or low import quotas.

trade bill ***Bill of exchange*** between traders. The value and acceptability of a trade bill depends on the standing of the accepting trader.

trade credit Credit one company or business gives to another, usually in the form of time to pay for goods or services supplied.

trade creditor Company or person to whom money is owed as a result of normal trading.

trade cycle Irregular pattern of movement in employment and prices, i.e. economic activity, which tends to go up (boom) and down (slump) cyclically.

trade debt Debt incurred by a company during the normal course of business as the result of non-payment of bills.

trade debtor Company or person who owes money for goods or services received.

trade deficit Excess of a county's imports over exports, resulting in a negative balance of payments.

Trade Descriptions Act 1968 UK legislation that bans misleading or false descriptions of goods or services – their contents, possible effects and price. It applies to advertising, packaging and even a verbal description.

trade discount Discount offered to trade customers, i.e. to customers who are likely to place large and regular orders. A trade discount therefore recognizes the value of the customer concerned.

traded months Months for which futures markets quote deliveries of commodities. Each market generally uses standard months in the year.

traded option Option, and not the contract to which it relates, that is bought or sold before its expiry date.

trade gap In an adverse balance of trade, the difference between the values of imports and exports.

trade-in offer Allowance against the price of a new product for an old model handed over to the seller, usually consumer goods for which the trade-in has only scrap value. A possible exception is the practice of accepting trade-ins in the motor retail trade.

trade investment Investment in capital goods related to existing business, or in a new business in an established sector.

trademark Logo or name (trade name) used to distinguish one manufacturer's product from another's. Registered trademarks may not be used by another manufacturer in the country of registration.

tradeoff Exchanging one thing for another. Goods may be traded off against each other, but so may many other things such as the terms of an agreement.

trade price Price a retailer pays to a manufacturer or wholesaler for goods to be stocked and sold.

trader Person who concerns himself or herself in trade. *See also* ***sole trader***.

trade references List of trading partners to whom a company may refer if it wishes to confirm the creditworthiness of a potential customer.

Trades Union Congress (TUC) Organization established in 1868 that represents UK trade unions nationally and internationally.

trade surplus Situation in which the value of a country's exports exceed those of imports (giving a positive balance of trade).

trade terms Special conditions (usually discount prices) available to people working in the same trade or industry.

trade union Organization that represents generally workers in negotiations with management and government. Other groups, such as students, may also form a trade union.

Trade Union Act 1984 UK legislation that requires trade unions to ballot members before calling an official strike and to elect (or re-elect) voting members every five years at least.

Trade Union Reform and Employment Rights Act 1993 UK legislation that, among other things, requires trade union members to give periodic written agreement to the deduction of union subscriptions at source (from their pay) and requires unions to give at least seven days notice of official industrial action.

trade war Retaliatory action, such as an embargo, by one government against another that has imposed tariff barriers against its exports.

trading Activity of a trader in all its meanings.

trading association Organization whose members are people or companies in the same sort of business, formed to represent them in, for example, dealings with local and national government.

trading at a discount Situation in the currency market when the quoted forward rate is lower than the spot rate.

trading at a premium Situation in the currency market when the quoted forward rate is higher than the spot rate.

trading bloc Group of countries with a mutual free trade arrangement, but with tariffs for imports from countries outside the bloc.

trading certificate Certificate handed to a new company by the Registrar of Companies to enable it to begin trading.

trading crowd Colloquial term for a group of traders interested in a particular security.

trading cycle Whole process that takes place between a company receiving an order and delivering it, and calculating the profit after it has been paid for.

trading day Day on which trading takes place on a stock exchange, i.e. all days except ***non-trading days***.

trading estate Area of land, usually cited just outside a town or city, set aside for warehouses and light industrial units. It is also known as an industrial estate or industrial park.

trading floor Area within an exchange building where trading takes place.

trading forecast Estimate of a company's sales figures and profits over the nest trading period (usually a year).

trading halt Temporary stoppage of trading on a securities or options market.

trading house US term for a company whose main business is the import and export of certain types of goods from certain countries or areas.

trading loss Loss incurred while taking a principal (trading) position in a market. It must be recorded in the profit and loss account of a company, but is therefore often disguised, where possible, by such tactics as "redefining" it as a fixed asset investment or including it as an extraordinary below-the-line item in the accounts.

trading post On the trading floor of the New York Stock Exchange, an area where dealers congregate to trade.

trading profit Difference between a company's revenue and its costs (including overheads), when the former exceeds the latter. *See also trading loss*.

trading risk Also called transaction risk, in a deal denominated in a foreign currency the risk that unfavourable changes in exchange rates may affect amounts of income or expenditure in the home currency.

trading stamps Discount given by a retailer to its customers in the form of stamps. The stamps have a redemption value (in cash or goods) and the discount is represented by this value.

Trading Standards Authority UK organization that enforces legislation relating to consumer protection (through its many trading standards officers).

trading standards officer Local council employee in the UK who checks that local businesses adhere to consumer protection legislation.

trainee Employee who, while at work, is being trained for a particular job.

Training Access Points (TAPs) Places in the UK, generally in public libraries or job centres, where people may find out about training schemes.

Training Agency UK government organization that coordinates national training schemes through such activities as Employment Training (ET) (for the long-term unemployed), ***Training and Enterprise Councils (TECs)*** and ***Youth Training Schemes (YTS)***.

Training and Enterprise Councils (TECs) Organizations established in the UK in 1990 to support business start-ups and coordinate local training schemes. Their members are local business people but the councils are financed by national government.

tranche Slice or portion; an instalment. In general, one of a series of payments which when put together add up to the total agreed.

tranche funding Funding by making available to a new company successive sums of money (tranches), often conditional on the attainment of targets in its business plan.

transchette Small block of gilt-edged securities issued to the market, as an addition to stock already on the market.

transaction Internal or external event that affects the finances or operation of a business, resulting in an accounting entry. Sales and purchases are examples of external transactions; depreciation of an asset is an internal transaction.

transaction charge Charge payable to the London International Financial Futures Exchange on each transaction made.

transaction costs Costs incurred by certain transactions, such as sales and purchases.

transaction risk Alternative term for ***trading risk***.

Trans-European Automated Real-time Gross Settlement Express Transfer (TARGET) System that is intended, after the establishment of ***European Monetary Union (EMU)***, to permit the transfer of euros directly between accounts held at a country's central bank.

transfer Legal movement of something (e.g. property, shares, etc.) from one owner to another.

transferable Generally an alternative term for ***negotiable***.

transferable credit Type of trade credit in which a ***letter of credit*** is opened by an importer in favour of an agent, who then transfers it to the exporter.

Transfer Accounting, Lodgment for Investors, Stock Management for Jobbers (TALISMAN) Settlement and clearing system for equities on the London Stock Exchange. Shares sold by market-makers are transferred into SEPON (Stock Exchange Pool Nominees) and buying orders are met from the same central pool. It was replaced by ***CREST*** in 1997.

transfer agent Organization that transfers shares from one owner to another on behalf of the issuing company, and keeps records of shareholders' names.

Transfer and Automated Registration of Uncertified Stock (TAURUS) Computerized share settlement system on the London Stock Exchange, but discontinued in 1993 in favour of ***CREST*** (established in 1996).

transfer deed Document that proves the sale of a property or registered stock. To make the transfer official, the seller must sign the deed. In the case of registered stock, the document is also known as a stock transfer deed or transfer form.

transfer payment Payment made by the UK government that is not in return for goods or services, such as state pensions and unemployment benefit.

transfer price Within a group of companies, the price at which goods or services are sold by one subsidiary to another.

transfer stamp duty Duty levied on the transfer of securities on the stock exchange; it is therefore a form of capital transfer tax. It is not imposed on government stocks, nor on securities bought and sold within one account.

transire Document carried and signed by the master of a coasting vessel detailing the goods being carried.

transmission of shares Automatic transfer of shares that does not involve a ***transfer deed*** but through the operation of law (as when executors of a will become registered shareholders after probate).

transnational corporation (TNC) Alternative term for a multinational company.

trans-shipment Movement of cargo from one ship (or other carrier) to another.

travel allowance Amount added to a person's salary to cover the cost of travelling to work, or for journeys undertaken in the course of work.

Treasury Government department that deals with national finance and government funding, and is responsible for the execution of the government's financial policy. Some large companies also have treasury departments.

Treasury bill In the UK, a government bill of exchange issued in £5,000 denominations to discount houses at a discount on its face value and repayable on a certain date (usually 91 days hence). In the USA, often abbreviated to T-bill, it is a short-term bill of exchange issued by the US Treasury in $10,000 denominations.

Treasury bill rate Interest rate that applies to Treasury bills bought in the money market.

Treasury bill tender Bank of England's weekly (every Friday) offer for sale of Treasury bills.

Treasury bond Alternative term for a ***government bond***.

Treasury investment growth receipts (TGRs, or **tigers)** Form of US ***zero-coupon bond*** in dollar denominations.

Treaty of Rome Treaty signed in 1951 that established the European Economic Community (EEC), now the EU.

trend Direction of movement in prices (or other parameter), which may be measured over periods of time, and possibly extrapolated into the future.

trickle-down theory Theory according to which the money put into the pockets of those who are already rich through government policy is thought to seep down into the hands of those who are less well off. Trickle-down is through to be a more effective method of redistributing wealth than are ***transfer payments***.

trigger point Point at which a take-over bid becomes mandatory because of the percentage of shares obtained by another company or person, or the percentage of shares held by one person that must be disclosed to the company (3 per cent of the voting rights).

trigger price Price of an import that is less than that charged in the producing country.

triple-A In the rating of US stocks and bonds, the highest rating a stock may achieve.

triple witching hour Colloquial expressions for the time when expiry dates of US stock index futures contracts, options on the contracts and options on individual stocks coincide.

truck Old term for barter, especially the practice of paying for labour in goods or tokens (exchangeable only at the company store) instead of cash, abolished by the post-1831 Truck Acts.

trust Term with three meanings:

1. Group of companies that join forces to create a cartel, or in some cases a monopoly. In the later sense it is more often used in the USA, e.g. in the term anti-trust law.
2. Sum of money or property placed in the care of a group of trustees, to be managed (although not necessarily invested) for the benefit of an individual or organization such as a charity.
3. In the securities industry, an investment operation that is managed by a group of trustees on behalf of other people, such as a unit trust.

trustbusting US government action taken to prevents trusts (in the US sense) forming, and to break them up if they are already in operation in an apparent effort to stimulate competition.

trust corporation Company (corporate body) legally authorized to act as trustee.

trust deed Legal document that transfers property into the hands of trustees and sets out the terms of the trust.

trustee Person (usually with others) who manages a trust.

trustee status Describing trustees authorized under the UK Trustee Investments Act 1961 to invest in ordinary shares (not previously permitted).

Truth in Lending Act US legislation that requires a lender to reveal fully the cost of consumer credit. It also allows a borrower a cooling-off period of three days in which to cancel a mortgage agreement.

TSA Abbreviation of The Securities Association. *See* ***Securities Association, The***.

TSE Abbreviation of ***Tokyo Stock Exchange*** and ***Toronto Stock Exchange***.

TUC Abbreviation of ***Trades Union Congress***.

turn Difference in the price at which a security is bought and the price at which it is sold. It is thus the gross profit on the transaction.

turnkey contract Contract, found especially in the computer and construction industries, in which a supplier provides a complete

T

customized package to a client (who has merely to "turn the key" and take over the package).

turnover Gross value of all sales made by a company during an accounting period; total sales revenue. The term is also used for the rate at which stock or some other asset is turned over (the turnover rate).

turnover rate *See* ***turnover***.

turnover ratio Accounting ratio that indicates the number of times a circulating asset has been replaced within a given financial period.

turnover tax Type of sales tax that is levied at each stage along the distribution chain. ***Value added tax (VAT)*** is an example.

turn-round rate On a commodity transaction, a charge consisting of the sum of the clearing fee and the broker's commission.

two-part tariff System of charges comprising two elements. In some cases, a fixed sum is supplemented by a variable sum (e.g. a taxi driver may make a fixed charge and then add a certain amount depending on the time of day and the time the journey has taken, or the distance travelled).

two-way market Market in securities in which brokers are as willing to sell at the quoted selling price as they are to buy at the quoted buying price.

tycoon Somebody who has amassed a large fortune and a great deal of personal and private power through business or inheritance.

U

UA Abbreviation of ***unit of account***.

Übernahme German for ***take-over***.

uberrimae fidei/fides Latin for in the fullest faith (usually translated as in utmost good faith), the legal principle that in all contract there is a complete disclosure of relevant facts (whether or not this is explicitly stated).

UCITS Abbreviation of ***Undertakings for Collective Investments in Transferable Securities***.

UDEAC *See* ***Central African Customs and Economic Union***.

UITF Abbreviation of ***Urgent Issues Task Force***.

ullage Difference between the capacity of a cask and the volume of its present contents (now called vacuity by Customs officials); or the actual contents of a cask (as used by Customs officials).

ultimate consignee Person overseas who finally receives an export for its designated end-use.

ultra vires Latin for beyond the power of, denoting an act that goes beyond or against an organization's objectives as defined in its terms of reference (such as a company's articles of association).

umbrella fund Offshore fund of funds that is invested in various other offshore funds.

umpirage In cases of arbitration, there may be more than one arbitrator. A group of arbitrators is governed by an umpire and in the event that the arbitrators are unable to reach a unanimous decision, the umpire's decision is always final. The act of referring to the umpire in this way is known as umpirage.

umpire *See* ***umpirage***.

unabsorbed cost Production cost may be allocated to each unit produced over a specified level of output and represented as a percentage of that unit's overall cost to the producer. If the specified level of output is not reached, then some of the cost is not paid for, and is known as the unabsorbed cost.

unappropriated profits Part of a company's profits not distributed as dividends or set aside for a particular use.

unbundling Colloquial term for ***asset stripping***.

uncalled capital Money owed to a company on partly-paid shares. It exists as a reserve to be called upon at any time by the directors of a company.

uncertified units In unit trusts, the dividends from the trust may be reinvested, to form new units. In most cases the dividends are too small to justify the issuing of a new certificate and so uncertified units are held on behalf of the investor until the units are surrendered.

uncommitted Describing a short-term international issue of, for example, euro-commercial paper that has no underwriting bank syndicate backing it.

unconscionable bargain Bargain that turns out to be unfair because one party has not had the time to consult an expert. Such bargains may be made void in law.

undated security Fixed-interest security that has no redemption date attached.

undercapitalization Financial situation of a company that does not have enough capital to take it through the initial burn-out period immediately after start-up.

under contract To be bound by the terms of a contract.

underemployment Situation in which people who nominally have jobs are not kept fully employed (and are paid very low wages).

underground economy That part of an economy controlled by organized crime. It is better controlled and more concentrated than the ***black economy***.

underlying security Security that is the subject of an options contract.

undertaking Agreement or promise to do something; or a loose term for an organization.

Undertakings for Collective Investment in Transferable Securities (UCITS) Unit trusts that may be traded in any of the EU countries.

underused capacity Part of an organization's capacity that is not utilized (at a given time).

undervalued currency Currency that has been oversold, i.e. its value has fallen below market value usually because of government intervention to make its country's export prices more competitive.

underwater Colloquial term to describe shares that drop in value after the initial public offering.

underwater option Stock option offered to US employees. The shares are normally offered at a discount on the market rate, but when the market price falls below the grant price, the option goes underwater.

underwritten Describing a euronote or other note that is backed by a bank, which guarantees to buy any unsold notes.

undisclosed principal Person represented in a business transaction by an agent or broker, and whose identity is therefore unknown to the person with whom the intermediary is conducting business.

undistributed profits Alternative term for ***retained earnings***.

undue influence If a party to a contract can be shown to have been influenced by a third party, such as a relative or close friend, so that the third party has some benefit from the contract, then undue influence may be declared and the contract made void.

unearned income Income not derived from work or fees of office (such as dividends on shares and interest on investments). It is liable for income tax in the UK, at the same rate as earned income. In the USA, the term denotes advances received from customers (i.e. money received before goods or services are delivered), also called deferred credit or unearned revenue.

unemployment benefit Commonly known as the dole, a benefit payment made in the UK to somebody who is out of work and has previously paid a certain number of ***National Insurance contributions (NICs)***.

unfavourable balance of trade Situation in which a country's imports are worth more than its exports.

unfair dismissal Removal of a person from his or her job for reasons that are unfair. To discover whether these reasons are indeed unfair, in the UK the case may be brought before an industrial tribunal.

Uniform Business Rate UK tax, set nationally but levied at a local level on businesses, to pay for services such as street cleaning and refuse collection.

uniform order bill of lading Negotiable ***bill of lading*** that is made to the shipper's order.

uniform reserve requirement Requirement that all US financial institutions should accumulate reserves according to the same rules.

uniform straight bill of lading Non-negotiable ***bill of lading*** that consigns goods directly to a named consignee.

unincorporated Describing a business that is not legally a company (such as a partnership or a sole proprietorship).

union See ***trade union***.

union recognition Granting of power by an employer to a union so that it can represent employees in negotiations with the employer. Under the terms of the Employment Act 1980 there is no obligation for a UK company to recognize a trade union (no matter how many employees belong to it).

unit One single item produced for sale; or a single area of production or retail space (e.g. on an industrial estate); or a share in an investment or series of investments.

unitary taxation System in some US states whereby a company is liable to pay tax not only on gains made from operating within that state but also on revenue generated elsewhere.

unit cost Cost of producing one item. It is calculated by taking the total cost of production and dividing it by the number of units produced. It is used mainly in determining the price that should be charged for a product. A unit costs may also be assigned to sales (as the cost of selling one item).

United Nations Monetary and Financial Conference 1944 Also called the Bretton Woods Conference (after its location at Bretton Woods, New Hampshire, USA), conference that considered post-World War II international financial relations and established the ***International Monetary Fund (IMF)*** and the ***International Bank for Reconstruction and Development*** (World Bank).

unitization Conversion of an investment trust into a unit trust.

unit of account (UA) Standard unit used in statements about the financial activities of international financial organizations, such as the European currency unit (ECU) used by the European Monetary System (EMS) and therefore not necessarily a tangible unit.

unit price Price paid per unit bought or price charged per unit sold.

unit trust Trust into which investors may buy by acquiring units. The capital collected in this way is invested in various securities in a wide range of markets. Contributors to unit trusts benefit from the diverse nature of the portfolio built up, and from the expertise of a fund manager.

universal agent Agent with unlimited authority to close contracts on behalf of the principal. *See also* ***special agent***.

unlimited company Company that consists of members who are all liable for the total of the company's debts. *See* ***limited company***.

unlimited liability Liability of the members of an unlimited company, or of the general partners in a partnership, or of the sole proprietor of a sole proprietorship. *See* ***limited liability***.

unliquidated damages Damages that are not specified in a contract but determined by a court.

unlisted company Also called an unquoted company, a company whose shares are not traded on a major stock exchange.

unlisted securities Also called unquoted securities or investments, securities that are not listed on a major stock exchange.

Unlisted Securities Market (USM) Former market for shares that do not fulfil the requirements for a full quotation on the London Stock Exchange, or that do not wish to be quoted, but which do fulfil certain less stringent requirements. It closed in 1996 to be replaced by the ***Alternative Investment Market (AIM)***.

unloading Practice of putting on the market large quantities of a certain product (or certain shares) at a low price. *See also* ***dumping***.

unofficial strike Strike of workers that is not sanctioned by their trade union at a national level.

unquoted Normally describing shares or debentures that are not quoted on a stock exchange.

unquoted company Alternative term for ***unlisted company***.

unquoted investment Alternative term for ***unlisted security***.

unsecured Describing something for which no formal security is held. If a loan is unsecured, there is no guarantee that it will be repaid.

unsecured creditor Person who has made a loan but received no security (and therefore has no protection against non-payment).

unsecured debenture Alternative term for ***simple debenture***.

unsecured debt Also called an unsecured loan, a loan made without any security, such as a charge on the assets of the borrower.

unsecured loan Alternative term for ***unsecured debt***.

unsecured loan stock Alternative term for unsecured debenture. *See* ***simple debenture***.

Unsolicited Goods and Services Act 1971 UK legislation introduced to protect consumers from the practice of ***inertia selling***. Thus a person does not have to pay for goods that were not specifically ordered, even if he or she does not return them.

up-and-in call/put option Option that is valueless until the underlying security's price rises above a defined level.

up-and-out call/put option Option that becomes valueless when the underlying security's price rises above a defined level.

up-market Describing a product that is aimed at customers with a lot of purchasing power. It is the opposite of down-market.

upside The bright side – describing an aspect where things will possibly get better.

upstairs deal Colloquial term for an agreement made behind closed doors – usually in the board room. Many take-overs are settled by upstairs deals.

upstream Describing the movement of funds from a subsidiary company to its parent company.

upstream activity Activity within an industry or company that extends beyond the basic manufacturing and marketing. Upstream activities are important in that they help to expand activities in general. Two examples of upstream activities are research and development in any industry; and exploration in the oil industry.

upstream pricing Practice of fixing the price (market value) of a commodity from which other products are made.

upstream vertical integration Alternative term for ***backward vertical integration***.

uptick Describing a transaction (such as a sale of shares) that is made at a higher price than the one obtained immediately before. It is also known as a plus tick. The term uptick is also used to denote a (short-lived) rise in a price or value.

uptrend Improvement of some general kind, for example in market prices.

Urgent Issues Task Force (UITF) Organization established in 1991 by the Accounting Standards Board to deal with urgent matters not already the subject of a standard.

usance Rate of interest on a loan, or ***unearned income*** derived from the ownership of wealth or capital.

useful economic life Time for which an asset provides economic benefit to its owner; the service life.

use of funds Any transaction that reduces a company's funds.

useful life *See* ***useful economic life***.

USM Abbreviation of ***Unlisted Securities Market***.

usufruct The right to the use of property belonging to someone else, but not the right to diminish its value in such use.

usury Moneylending at an excessive rate of interest, not in itself illegal. *See also* ***moneylending***.

utility Industry that provides basic necessities such as power or a clean water supply.

utility stock Share in a company that provides utilities such as water, electricity and gas.

utmost good faith *See* ***uberrimae fidei/fides***.

V

valeur au porteu French for ***bearer bond***.

valeur non-cotée French for ***unlisted security***.

valium picnic Colloquial term for a quiet day on the New York Stock Exchange.

valorize Governmental practice of setting an artificial price for a commodity (rather than allowing it to attain a market price determined by supply and demand).

valuation Estimate of what something is worth. More particularly, it is a summary of the value of a portfolio of investments at a given time.

value Term that is not as precise as it may seem. The value of something is the price a buyer is prepared to pay for it, but this can fluctuate according to all sorts of variables, for example whether it is a buyer's market or a seller's market, to what use the buyer will be putting the item, and so on. Usually the term is qualified, to minimize possible confusion.

value added Difference between the price a company or industry pays for its materials and the price at which it sells finished goods. For example, a used-car dealer may acquire a car, recondition the engine and repaint the body. When the dealer sells the car, the added value is the value of these operations as reflected in the new (higher) selling price of the car.

value added tax (VAT) Form of indirect taxation in which the producer, seller and consumer pay a percentage of the value added to the product or service. For example, if a manufacturer buys raw materials at £10 per unit and sells each unit of product for £20, the value added is £10. The manufacturer is required to pay a percentage of the £20 in VAT, and can claim back the VAT paid on the £10-worth of materials. VAT in the UK is 17.5 per cent for most things (since April 1991), although some goods and services are exempt and some zero-rated.

value analysis Also called value engineering, an analysis of every aspect of a product, usually to determine if there are any opportunities for cost cutting (through, for example, simplifying design or using cheaper components or materials).

value at par Face or nominal value of a share.

value broker Broker who charges a commission on a total transaction, rather than per share.

value engineering Alternative term for ***value analysis***.

value in exchange Value of something as form of exchange, rather than as an object of use. For example, precious stones are worth virtually nothing in terms of real value in use but because they are rare and desirable, they command a high price. *See also* ***value in use***.

value in use Value of something to the person using it, which may be different to the sale value of the object. For example, a machine may be valuable to its owner because it produces goods for sale, whereas it may be valueless in itself, perhaps because it cannot be moved. In accounting terms, an asset's value in use can be calculated by discounting the future cash flows that would accrue from its continued use. *See also* ***value in exchange***.

value paradox An object or commodity may be valuable in terms of exchange, but totally worthless in terms of use. Equally, a thing may be extremely valuable in use but is inexpensive to acquire. For example, salt or water are very useful commodities, but are fairly cheap. Most precious stones may be said to be totally useless, but are expensive to buy because they are so rare. The value paradox is this apparently illogical assignment of value. *See also* ***value in use; value in exchange***.

variable cost Also called direct cost, an expense that varies with the level of activity, such as costs incurred in production that vary depending on the quantity of output.

variable cost per unit Total of all variable costs involved in production divided by the number of units produced.

variable levy (VL) Tariff that is changed in line with changes in world market prices (to maintain a constant post-duty import price).

variable overhead cost Part of a product's indirect costs that vary in proportion to the quantity produced or sold. Consumable materials and salesperson's commission are examples of variable overhead cost.

variable rate Rate of interest that may be varied to suit conditions on the money market.

variance In standard costing, the difference between actual results obtained and those budgeted for or expected. If the former is larger than the latter, it is a favourable variance; if the latter is greater than the former, it is an unfavourable variance.

variation analysis In standard costing, the examination of variances to determine why they occurred.

VAT Abbreviation of ***value added tax***.

VATman Colloquial term for a Customs and Excise employee who deals with ***value added tax (VAT)***.

VAT Abbreviation of ***value added tax (VAT)***.

VAT-registered Describing a trader or organization that is registered (with Customs and Excise) for payment of ***value added tax (VAT)***.

VCTS *See* ***Venture Capital Trust Scheme***.

vehicle currency Currency used to make payments and quotations in international investment and trade, most often the US dollar.

vendor Person who sells goods or services.

vendor placing When a company issues shares in payment for another company, the practice of disposing of those shares (by the selling company) through a stockbroker (rather than selling them on the market, where a large block of shares may adversely affect the price).

venture capital Also known as risk capital, capital invested in a venture (usually a young company, often in high technology areas) that presents a risk.

Venture Capital Trust Scheme (VCTS) Scheme established in the UK in 1993 that gives incentives (such as tax-free dividends) to corporate investors in unquoted companies.

VER Abbreviation of ***voluntary export restriction***.

verba chartarum fortuis accipiuntur contra proferentem Legal maxim that means that where the wording of a contract is imprecise and open to misinterpretation, it will be taken in the sense that goes against the party that drew up the contract. It is also known as the *contra preferentem* rule.

verbal warning First stage in the sequence that, under UK employment law, can lead to the valid dismissal of an employee (for actions that do not justify ***summary dismissal***).

Verfall German for ***redemption date***.

verification Method used by an auditor to check the accuracy of a financial statement by, for example, tracing documentary evidence that gave rise to an entry. The auditor may also seek ***confirmation*** from outside sources.

Verkehrswert German for ***market value***.

vertical diversification Diversification into industries or businesses at different stages of production to the diversifying company. *See also* ***horizontal diversification***.

vertical integration Amalgamation of companies involved in different stages of production in the same industry, for example to form one company capable of extracting raw materials, using them to produce goods and then distributing and selling the manufactured product.

vertical spread Combination of a long call (or put) option and a short call (or put) option of the same expiry date.

vested interest Reason (e.g., an investment) or possible benefit that a person may have for maintaining a certain state of affairs.

viability Ability of a person, a company or even a country to support itself; or of a product to survive in a market and generate a profit.

vicarious liability Legal responsibility of an employer for the actions of employees at work.

vicarious performance Situation that occurs when a party who has contracted to supply something passes the work to a third party to be completed. In this case, the legal responsibility under the contract still lies with the original supplying party.

vigilantibus non dormientibus jura subveiunt Legal maxim meaning that if people think they have a claim to make, they should go ahead and make the claim – as soon as possible.

virtual enterprise Organization that has few tangible assets, usually subcontracting for asset-requiring facilities and conducting its business electronically.

visible Also termed tangible, describing something that can be seen, identified or counted, such as visible assets, exports and imports (as opposed to invisible or intangible).

visible exports Also known as visibles, goods sold to foreign buyers and shipped abroad. The difference between the value of visible exports and visible imports is the balance of trade.

visible imports Tangible products that are imported; imports of goods rather than of services.

visibles Alternative term for ***visible exports***.

visible trade Trade in ***visible exports*** and ***visible imports***.

VL Abbreviation of ***variable levy***.

voice broker Broker of foreign exchange who deals only by telephone.

voidable contract Contract that may be voided by one or other of the parties to it. For example, if one party fails to make known all information relevant to the contract, it may be deemed voidable. *See also* ***void contract***.

void contract Contract that is deemed by law never to have existed (perhaps because one of the signatories did not have the authority to sign). *See also* ***voidable contract***.

volatility Measure of the stability of a particular financial instrument. If, say, a share price or a market index moves often and oscillates wildly, it is said to be volatile.

volume Number of units traded (as opposed to turnover, which is the value of the units traded, although the terms are sometimes interchanged).

voluntary arrangement Procedure, which must be subject to a court order, whereby a person (or company) can avoid bankruptcy (or winding up) if an insolvency practitioner agrees a plan for paying outstanding debts.

voluntary export restriction (VER) Limitation on certain types of exports from one country to another (or group of countries) in order to forestall the imposition of import quotas or other restrictions by importing countries. It is often preceded by a voluntary restraint agreement, stating that this is what the exporting country intends to do.

voluntary liquidation Also termed voluntary winding-up, the liquidation of a company that has decided to cease trading, rather than one that has gone bankrupt.

voluntary restraint See ***voluntary export restriction (VER)***.

voluntary winding-up Alternative term for ***voluntary liquidation***.

vorläufige Dividende German for ***interim dividend***.

Vorstand German for ***board of directors***.

vostro account Account opened for a depositing bank from another country.

voting rights Rights of a shareholder to vote at a company's ***annual general meeting (AGM)***. This right depends on which type of shares are held; generally, ordinary shares carry voting rights whereas debentures do not. The articles of association and the company's prospectus detail which shares carry voting rights and which do not.

voting shares Shares that carry ***voting rights***.

voucher Document (such as a receipt or invoice) that supports or proves entries in a book of prime entry. A voucher is also the name given to a paper given in place of money (such as a gift voucher or a luncheon voucher).

voyage charter Charter agreement (relating to a ship or its cargo space) for a particular voyage.

vulture capitalism Pejorative view of ***venture capital***, whereby investors lure talented people away from established companies, encourage them to set up on their own, work hard and be ingenious, and then face a demand for a high return on the investment.

W

WACC Abbreviation of ***weighted average cost of capital***.

wage Payment made to a worker, normally at a fixed rate per hour, day or week (and usually paid weekly). *See also* ***piece rate***; ***salary***.

wage differential Difference between levels of wages, caused by many variables, such a s occupation, industry, sex and age of employee, geographical location, experience and qualification of the employee, and so on.

wage freeze Situation in which wages are fixed for a certain period of time, either by government authority on a national level or by agreement within a single company or industry.

wage-price spiral Form of inflation. If a producer is forced to increase wages, he or she must increase the price of the product to cover the increased wages cost, which in turn leads to new wage demands by workers.

wage restraint Voluntary agreement between government and trade unions that wage increases will be modest in an attempt to combat inflation. It is generally a more acceptable policy than a ***wage freeze***.

wages councils Former independent UK government-appointed organizations that fixed minimum wages for certain industries and types of work (particularly those that were low-paid). They were abolished in 1994.

waiter Person on the London Stock Exchange or at Lloyd's who runs errands, takes messages and looks after the day-to-day running of the exchange. Historically, the first waiters were those in the coffee houses at which dealing first took place.

waiting time Time an employee spends not working, i.e., waiting for a machine to warm up or be repaired, or waiting for another employee to finish the previous stage of a job.

waiver Formal giving up of rights in a contract (and requiring a new contract to be drawn up if the parties so desire).

wallflower Colloquial name for a stock that is no longer favoured by stock market investors.

Wall Street Brief name for the ***New York Stock Exchange*** (which is located in Wall Street, Manhattan). Sometimes the name is further abbreviated to The Street.

Wall Street Journal Daily US business newspaper published by the Dow Jones company, which produces the main share index the New York Stock Exchange.

warehouse club Organization open to the general public (who pay a membership fee) that allows them to buy groceries and household goods at discounted prices. It is similar to a ***cash and carry***, which is generally accessible only by traders and caterers.

warehouse receipt Also termed a depository receipt, a document that gives details of goods (commodities) delivered to a warehouse

warehousing Term with three meanings:

1. With reference to shipping, it is the business of storing, examining and sorting imported goods, which takes place in a warehouse before they are released into the country in question.
2. In more general terms, it is the storage of goods on behalf of a manufacturer, distributor or retailer.
3. On the stock market, it describes using funds invested in insurance or unit trusts to buy shares that are falling in price, often as a precursor to a take-over bid.

warrant (WT) Term with three meanings:

1. Receipt that describes goods held in a warehouse, transferable by endorsement. In this sense a warfinger warrant (also known as a warfinger receipt) is a similar receipt describing goods on a warf.
2. It is a long-dated option.
3. It is a security of a specific market value that may be exchanged for a certain share at a predetermined price. The warrant's value lies in the difference between the predetermined conversion price and the current market price of the share.

warranty Promise by a manufacturer or seller to correct any defects in goods sold. In some manufacturing companies, an amount is estimated as possible warranty expense and treated as a liability.

warranty of authority Power given to an agent to act under the instructions of a principal.

wash sale US term for the sale and then simultaneous repurchase by a single investor of a block of securities, perhaps to give a false impression of active trading in that security. It is illegal if done between two brokers in order to avoid paying tax.

wastage Also known as spoilage, the materials lost during a production process. Normal loss is an acceptable level of wastage.

wasting asset Asset that has a limited useful life (such as a natural resource that becomes depleted as it is consumed).

watered stock Stock that has become a smaller percentage of a company's total share capital because of a subsequent share issue.

waybill *See* ***consignment note***.

ways and means advance Advance paid by the Bank of England to the consolidated fund.

WCL Abbreviation of ***World Confederation of Labour***.

wealth Total of a person's or a country's assets, both tangible and intangible.

wealth tax Tax levied annually on wealth (which is notoriously difficult to define). It is used in some European countries but not in the UK.

wear and tear Popular and legal term for ***depreciation***. It is the decrease in value of an item due to deterioration through normal use rather than through accident or negligence.

weather working days Working days (particularly in the construction industry or at a port) when work can be done because the weather conditions are favourable.

weekend effect Theory that the prices of stocks and shares do better on a Friday than on a Monday, because of such influences as the way in which dealers time their settlement of purchases, etc.

weighted average cost of capital (WACC) Way of determining a company's cost of capital by assigning a required rate of return to each source of funds on its balance sheet. The size of the source is then used to weight the required return and the WACC expressed as a percentage by dividing the total return by the total weights.

weighted ballot Ballot (for shares) that is in some way biased towards a certain type of investor (e.g. an institutional investor or a small investor).

Weights and Measures Act 1963 UK legislation that made it illegal to sell goods whose weight or volume was less than that stated on them.

Weights and Measures Act 1985 Variation of the ***Weights and Measures Act 1963*** that allowed for the use of metric measures.

Wertpapier German for (a) ***security***.

Wertzuwachs German for ***capital gain***.

wharfage Payment charged for placing goods on a warf during loading or unloading a vessel.

wharfinger Person who is responsible for running a warf at the docks, similar to a warehouseman.

wharfinger recipt *See* ***warrant***.

whipsaw Colloquial term for a violent movement (or series of movements) in prices on any market.

white-collar Describing an employee who does office work rather than factory work. In contrast, a person who does manual work is called a blue-collar worker.

white goods Retailing term for domestic appliances such as cookers, dishwashers, freezers, refrigerators and washing machines.

white knight When a company finds itself the target of a take-over bid, it may seek an alternative company or person to whom it offers to sell itself in preference to being taken over by the original bidder. This friendly company is known as a white knight and the tactic as a white knight defence.

white knight defence *See* ***white knight***.

white squire defence When a company finds itself the target of a take-over bid, it may place a significant number of its shares with a friendly party in order to prevent the raider from acquiring them. This tactic is known as a white squire defence.

wholesale market Interbank money market, especially for short-term loans.

wholesaler Person who buys goods in bulk from a producer and then sells them in smaller quantities to retailers or other wholesalers, earning a profit either by charging a commission to the retailer or by adding to the manufacturer's price. *See* ***mark-up***.

wholly owned subsidiary Subsidiary whose shares are all owned by the parent company.

wide band In the European Monetary System (EMS), option that permits a currency to vary above or below its central rate by up to 6% (narrow band is only 2½%).

wildcat strike Sudden unofficial strike action by workers.

windbill Alternative name for an ***accommodation bill***.

windfall gains and losses Gain or loss resulting from circumstances outside the control of the recipient (such as changes in the net present value of earnings because of changes in discount rates).

windfall profit Profit resulting from fortuitous circumstances outside the control of the recipient, such as that caused by a rise in stock prices or an inheritance.

windfall tax Once-only tax levied on British privatized companies under the terms of the budget of 1977 (it was 23%, payable in two annual instalments). The term has been extended to include other such taxes.

winding-up Cessation of a company's business activity and the start-up of its liquidation.

windmill Alternative name for an ***accommodation bill***.

window Normally short time for which particular funds are available, as with special lending by a central bank.

window-dressing Creative accounting, in which a favourable account sheet is created (without resort to actual fraud).

witching hour Time that an event affecting the whole securities market takes place (such as the hour before a stock-index option expires).

WIP Abbreviation of ***work in progress***.

wire house Informal US term for a large stockbroking firm.

withdrawable repurchase agreement (RP) Repurchase agreement that a dealer can cancel by giving notice to the US Federal Reserve by 1.30 p.m. on the day of cancellation.

withdrawal of labour Euphemism for a strike.

withholding tax Tax on the interest on a deposit or investment deducted at source (the depositor or investor receives net interest).

without recourse Note on a ***bill of exchange*** that indicates that in the event of non-payment of the bill, the current holder may not blame the person from whom he or she bought it. It is sometimes written in French as *sans recours*.

with recourse Note on a discounted ***bill of exchange*** that indicates that in the event of non-payment of the bill, the discounting bank has the right to reclaim the bill's amount from the customer.

worker participation Involvement of employees in the planning and management of an organization.

workers' cooperative Business (usually labour-intensive) that is owned and controlled by the people who work for it.

work-in Industrial action in which redundant staff continue to work for a defunct company (in order to attract a possible buyer).

working assets All the assets of a company except its ***capital assets***; current assets less current liabilities. They include outstanding debts, stocks of raw materials, work in progress, stocks of finished goods and cash in hand.

working capital Capital available for the day-to-day running of a company, used to pay such expenses as salaries, purchases, and so on.

working-capital ratio Alternative term for ***current assets ratio***.

working days In shipping, each weekday except Sunday and bank holidays; in some places Saturday is also excluded.

working director Director who takes an active part in the management of a company.

work in progress (WIP) (Value of) goods currently under manufacture or services being supplied, but not completed at the end of an accounting period.

workout loan Loan that is not being repaid according to the terms of its contract (e.g. payments may be overdue).

work permit Document issued by a host country that gives permission for a foreign national to take paid employment in that country.

works council Discussion group whose members include management and employee's representatives that looks at the company's plans and suggests shop-floor improvements (but does not deal with matters, such as pay and conditions, that are normally dealt with through a trade union).

work study Study carried out to minimize effort put into a particular task; similar to a time-and-motion study.

work-to-rule Industrial action in which workers refuse to do anything that is not exactly defined in their contract of employment.

World Bank Central bank of the United Nations, formally the ***International Bank for Reconstruction and Development***.

World Confederation of Labour (WCL) Organization established in 1920 (as the International Federation of Christian Trade Unions) to represent the interests of workers throughout the free world.

World Trade Organization (WTO) Free trade organization encompassing more than 100 countries which superseded the ***General Agreement on Tariffs and Trade (GATT)***.

write down To take the cost of an asset and deduct the amount by which it has depreciated in capital terms. This gives its written-down or book value. *See also* ***depreciation***.

write off To charge the whole of the value of an asset to expenses or loss (i.e., assign it zero value on the balance sheet). It is also known as charge off in the USA. ***Bad debts*** may also be written off.

writer Person who issues (sells) an option.

write up To increase the value of an asset without recording any spend on it (i.e., there is no corresponding transaction).

written warning Second stage in the sequence that, under UK employment law, can lead to the valid dismissal of an employee (for actions that do not justify ***summary dismissal***).

writing-down allowance Another term for ***capital allowance***.

wrongful dismissal ***Redundancy*** that a court of law decides was illegal. A company responsible for wrongfully dismissing an employee is normally expected to re-employ the person concerned, and may also be liable to pay some form of compensation.

WT Abbreviation of ***warrant***.

WTO Abbreviation of ***World Trade Organization***.

Y

yankee Colloquial term of the ***London Stock Exchange*** for a US security.

yankee bond Bond that is written in dollar denominations to attract US investors.

yearling bond UK fixed-interest security that has a life of less than five years. Such bonds are issued through banks and stockbrokers on a weekly basis.

year's purchase Method of calculating the value of a purchase (of, say, a company) by relating it to the anticipated year's income from the purchase; i.e., the price of a business in relation to its average annual profits or the price of a property in relation to the average annual rent.

year to date Total of figures for the months of the (financial) year that have elapsed up to the present date.

Yellow Book Popular term for a publication entitled *Admission and Securities Listing*, issued by the London Stock Exchange Council, setting out regulations for admission to the Official List and the obligations of securities admitted.

Yellow Sheet Daily US publication that lists prices of bonds and names firms that are in the market for them.

yield Return on an investment, taking into account the annual income and the capital value of the investment, usually expressed as a percentage. There are also various other methods of calculating yield.

yield curve Usual tendency for a security's yield to rise with increasing maturity.

yield gap Difference in average yield between investments in ordinary shares and in gilt-edged securities.

yield to maturity Alternative term for ***redemption yield***.

York-Antwerp Rules Voluntary code, drawn up in 1877, for those involved in shipping cargo by sea.

Youth Training Scheme (YTS) UK training scheme for unemployed school-leavers, organized through local ***Training and Enterprise Councils (TECs)***.

yo-yo stock Colloquial term for stock whose price fluctuates widely in an unpredictable way.

YTS Abbreviation of *Youth Training Scheme*.

Z

Z-account Account at the ***Bank of England*** that allows rapid over-the-counter certification and registration of transfers of gilt-edged securities (for discount houses, gilt market-makers and insurance companies).

zaitech Company's investment in financial markets to supplement earnings from its usual activities (from Japanese *zai* = wealth and *tech* = technology).

ZBB Abbreviation of ***zero-based budget***.

zebra Form of ***zero-coupon bond*** for which the accrued income is taxed annually (rather than at maturity).

zero Shorthand for ***zero-coupon bond***.

zero-based budget (ZBB) Budget calculated as through it were being prepared for the first time using a zero base (with no initial commitment to spend on any activity).

zero-coupon bond Bearer bond that pays no dividend, but is issued at a substantial discount. A capital gain is made by the bearer when the bond matures, and so tax on the proceeds is paid at a lower rate than if the proceeds were drawn in the form of dividends.

zero defects Aim of manufacturing products of perfect quality every time, not achievable in practice within restraints of cost.

zero-dividend preference share Type of share sold by an investment trust that pays no dividend to the investor, who receives payment only when the trust is wound up.

zero-hours contract Contract of employment that defines the number of a worker's weekly hours as zero, so that the employer can inform staff at the beginning of the week what hours are to be worked.

zero-rated goods and services Goods and services that are liable for ***value added tax (VAT)*** but are currently rated at zero tax.

zero salvage value Under US tax regulations, a depreciable asset whose salvage value is estimated at less than 10% of its cost can be assigned a salvage value of zero.

Zins German for ***interest***.

Zinssatz German for ***interest rate***.

Zinsschein German for ***coupon***.

Appendix: World Currencies

Country	Currency	Abbreviation	Subunits
Afghanistan	afghani	Af	100 pule
Albania	lek	Lk	100 qindarka
Algeria	Algerian dinar	AD	100 centimes
Andorra	French franc	Fr	100 centimes
Angola	new kwanza	KW	100 lwei
Antigua and Barbuda	East Carribean dollar	EC$	100 cents
Argentina	nuevo peso	A$	100 centavos
Armenia	dram	Dr	100 luma
Australia	Australian dollar	A$	100 cents
Austria	Schilling	Sch	100 Groschen
Azerbaijan	manat	Rub	100 gopik
Bahamas	Bahamian dollar	Ba$	100 cents
Bahrain	Bahraini dinar	BD	1000 fils
Bangladesh	taka	Tk	100 poisha
Barbados	Barbadan dollar	BD$	100 cents
Belarus	rouble	Rub	100 kopecks
Belgium	Belgian franc	BFr	100 centimes
Belize	Belize dollar	Bz$	100 cents
Benin	CFA franc	CFA Fr	100 centimes
Bermuda	Bermudan dollar	Bda$	100 cents
Bhutan	ngultrum	Nu	100 chetrum
Bolivia	boliviano	Bs	100 centavos
Bosnia Herzegovina	dinar	Din	100 paras
Botswana	pula	P	100 thebe
Brazil	cruzeiro real	Cr	100 centavos
Brunei	Brunei dollar	B$	100 cents
Bulgaria	lev	Lv	100 stotinki
Burkina Faso	CFA franc	CFA Fr	100 centimes
Burundi	Burundi franc	Bur Fr	100 centimes
Cambodia	riel	C Rl	100 sen
Cameroon	CFA Franc	CFA Fr	100 centimes

Country	Currency	Abbreviation	Subunits
Canada	Canadian dollar	Can$	100 cents
Cape Verde	escudo	CVEsc	100 centavos
Central African Republic	CFE franc	CFA Fr	100 centimes
Chad	CFA franc	CFA Fr	100 centimes
Chile	Chilean peso	Ch$	100 centesimos
China	yuan	Y	10 jiao = 100 fen
Colombia	Colombian peso	Col$	100 centavos
Comoros	CFA franc	CFA Fr	100 centimes
Congo	CFA franc	CFA Fr	100 centimes
Costa Rica	Costa Rican colón	CR¢	100 céntimos
Côte d'Ivoire	CFA franc	CFA Fr	100 centimes
Croatia	kuna	Din	100 paras
Cuba	Cuban peso	Cub$	100 centavos
Cyprus	Cyprus pound	C£	100 cents
Czech Republic	koruna	Kcs	100 haleru
Denmark	Danish krone	DKr	100 øre
Djibouti	Djibouti franc	DjFr	100 centimes
Dominica	East Carribean dollar	EC$	100 cents
Dominican Republic	Dominican Republic peso	RD$	100 centavos
Ecuador	sucre	S/.	100 centavos
Egypt	Egyptian pound	£E	100 piastres = 1000 millièmes
El Salvador	colón	ES¢	100 centavos
Equatorial Guinea	CFA franc	CFA Fr	100 centimes
Eritrea	birr	Br	100 cents
Estonia	Estonian kroon	Kr	100 kopecks
Ethiopia	Ethiopian birr	Br	100 cents
Fed. States of Micronesia	US dollar	$	100 cents
Fiji	Fiji dollar	F$	100 cents
Finland	markka	Fmk	100 pennia
France	franc	F	100 centimes
Gabon	CFA franc	CFA Fr	100 centimes
Gambia	dalasi	D	100 butut
Georgia	lari	Lr	100 kopecks

Country	Currency	Abbreviation	Subunits
Germany	Deutschmark	DM	100 Pfennig
Ghana	new cedi	C	100 pesewa
Greece	drachma	Dr	100 lepta
Grenada	East Carribean dollar	EC$	100 cents
Guatemala	quetzal	Q	100 centavos
Guinea	Guinean franc	FD	100 centimes
Guinea-Bissau	Guinea-Bissau peso	GB P	100 centavos
Guyana	Guyana dollar	G$	100 cents
Haiti	gourde	G	100 centimes
Honduras	lempira	La	100 centavos
Hungary	forint	Ft	100 filler
Iceland	Icelandic króna	Ikr	100 aurar
India	Indian rupee	R	100 paise
Indonesia	rupiah	Rp	100 sen
Iran	Iranian rial	RI	100 dinars
Iraq	Iraqi dinar	ID	1000 fils
Ireland	Irish pound (punt)	Ir £	100 pence
Israel	new Israeli sheqel	IS	100 agorot
Italy	lira	Lit	100 centesimi
Jamaica	Jamaican dollar	J$	100 cents
Japan	yen	¥	100 sen
Jordan	Jordanian dinar	JD	1000 fils
Kazakhstan	tenge	Tg	100 kopecks
Kenya	Kenyan shilling	KSh	100 cents
Kiribati	Australian dollar	A$	100 cents
Kuwait	Kuwaiti dinar	KD	1000 fils
Kyrgyzstan	som	S	100 tyiyn
Laos	new kip	NK	100 at
Latvia	lat	L	100 santami
Lebanon	Lebanese pound	L£	100 piastres
Lesotho	loti (plural maluti)	L	100 lisente
Liberia	Liberian dollar	L$	100 cents
Libya	Libyan dinar	LD	1000 dirham
Liechtenstein	Swiss franc	SFr	100 centimes

Country	Currency	Abbreviation	Subunits
Lithuania	litas	L	100 kopecks
Luxembourg	Luxembourg franc	LFr	100 centimes
Macedonia, F. Y. Rep. of	denar	D	100 deni
Madagascar	Malagasy franc	Mal Fr	100 centimes
Malawi	Malawian kwacha	M Kw	100 tambala
Malaysia	ringgit	M$	100 sen
Maldives	Maldavian rufiyaa	Mv Ru	100 laari
Mali	CFA franc	CFA Fr	100 centimes
Malta	Maltese lira	Lm	100 cents = 1000 mils
Marshall Islands	US dollar	MI$	100 cents
Mauritania	ouguiya	UM	5 khoums
Mauritius	rupee	Mau R	100 cents
Mexico	new Mexican peso	Mex$	100 centavos
Moldavia	leu	L	100 bani
Monaco	French franc	F	100 centimes
Mongolia	tughrik	Tug	100 möngös
Morocco	Moroccan dirham	Dh	100 centimes
Mozambique	metical	Mt	100 centavos
Myanmar	kyat	K	100 pyas
Namibia	South African rand	R	100 cents
Nauru	Australian dollar	A$	100 cents
Nepal	Nepalese rupee	NRe	100 paisa
Netherlands	Netherlands guilder	Gld or Fl	100 cents
New Zealand	New Zealand dollar	NZ$	100 cents
Nicaragua	gold córdoba	C$	100 centavos
Niger	CFA franc	CFA Fr	100 centimes
Nigeria	Nigerian naira	Na	100 kobo
North Korea	won	Wn	100 chon
Norway	krone	NKr	100 øre
Oman	rial	RO	1000 baiza
Pakistan	rupee	Pre	100 paisa
Palau	US dollar	$	100 cents

Country	Currency	Abbreviation	Subunits
Panama	balboa	B	100 centesimos
Papua New Guinea	kina	K	100 toea
Paraguay	guarani	G	100 céntimos
Peru	neuvo sol	S/.	100 centavos
Philippines	peso	P	100 centavos
Poland	zloty	Zl	100 groszy
Portugal	escudo	Esc	100 centavos
Qatar	Qatari riyal	QR	100 dirham
Romania	leu (plural lei)	L	100 bani
Russia	rouble	R	100 kopecks
Rwanda	franc	RF	100 centimes
Saint Kitts-Nevis	East Carribean dollar	EC$	100 cents
Saint Lucia	East Carribean dollar	EC$	100 cents
St. Vincent & Grenadines	East Carribean dollar	EC$	100 cents
San Marino	Italian lira	Lit	100 centesimi
São Tomé & Príncipe	dobra	Db	100 cêntimos
Saudi Arabia	Saudi riyal	SR	100 halalah
Senegal	CFA franc	CFA Fr	100 centimes
Seychelles	rupee	SRe	100 cents
Sierra Leone	leone	Le	100 cents
Singapore	Singapore dollar	S$	100 cents
Slovakia	koruna	Sk	100 haleru
Slovenia	tolar	SIT	100 stotins
Solomon Islands	Solomon Islands dollar	SI$	100 cents
Somalia	Somali shilling	So Sh	100 cents
South Africa	rand	R	100 cents
South Korea	won	W	100 chon
Spain	peseta	Pta	100 céntimos
Sri Lanka	Sri Lanka rupee	SC Re	100 cents
Sudan	pound (dinar)	LSd	100 piastres
Suriname	guilder	Sf.	100 cents
Swaziland	lilangeni	Li	100 cents
Sweden	Swedish krona	SKr	100 öre
Switzerland	Swiss franc	SwF	100 centimes

Country	Currency	Abbreviation	Subunits
Syria	Syrian pound	S£	100 piastres
Taiwan	new Taiwan dollar	NT$	100 cents
Tajikstan	ruble	R	100 tanga
Tanzania	shilling	TSh	100 cents
Thailand	baht	B	100 satang
Togo	CFA franc	CFA Fr	100 centimes
Tonga	pa'anga	T$ (=A$)	100 seniti
Trinidad & Tobago	Trinidad & Tobago dollar	TT$	100 cents
Tunisia	dinar	D	1000 millimes
Turkey	Turkish lira	TL	100 kurus
Turkmenistan	manat	M	100 tenesi
Tuvalu	Tuvaluan dollar	$T (=A$)	100 cents
Uganda	shilling	USh	100 cents
Ukraine	hryvna	G	100 kopiykas
United Arab Emirates	UAE dirham	Dh	100 fils
United Kingdom	pound sterling	£	100 pence
United States	US dollar	$	100 cents
Uruguay	peso	N$	100 centesimos
Uzbekistan	som	S	100 tyiyn
Vanuatu	vatu	VT	100 centimes
Vatican City	Vatican lira	VL (= Lit)	100 centesimi
Venezuela	bolivar	B (plural Bs)	100 centimos
Vietnam	dong	D	10 hao = 100 xu
Western Samoa	tala	WS$	100 sene
Yemen	Yemeni rial	YD	1000 fils
Yugoslavia	dinar	Din	100 paras
Zaire	zaïre	Z	100 makuta
Zambia	Zambian kwacha	ZKw	100 ngwee
Zimbabwe	Zimbabwe dollar	Z$	100 cents